The Galway Races

Jack Mahon

BLACKWATER PRESS

Acknowledgements

When I first mooted the idea of this book on the Galway Races, I received nothing but help and courtesy from the Galway Race Committee and its Office staff, Mr John Moloney, Secretary-Manager, Mrs Dolores Gillen and her able helper Annette Walsh. At the Galway September meeting of 1994 I received much good advice from leading trainer Mr Jim Bolger. My gratitude to the *Connacht Tribune* for permission to use many of their black and white photographs and also to Liam Healy, Listowel for the colour photographs supplied. Visiting the different stables was a labour of love despite the long miles of travel. Buíochas, too, to Paddy and Florrie Barrett for their great patience and enthusiasm in the typing and layout of the book and to Susannah Gee and Anna O'Donovan and to all at Blackwater Press for their co-operation. Finally my thanks to John Welcome and Fergus A D'Arcy for their invaluable assistance.

Editor
Susannah Gee

Layout
Paddy Barrett

Design
Gabrielle Stafford

ISBN
0 86121 727 6

Produced in Ireland by
Blackwater Press
c/o Folens Publishers
8 Broomhill Business Park,
Tallaght, Dublin 24.

Contents

Foreword

You have to be from Galway to really appreciate what the Galway Races mean to the City of the Tribes and to the West of Ireland generally. It is the biggest Irish festival race meeting of the year and is the high point of Summer in the West. People tend to make it their annual holiday and there is an atmosphere in Ballybrit that is unique.

As youngsters we heard a lot about the Galway Races and longed for the day we could join the long queue of cars which annually trekked through my home town Dunmore *en route* to Ballybrit. When that day came my most abiding memories are the sounds of the horses hooves hitting the turf as they passed the Stands always teeming with people it seemed.

It was only a two-day event in my young days. Now and for some time, it is a week-long Summer Fiesta — a Mardi Gras as Tom Bourke calls it in this book. This year is the 125th running of the Galway Races at Ballybrit. The Galway Plate and Hurdle are still the two main events but all the other events are closely contested and the Galway Races now attracts the quality flat horses as well as the top National Hunt ones. I love Galway Races time. Like everybody else here in Galway I tend to measure the year by the Races and there is a flat feeling after it is all over for another year. A lovely cross-section of people flock to the Galway Races annually. They are very welcome visitors for the week and help in no small way to make it the week of the year in Galway. I hope this book captures the unique flavour of the Galway Races and that more and more people will enjoy the sound of the hooves hitting the turf and the thrill of backing a winner in Galway.

Jack Mahon — June 1995

The Glory and the Magic

From The Horse's Mouth

Arthur Helliwell in **The People**, *Sunday August 4 1957.*

Crazy Carnival. No sleep for twenty-four hours but it was worth it.

"I was told that Galway race week was one of Ireland's mad-dest frolics. So on Wednesday I flew to the west coast to see the fun — and discovered this was a classic understatement.

Personally, I found the meeting with its mixed crowd of tweedy 'gintry', lovely colleens, sporting priests, slick con men, wandering minstrels and colourful tinkers quite enchanting. I have been racing at fashionable Longchamps, exotic Hialeah Park, and at tracks in the Bahamas, South America, India and Australia, but none has matched the charm of this Galway course.

What a welcome they gave me, from dapper little Colonel Dan Corry, captain of the Irish army jumping team and one of the world's finest horsemen, to silver-tongued Tom McNally, king of the roustabouts, who once convinced a mag-istrate's court that the three-card-trick was legal!

Tommy, whom I last met at Puck Fair, spotted me on the popular side of the course and roared a welcome through his megaphone that they must have heard in the hills of Connemara."

1

Pure Magic

I've a little racing mare called Sweet Marie,
And the temper of a bear has Sweet Marie,
But I backed the mare to win and on her I've all my tin,
So we'll take a trial spin Sweet Marie.

Chorus

Hold your holt, Sweet Marie, If you bolt, Sweet Marie,
You will never win the Galway Plate for me.
Every daisy in the dell ought to know me mighty well,
For at every fence we fell, Sweet Marie.

The gods looked down on Galway's Summer Festival of Racing 1994, weather-wise at least. It started off dull and misty on the Monday night and finished off on the Saturday in similar fashion. In between there was beautiful balmy July racing weather, a perfect time for the fair sex to display their style and wares, with a fresh breeze blowing in from the Atlantic to cool everybody off. Any rain that came fell during the night. And it absolutely bucketed in Galway late on Saturday night. I'm sure John Moloney, the Racecourse Manager and organiser-in-chief of the whole show, heaved a mighty sigh of relief after it was all over. This was the most successful ever of what has now become recognised and accepted as Ireland's greatest racing extravaganza. New financial records were broken yet again — largest ever crowds and despite all this and the ever increasing danger emanating from the growth in the corporate hospitality circle and what may be termed the growing helicopter brigade, preserving an intimacy peculiar to Galway. Let that intimacy be preserved at all costs.

DERMOT WELD

It was a time for swimming daily in the bracing Atlantic waters of Salthill. On the mornings those of us who swim daily in Blackrock, Salthill, swapped tips galore. The first time I ever met Dermot Weld was after Dermot himself had taken time off on a Summer race day to cool off with a dip in Salthill. Any talk of Galway must include Weld. Despite rumours of the presence of a virus in certain stables, including Dermot's, he was early off the mark on the Monday evening with his one hundredth Galway Festival winner in *Union Decree* and moving into the second century on *Sprint for Gold* both under the expert guidance of Mick Kinane. You usually don't win too much money following Weld in Galway but it has become a safe course to follow. This mighty man of Irish racing has literally grown up on Galway. He celebrated his forty-sixth birthday on the Friday. Thirty years before to the day, bar one, he had his first ever winner as a jockey on the course. He was only a young gasúr then, an overgrown school boy. The horse's name was *Tirconderoga*. I remember it well for I had two bob on it and the event was the feature event of the evening, the Player/Wills Amateur Handicap. Since those early days as an amateur jockey Galway has become special to Dermot and he saddled ten winners at the 1994 festival, to equal the feat he achieved in 1993. What an amazing man!

CLASSLESS RACING

Everybody that was anybody was in Galway in 1994. Fianna Fail had their own corporate hospitality marquee and Government Ministers were two-a-penny. Albert Reynolds, our Taoiseach then, was there but he has always been a racing man. Charlie McCreevy, another racing man, arrived for a day or two also. The President, Mary Robinson, paid a short visit on the Saturday and received a warm welcome. In Galway you can meet anybody really. Sean Purcell, great footballer of yore, casually introduced me to Dessie Hughes, former jockey supreme, then having a bad run as a trainer. A lovely man, he smiled through it all. In racing you learn to take the rough with the smooth. Luck changes often. Brian Geraghty, an old friend from Oughterard and a racing aficionado for years, introduced me to Willie and Jackie Mullins, Richard Dunwoody, champion jockey over the jumps across the water for 1993-1994, Joanna Morgan, and John Queally former amateur jockey now trainer, among others. The secret of Galway racing success according to Lord Killanin, that lovely gentleman who is so much part of Galway's racing scene and who celebrated his eightieth birthday shortly before then, is that you have in Galway, what he termed, classless racing. But danger signs loom. There has been a continual growth in the provision of corporate entertainment at the Galway Races. In such a corporate marquee, the client need not leave to have a wager. Everything is laid on. Thankfully I like mixing with the crowds and so it seems do all the racing set themselves. But this growing phenomenon of class division through affluence or keeping in step with the Jones's syndrome may very well choke the homeliness and intimacy out of the Galway Races.

I spent part of one day in the infield free area, once a hive of activity, now becoming largely a thing of the past. No corporate hospitality here but a better chance to stop and chat. Much more space. More fun and games. No shelter from the elements if needed. Plenty of activity still for young and old. The three-card-trick man and his entourage of friends much in evidence. Once I saw one with a distinct Limerick accent set up shop near the parade ring, orange box, covering cloth, the same old spiel but the gang was quickly ushered away. I applaud the Race Committee for preserving this free open area for those who still want to ramble in for nothing, to hear the sound of the hooves at close range, to bet in comfort and to get close to the jumps now and again, such as at the famous two jumps at the Moneen (the last two jumps before the finish).

RECORDS GALORE

Every year it seems produces its own set of records for Galway. 1994 was no different. The Tote takings on the Monday evening were £308,727, up over £30,000 on the same day the previous year. This marvellous first day attendance set the tone for the rest of the week. Galway now holds every betting and attendance record for Irish racing. Let's put that in sharp focus. In the first four days punters backed a total of £3,495,000 with the Bookies and £1,917,000 on the Tote. The Galway Plate alone drew a sum of £127,826 on the Tote, four times the total Tote takings at race meetings in Ireland any day of the week. I'd hate to see the demise of any race track in Ireland but it is nice to have Galway to prop them all up. Thursday's Guinness Hurdle or The Galway Hurdle as it has been known for donkeys' years drew a Tote betting figure of £137,800 an all-time record for any single race in Ireland, while bettors laid £201,000 with the bookmakers for the same race. That record Tote figure surpasses the entire Tote takings on two of the Classic days at the Curragh in 1994 for all seven races on the card and the prize-money for the Galway Hurdle was a mere £40,000 in total. The attendance of 24,000 in the enclosure on Galway Hurdle day is also a national record. Add in another 8,000 in the Free area and at the very traditional Moneen fence area on the Galway side and you have the full picture. Statistics and records of attendance make cold reading but any book on the Galway Races must of necessity include these facts.

LONG QUEUES

There are some people in Galway who dread the advent of the Summer Racing Festival, for it spells long queues of cars everywhere, crowded bars and restaurants and the real start of the busy tourist season in the West. The new bridge across the Corrib has tended to alleviate traffic congestion in a huge way. Up to recently Salthill was the place to go after the Races but in recent years many punters stay around Galway and night life has tended to shift to the inner city. Such trends tend to change. In 1994 the Galway Races started the busiest ever tourist season for Salthill, Galway, and the West generally. But if the Races bother some people, the vast majority welcome the financial boom and massive injection of cash that comes to Galway as a result, and the great activity, air of gaiety and life that follows it. For the racing set are the finest of all. Big spenders, out for a good time, having a ball and literally no bother. I love this time in Galway and I've seldom seen any aggression over the years. As to the Races themselves, their very popularity creates the greatest problems. It is difficult to move around with ease on the big days. Long queues at the Tote almost always. Sometimes you're just in time with your bet and you miss seeing the race. But you tend to get wise.

The Race Committee keep improving the place. In 1994 the traditional grass banks around the Parade Ring were replaced with concrete terracing fit to accommodate two thousand people and two hundred and fifty pod seats were placed around the Parade Ring's perimeter fence. A few extra Tote windows near the Parade Ring would help on the big Festival days. The new facilities were excellent and the atmosphere at the Parade Ring was enhanced.

FEATHERED GALE

The Galway Plate for 1994 was won by *Feathered Gale* ridden by Frankie Woods and trained by Arthur Moore, son of the great Dan, who just got up to beat J P McManus's *Minister for Fun* and a fast finishing *Mubadir* trained by Galway specialist Noel Meade, third. It was a great finish and the winning trainer relished it all, for his father Dan rode the winner of the Plate fifty-two years before for trainer Dorothy Paget. It was for me a reminder of the first time I took notice of the race. The winning horse you see was *Golden Jack*. Now how could I not take notice! *Oh So Grumpy* won the Hurdle ridden by Mark Dwyer but the locally trained *No Tag* hadn't the best of luck. Jessica Harrington became the first ever lady trainer of a Galway Hurdle winner. An English challenger *Royal Print* was second. In Galway we love a local success and there were plenty of smiles when Herb Stanley's *Cable Beach* and Sean Creaven's *Open Market* opened proceedings on Plate day, the first ridden by Richard Dunwoody, the latter by Adrian Maguire. These are the two most successful jump jockeys in the world and their amazing fight for the 1993-1994 champion jockey title brought life to the sport in England. This duel was acknowledged in Galway when both jockeys received a presentation to honour that now historic competition. Dermot Weld finished off the Saturday with two more winners *Bryn Clovis* and *King Leon* where the absolute riding skills of Mick Kinane were applauded on all sides. In between, this man had been to Glorious Goodwood. That didn't stop him winning the Top Flat Jockey of the Week Award and as generally expected Charlie Swan won the Top Jump Jockey Award of the Week. The new big man of Irish racing Aidan O'Brien of Piltown, County Kilkenny, had a winner in Galway on the Tuesday in *Bob Barnes* and rode and trained *Kelly's Pearl* to victory in the last race on Plate day. The English based jockeys all bade adieu to Galway on the Thursday.

Their season, beginning a few weeks earlier than usual, was to begin in Bangor (Wales) the following day and was to be followed by Newton Abbot on Saturday. The show goes on for the jockeys from day to day. "I love the Galway scene. Great buzz here but I have to leave today," was how R. Dunwoody put it to me before he left sunny Ballybrit.

OVER FOR ANOTHER YEAR

And so Galway's Summer Festival came to an end for another year. Thursday was as always Ladies Day, or Fashion Day. There was much style in evidence and all the social pages of the dailies were sprinkled with photographs of lovely girls in floral outfits under all shapes of hats. Competitions for the best dressed lady drew much attention and local couturier the late Fergus Foley looked a happy man. The catering facilities at the course were outstanding. On the two big days Des Scahill conducted interviews with many racing personalities past and present *à la* Ian Carnaby in Cheltenham at their Festival meeting. I really enjoyed the interview with those folk legends of yore Martin Molony and Aubrey Brabazon. This innovation — the brainchild of Manager John Moloney — will take off in the future with a little improvement in the PA system. Those seated around the ring had difficulty in hearing the interviews. As I left Ballybrit on the Saturday there was a reluctance among people to go home. A kind of sadness that it was all over. Over in Tuam on the Wednesday night one local punter, Sean Holian, who loves the races, put it well: "I'm always sad when the last race is over and I have to go home. But there is always tomorrow". That was Wednesday night. How must he have felt on Saturday? Joe Connolly, Galway's hurling captain of 1980 was having a drink with his father when who joined our group but former Dublin footballer Anton O'Toole. Anton was off on the morrow to see Dublin play Meath in the Leinster final. John Moloney, Racecourse Manager talked of his thoughts as he gets up on the Sunday morning after it is all over "When I rise and look out at the absolute quiet of it all, no crowds, buzz gone, litter everywhere, just the odd car, it is an awful comedown."

When we started off to race my Sweet Marie
I had backed you for a place my Sweet Marie
But you barely hit the dawn, I fell off and you went on
Now my money is all gone, Sweet Marie.

Chorus

Hold your holt, Sweet Marie, if you bolt, Sweet Marie
Now you've gone and lost the Galway Plate for me
You're a stayer too I find, but you're not the proper kind
For you stay too far behind, Sweet Marie.

— by Percy French in **Prose, Poems and Parodies** *(1925).*

From The Horse's Mouth

Drogheda

Drogheda owned by Mr G F Gradwell from near Drogheda, won the Galway Plate in 1897 and subsequently won the Aintree Grand National, owned then by R C Dawson. The Aintree race was run in a snowstorm. The winning horse was ridden by J Gourley. Mr Gradwell later became Clerk of the Course in Galway until 1929.

Irish Horse-racing *by J Welcome (Gill and MacMillan).*

2

Over to you, Mícheál

"No racing to compare with the Galway Festival"
— Mícheál O'Hehir.

Mícheál O'Hehir, the greatest radio commentator this country has produced became as synonymous with racing as with the GAA. His part in the radio commentary of the Aintree Grand National became part of that event for all of us as he took over from Peter O'Sullevan with an injection of excitement only his voice would generate. The Galway Plate and Hurdle commentaries of O'Hehir were part of our growing up. I well remember leaving a hayfield on two successive sunny days at Corcoran's farm in Adrigoole, Dunmore to listen to Mícheál's commentaries. Another time on a bus journey from Achill to Westport, the driver allowed all of us hear Mícheál's commentary in a pub in Newport. The year was 1959 and *Highfield Lad*, trained by Charlie Weld, won the race. Mícheál thankfully is still with us. He penned these notes on the Galway Races in a special Galway Race Week Magazine of 1983, two years before illness cut short his wonderful broadcasting career. His two sons Tony and Peter carry on his tradition of commentating and writing on the racing scene.

"What is it makes this week so special? Truly it is difficult, almost impossible, to diagnose the attraction, yet there are hundreds of people who will go racing nowhere else and many more, living abroad, who annually time their holiday 'at home' to coincide with Ballybrit's racing. One will find also among the *cognoscenti* of holiday racing an avowed preference for the meeting over any other, except of course amongst that small group who must have virtual solitude and an air of superiority over everybody in sight to feel that they are enjoying 'racing'.

"To me, and to thousands more, Galway Races are many things. The companionship and good humour of the crowd. The people themselves, the ordinary Irish folk, with a sprinkling of foreign holiday makers, out to enjoy themselves without any edge or artificial airs. These are some of the basic attributes of the Galway meeting.

"For the racing 'expert' there is much to add to the atmosphere also, for while some time ago there were the Plate and the Hurdle, and support races which were third-rate in many cases, now it is a case of every race being a competitive event with horses, who may well be seen on the world's tracks, and not merely the jumpers but flat racers as well. *Cairn Rouge* was an example.

"Mind you not so long ago I recall canvassing trainers whose horses had run on one day and were still engaged the following day to please run again just to make up a field. This happened as recently as the sixties when Television came to the course and despite objections at the time from some sections who claimed TV would kill the crowds, the medium has proved the biggest boost possible for the meeting. Sponsors, so eager for TV coverage, are now part of the life of the meeting and the crowds are bigger, not smaller, than ever.

"The recent addition of the new stand, the extension of the meeting to six days in 1982 and the fine Chairmanship of Lord Killanin are all major aspects of the surge of not merely nationwide but much wider recognition of the meeting. I am convinced that the time is near when there will be a mass invasion of cross channel runners, not merely for the Plate and Hurdle but for the other events as well."

How right Mícheál was in his predictions, though the simultaneous running of the Glorious Goodwood meeting tends to keep the flat racer in England. But many of the top English National Hunt jockeys make Galway their home. Subsequently in an article Mícheál wrote of times past with nostalgia for men like Harry Ussher, Barney Nugent, Phonsie O'Brien, Paddy Sleator, Jonjo O'Neill, Dermot Weld, Paddy Powell and included these lovely vignettes from the old days.

ABOUT HARRY USSHER: "I well recall, when the broadcasting box was down on the ground alongside the track — within conversation range of the riders as they went to the post — how the jockeys came out in single file and did a parade of respect for Harry Ussher, on the day in

15

1957 when the news of his death arrived."

ABOUT BARNEY NUGENT: "Barney typified the enjoyment of Galway Races in the two-day meeting days. A thorough professional at his job, good humoured, popular, he enjoyed every moment. I recall one day at Tuam Races, which for decades followed the Galway meeting, a slightly dishevelled Barney asked me,'For heaven's sake, will you stop the stand from going round and round'!"

One of the first times I went to the Tuam Races, I remember meeting Mícheál O'Hehir between races and getting a tip from him which won. It was in the late fifties. I had come to know Mícheál O'Hehir through my GAA association and the horse's name was *Olave* or close to that.

(Bookie, laden down with bets in an aside to Mícheál alongside the stands.) "It was like as if all the people from the hills around Galway came down with fists full of money, just having a good time."

Galway is still very much as you predicted. But a lesser place without you, Mícheál….

 From The Horse's Mouth

A Sane Madness.

"It is impossible to pinpoint exactly what sets Galway apart. This is not just another race meeting. It is not just another festival. Here is a different world. An abstract. It is a frame of mind. An ideal. A sane madness."
— *Donn McClean,* **Sunday Independent** *July 31 1994.*

3
Handing on the Reins

"I used to love going to Toft's in Eyre Square after racing"
— Tony O'Hehir (RTE).

Tony O'Hehir, eldest son of Mícheál took to broadcasting and to racing like a duck to water but then where would he leave it. What was it like to grow up in the O'Hehir household?

"It was a very much sports oriented home from the very beginning. Particularly at weekends when there was always a match of some description, whether it was a local club game, when my grandfather used to bring me on the carrier of his bicycle, or an inter-county game. Then came the realisation that the voice on the radio was that of my father. My grandfather was the man who trained the Leitrim team of 1927 to win their first ever Connacht title. He trained the Clare hurlers as well, was involved with the Civil Service Club and was actually President of the great Saint Vincents when they won their first ever Dublin championship in 1948. When he died in the late fifties, I missed him greatly. I was born in 1950 and during the fifties my father was racing correspondent for the *Irish Independent*. This involved his going to all the Irish meetings and the bigger meetings in England. The weekends were the most hectic, with racing on the Saturday and either football or hurling every Sunday. So sport was definitely ingrained in me from an early age. I used to drive my mother mad as a youngster as I couldn't go out in the back garden or on the street with a ball, even when on my own without doing a commentary — even when I was down in Lecanvey in County Mayo on holidays. And it didn't matter what game we were playing. I would not be consciously copying my father's voice. To me it simply was not football or hurling unless there was a commentary with it.

DAD'S SPORTING LIFE

"From our point of view we went to games every Sunday. Racing wasn't as child friendly then as now and we'd be brought to racing occasionally. Everyone of our family of five, Peter, Michael, Mary, Ann and myself went through the phase of keeping the scores of games in the commentary box for Dad on the Sundays. That worked its way in the family all the way down starting with me, finishing with Ann my youngest sister. You know the format: John Keenan, a Galway point second minute; James McCartan, a Down punched goal, sixth minute. This page was available to him for a half-time run down on the scores. But we would have it well planned beforehand. He always said his two favourite sports were hurling and jump-racing. Though he enjoyed Gaelic football and the flat, that love for hurling and the jumps persists with him today.

AINTREE

"He looked forward greatly to the Aintree Grand National every year. Still does. He was involved with the BBC on the commentary of the National from the late forties, first with radio then with a radio and television combination and then when television went its own way in the seventies he went back to radio again. In many ways one of the biggest kicks I got out of commentating was to be asked to take over the Aintree broadcast on radio for the BBC after my Dad got his stroke in 1985. This year 1995 was my tenth such broadcast. Where Aintree is concerned it was definitely a case of 'handing on the reins' so to speak. Commentating and keenness on sport was in all our veins and my brother Peter is involved as well. Not so much in the broadcasting side as in the journalistic end. He used to write for the *Irish Press* but for some time now operates freelance working for the *Irish Field, Cork Examiner,* Irish tips and racing news for the *Daily Mail* as well as doing the Form Book for the Turf Club.

"The commentary my Dad is best remembered for is of the 1967 Grand National and the pileup at the fence after Beecher's Brook, the twenty-third fence in fact, when the loose horse ran across the jump and they all milled into him. I was actually at that Grand National as a kid. Two or three years before that he brought me to Aintree first as there was a big doubt at the time about the future of the National and he said to me 'whatever happens you're coming because you might not see another'. So he brought me over for 'the first of the last Grand Nationals' and I got a trip out of it for another few years after that. I was in the box with him when that *Foinavon* business happened, literally looking straight down on it. A rare achievement to be spot on in all the mayhem. The All-Ireland finals were other big occasions. Depending on who was involved or where they were staying he might go to the hotels to meet the teams and get the latest, up to the minute, news. Be it racing or games my father always went early. He just had to be there in good time. Often we arrived at a Racetrack and the gates would just have been opened. In Croke Park he would be there an hour and a half before going on air.

EARLY GALWAY MEMORIES

"We used to go on our Summer holidays down to the West of Ireland to a place called Thornhill, Lecanvey near Murrisk and Croagh Patrick in County Mayo, where my grandparents built a house in the thirties. My mother and her brother used to spend their Summers there and when she got married, we continued the custom. My father would come down the weekend before the Galway Races. We wouldn't see that much of him as the Summer was his busiest time and he'd be off to Galway and to Croke Park for all the All-Ireland semi-finals. The first time I went to Galway was in 1958 and *Hopeful Colleen* won the Plate ridden by Johnny Mahony, trained by Jimmy Brogan, father of Barry. I was eight years old at the time. I was brought into the commentary box that day of course. I remember being brought into the old Weighroom to help the man handing out the number cloths to the jockeys. For a few years that was my job in Galway. I'd be trying to anticipate him with the colours and tell him what numbers to give the jockeys. Francis Flood was riding as an amateur in those days. He'd come out and I'd say, 'Number three,' to him and he was quite impressed. He'd say to me, 'Is your mother here?' and when I said, 'Yes,' he'd tell me to tell her to have 2/6 each way on himself in that race. I used to make sure to tell her and I often think I should have organised something for myself at that time.

"My father always liked Galway. There weren't that many race meetings on the radio in those days. I remember hearing a commentary on the Galway Plate before seeing it. Apart from the Irish Grand National or the Guineas it was unusual to have midweek broadcasts of racing. In those days too I remember a man from Galway Mícheál Ó Raifteiri introducing the Races from Galway tré Ghaeilge.

BROADCASTING START

"It was the last race of one of the days in 1969. It was won by a horse owned trained and ridden by Archie Watson, who is long since dead. I just did the last race without any blow about announcements or that. I had done a few tests beforehand. So my first live broadcast was of a bumper in Galway. I was confident enough I'd know the colours but didn't know what it would sound like. It comes reasonably easily to me now but I have had plenty of experience since. From 1970 until 1985 I did most of the course commentaries all over Ireland. I was also doing the Form Book and some work for the *Sunday Press*. Since I stopped doing the course commentaries in 1985 when I started working with the *Racing Post*, I only do work for RTE mostly at the weekends and as a result, I have to work harder on the colours now than before. Before 1985 I saw them every day. But I have a contract with RTE for race commentaries on races covered by them.

THE SUCCESS OF GALWAY

"I can only comment on what I have seen Galway become since going there first. As far back as I can remember the Plate and Hurdle were broadcast and I cannot account for how they became big name races. The thing about Galway that fascinates me is that I know Irish people everywhere who wouldn't go to a race meeting anywhere else but Galway. I know one particular fellow who lives fifteen minutes from Kempton Park and has never set foot in it. Yet he never misses the Galway Festival week, and he isn't a Galwayman. Once Punchestown is over, everything looks towards Galway. It hasn't got much to do with the quality of the horses basically. It is just a big party. It is a mixture of different things really. The course has improved immensely from the old days. I don't see the Festival week expanding much more. The possibility of it starting and finishing on Sunday would probably make some sense but I would not see it expanding beyond that. Further expansion would kill it. I look forward to Galway a lot. When I was doing the course commentaries I got into a routine and everyday was pretty much the same, but I would always pick up a gear or two for Galway. The horses weren't the only ones trying hard in Galway. I always felt that with the huge attendances you had to perform well. On your toes really, not just going through the motions.

"I had one particularly bad bloomer in Galway the year in fact Paddy Mullins won the Galway Hurdle with *Prince Tammy*. Two races later on the same day the same owner had a horse running in a mile handicap or something like that. This is one of the most difficult things for a commentator on a race. Not mixing up the individual horses in a race but looking at these colours and getting the wrong horse for a particular colour. On that day *Prince Tammy* made all in the mile handicap two races after winning the Galway Hurdle! Some horse *Prince Tammy*! The actual name of the horse was *Brandon Hill*. A particular trainer cast all sorts of aspersions on me coming down off the Stands that day asking was I drunk or what not, but I got over that one. The old commentary box used to be in the top right hand corner of the top open stand and was nearer the last hurdle than the finishing post. When that was done away with they introduced some improvements. They used to have a race card seller's box tied down to the roof of the Stand and I remember swaying around in the breeze in it more than once and complaining to Luke Mullins that myself and the box would take flight some day. However that was replaced too.

MICHEAL TODAY

"He's in reasonable form all things considered. Still takes an interest. Last year he received an honour at the Killarney Races and that was a good day for him meeting so many old acquaintances. Galway would be a particularly traumatic time for him for it was the last meeting he worked at before he got the stroke in 1985.

"Nowadays I'm full time with the *Racing Post* since it came into being in 1986. They have no objections to me working for RTE. But I'm immersed absolutely in racing. Commentaries would be my first love really but being the Irish racing correspondent for the *Racing Post* keeps me busy and brings me all over the world. I have never been to Glorious Goodwood because it clashes with Galway, but another memory is of travelling to Galway for the races annually and pulling into the side of the road to hear Peter Bromley's commentary of the Stewards Cup from Goodwood and it seemed to be always the same thing every year. 'Over the brow and the shimmering sunlight'. He painted the picture well and I'd be doing this to myself in Galway before I'd come on. As a child we used to love going to Toft's in Eyre Square after the Races for rides on this and that and seeing the Wall of Death.

"I have been lucky in getting round quite a bit to all the major racing events. Liverpool, Cheltenham and the Epsom Derby, Royal Ascot, the Prix de l'Arc weekend in Paris and the Melbourne Cup in Australia. I have covered them all for the *Racing Post*. It was great to be in Melbourne when *Vintage Crop* won — probably my greatest racing thrill because the two horses to go over there were the first ever to go from Europe for the race. To see the reaction of the Irish people there to Dermot Weld's triumph was something else. Dermot Weld is his own best PR man and he was quite outstanding after that success. At the press reception he went down really big. It went like this. 'This triumph fulfilled an ambition I have had since I was a child and I have always had a soft spot for Australia since I got a present from some owner of my father's of a book of Banjo Patterson's poetry and I have always been a great fan of Banjo ever since.' All the experienced and battle scarred pressmen were nudging each other more or less saying we have heard this before but they underestimated our Dermot who astonished them by putting his hands behind his back and reciting four or five verses of *The Bush Picnic* by Banjo Patterson. So D K Weld and *Vintage Crop's* success will never be forgotten down under. As for the other meetings, it is great to be involved. I enjoy Paris and the Prix de l'Arc. It was there I met my wife, Phil, so it has to be special. We have four in the family, Paul, Niamh, Fiona and Gillian. Niamh is mad on horses. I rang her from Cheltenham earlier this year and she told me she listened to the Champion Hurdle during a French class using leads etc. Paul says he fancies going into sports journalism. So it could happen that I might be handing on the reins to one of them."

4

My Favourite of All Racecourses

"Galway has always been special to me"
— Colm Murray, RTE News.

Colm Murray is a well-known TV face from the RTE Newsdesk and Sport. A native of Moate, County Westmeath, he has long been a devotee of Galway, Race Festival Week being a very special time annually. Colm has more than a passing interest in racing and in sport generally. His work with RTE has copper-fastened that interest and for years now he has in his professional capacity covered the racing scene at Galway, Punchestown, Cheltenham *et al*.

"I remember going to the Galway Races first with Mum and Dad in 1959. I was overwhelmed by the crowds, the colour, the atmosphere and the sheer size of it all. The Parade Ring really impressed me. The jockeys hopping up on to the horses and their lovely colourful silks. After that came the teenage years, again with my Dad, a man who never missed Galway but whom you'd hardly describe as a racegoer. My first memory of the Galway Plate was when *Royal Day* won it for Paddy Sleator in 1967. But what really impressed me was viewing the Plate from the uncovered top of the Main Stand, a marvellous vantage point with quite a magical vista.

UCG

"My University days in UCG cemented my love of Galway, and I have always felt so much at home there. I got married in July 1978 and Ann and myself decided to spend the first few days of our honeymoon in Ireland before we flew off to Portugal. We planned a mystery tour to the West which ended in Ballybrit. Ann wasn't over the moon with my idea of mystery destination. In we went and I remember backing five pounds on Charlie Haughey's horse *Blasket Sound* at 7/2 and it won, but when we met over half our wedding guests, I had great difficulty in persuading her to stay.

"Now the Galway Racing Festival is Wedding Anniversary time and we never miss it. But the greatest Galway memory has to be seeing *Magic Oats* win the three-mile Hurdle on Galway Hurdle Day 1990. A group of us, comprising David Furlong, Tony Deane, Frank O'Toole and myself, had leased this mare through trainer Willie Mullins. So I laid twenty-five pounds each way on the Tote and a few bob also on her in the ring. She won at 25/1 odds in the ring and at 67/1 on the Tote. I had such little faith in her winning that I had agreed to do a radio interview immediately after the race with Mick Kirby from Castletown Geoghegan in Westmeath on the tourist potential of Lilliput. So when Ronan Collins handed over to me on top of the uncovered section of the Stand, it was difficult for me to concentrate. In my mind I could hear the announcements of the odds in the background, the winner alright, then the Tote prices and I was calculating my winnings in the middle of all the questions. Down in the Parade Ring the lads and Willie were waiting for me to lead in the horse but my lack of faith denied me the prize. That evening is one I'll always cherish. The first time we ever hosted a champagne celebration. That night I counted a cool £1,975 winnings on *Magic Oats*.

"Nowadays I wouldn't miss Galway Festival Week for anything. Over the years I've covered the scene for RTE television and radio, have done Parade Ring presentations for the Galway Race Committee and last year gave some hopefully informed tipping for some corporate guests who had come to enjoy greatly the superb facilities in Galway. Galway Race Week is a mixture of a race week with the coming together of the clans and is the closest thing I know to the great GAA All-Ireland occasions every September. Galway has always been special to me."

Racing Folk

From The Horse's Mouth

Statistics in Galway since January 1 1988.

Leading Flat Trainers -
>D K Weld 61
>J S Bolger 20
>P J Flynn 14
>C Collins 14
>John M Oxx 13
>T Stack 9

Leading Irish National Hunt Trainers -
>D K Weld 13
>Noel Meade 12
>Arthur Moore 10
>A P O'Brien 10
>Anthony Mullins 8
>Paddy Mullins 7

Leading Flat Jockeys -
>M J Kinane 58
>P Shanahan 19
>S Craine 18
>J P Murtagh 13
>C Roche 12
>P V Gilson 11

Leading Irish National Hunt Jockeys -
>C F Swan 20
>B Sheridan 13
>M Flynn 8
>K F O'Brien 8
>G M O'Neill 7
>C O'Dwyer 7

5
Dermot Weld

"It takes a good horse to win in Galway."
— D K Weld

Harry Ussher may have been Galway's darling trainer of the past. Phonsie O'Brien and Paddy Sleator were also big in Galway in their day but it is fair to say that Dermot Weld, who trains close to the Curragh Racecourse, is the real darling of Galway for years past. I remember him coming to Galway as a schoolboy and riding his first winner. In between we have all watched him grow in stature in the racing world and Galway holds a very special place in his racing heart. He has now become part of Galway racing and every horse he runs in Galway is highly favoured. He trained his hundredth Festival winner at the 1994 meeting.

I visited D K Weld at his home in The Curragh on a bright Winter's day some months back. The flat season was over and the National Hunt scene was hotting up for Cheltenham. *Vintage Crop*, Dermot's prize horse in an illustrious yard, was safely back from his second Australian trip. The mishap which caused the injury and required fourteen stitches to his leg, was fading away. The horse was out in a field with his companion pony. Hard to believe this was one of the most prized equine possessions in the land, the only horse from Europe ever to win the Melbourne Cup. I found Dermot the perfect host, a modest and unassuming man, delighted to talk about racing in general and his association with the Galway Races.

I asked him if he was bred into racing and if it was always going to be his career.

"I think it was inevitable. I was always associated with horses and from an early age it was my intention to be involved in some way with them. After leaving school in Newbridge College, I became a veterinary surgeon, qualifying from UCD at the age of twenty-one.

EARLY YEARS

"The first time I remember being in Galway, was the year *Highfield Lad* won the Galway Plate (1958). I have a nice photograph of myself leading in the winner owned and trained by my father, Charlie Weld, and ridden by Johnny Lehane. My current head man, Joe Malone, used to look after the horse. So my first memory of Galway was of our own horse winning the Galway Plate. Great excitement and enjoyment. As a boy I used to go to the in-field regularly and enjoy all the amusements there and the festivities associated with that unique area, I always made a beeline for it and enjoyed it all, even seeing the three-card-trick men in action, though I was wise enough never to be conned into participating.

"Obviously I was going to Galway for a few years before the *Highfield Lad* triumph, but the latter is my first real memory. Seeing Johnny Lehane jumping the last fence and the roar of the crowd, that is the precise one. And then, of course, leading him in. I was in Newbridge College at the time and in that photograph of the lead in was another boy with me named Maurice Aherne. I hadn't met Maurice for many moons until I met him at the September 1994 Leopardstown meeting and, of course, it reminded me of 1958. My father was very successful with his horses in Galway and I remember it mostly as a three-day event and then going on to Tuam on the Friday. We always stayed in the Golf Links Hotel, owned by Mr Matt Cheevers, right opposite the swimming area of Salthill. A very nice clientele used to stay there. Always full and pretty much the same set of regulars. I met a man there who went on to be one of Ireland's leading bookmakers but more importantly he was one of the nicest and most intelligent people I've been fortunate to meet in my life. Tom Tormey, the man I refer to, and his brother stayed there annually. Tom was a brother-in-law of Captain Michael Byrne, the Flat Handicapper. Another great attraction was the proximity of the Salthill swimming area. I loved swimming and it was so nice just to walk across and have a dip.

FIRST RIDING EXPLOITS

"I started riding very young and was fifteen when I rode my first in Ballinrobe when I came fourth on a horse called *Wild Knight* trained by my father and owned by Michael Foley. Michael Foley and Herbert Shouler owned the horse jointly. Michael hailed from Kells and Herbert was a Yorkshire man. My father was noted as always having very good young bumper horses, and as I was beginning to develop, I was fortunate to ride many of them. My second or third ride was in Galway on *Tirconderoga* and he was my first ever winner as a jockey. It was in the Player Wills Amateur Handicap on the Tuesday night of the 1964 Race week. It was a great occasion for me. I remember he won at 100/7. *Tirconderoga* was a good horse. That was and still is regarded as one of the top two-mile flat handicaps of the year in Ireland. It was regarded as the Amateur's Derby and still is the most prestigious amateur race to win in Ireland. I was fortunate to be the only amateur to win it four times. I was beaten twice in that same event and believe I should have won it on both those occasions. My father had Tony Cameron booked for the ride. Tony was then one of the top amateur jockeys but whatever happened Tony opted for a more fancied horse and I got the ride. Luck has always played a part in my life. Vivian Lynch, a great friend of mine, who fancied the horse, almost had second thoughts when he saw young Weld was the jockey but he placed his trust in the horse whatever about me! The day of the race was my sixteenth birthday — July 29 — or one day either side.

"The race itself went pretty much as planned. I was always conveniently handy on him and when I really asked him to quicken in the last furlong and a half he picked up well and I beat two great rivals. Kevin Prendergast was second on a horse called *Running Rock* and Bunny Cox, the great amateur jockey, finished third on a horse called *Old Mull*, who was the favourite, all very good horses. It was the Championship and these were the best two-mile handicappers Ireland had at the time. *Running Rock* trained by the late Paddy Norris and *Old Mull* trained by the late Willie O'Grady were very good horses and ridden by two of the best amateur jockeys of that era. That made headlines on the front page of the *Irish Independent* next day. The presentation photo included my late father. *Tirconderoga* was a smallish horse but very tough and courageous. He gave me one of the happiest moments of my life that day.

TIRCONDEROGA

"*Tirconderoga* taught me at a very early age the highs and the lows of racing. It's a wonderful sport and business but you have triumph and a consequent elation and success alongside tragedy in this rough hard business. The following year *Tirconderoga* was to go for the Galway Hurdle and I was looking forward to riding him then but my father, probably prudently at the time, decided I was too young and opted for Paddy Powell instead, who then won the Galway Hurdle with him. My father had intimated to me that I was likely to be riding him in Galway so I was a wee bit sore. Paddy rode him in Galway and he won there. I rode him two weeks later in the Carroll Hurdle in Dundalk and came in fourth there. Sadly then I rode him in the Double Diamond Hurdle in Listowel sponsored by Smithwicks, which is still run there, but now called the Smithwicks Beer Extended Handicap Hurdle. I always remember I was cantering on him over the far side in Listowel, about fifth and going very easily. They had gone very fast and I had taken my time and made steady progress through the field, literally cantering. A horse called *K.O.*, trained by Charlie McCartan, fell and I just couldn't get out of his way and fell over him. I got a very bad fall, but much worse *Tirconderoga* was killed. It taught me both the triumph and the tragedy of racing within a year. Winning the Player Wills at sixteen, being jocked off for the Galway Hurdle but then losing him altogether in Listowel. So at seventeen I had seen it all. *Tirconderoga* was my favourite horse, then. The fall was bad for me in that I was knocked unconscious but losing *Tirconderoga* was the deepest hurt. I well remember the long journey from Listowel as far as the Regional Hospital in Limerick. I had regained consciousness fairly quickly in the ambulance room and was suffering from concussion. The journey home in the back of the car was a long one with me getting sick repeatedly. My father was worried and the doctor in the Regional Hospital in Limerick diagnosed me as having delayed concussion and said I'd be alright. Really it was the loss of the horse that bothered me.

"The horse had been looked after by a man called Paddy Kiersey, a great stable-man and horseman from Kilmacthomas, County Waterford, who had spent his life in England and Ireland with horses and worked for many years for my Mam and Dad. Paddy really loved *Tirconderoga* and I remember Paddy didn't come home from Listowel for a week. He arrived in the following Monday week and my father never said a word to him. He just went about his job as if he had been there every day. That was another little lesson I learned about life from my Dad. How to handle situations and how to understand people. We, Paddy and I, never spoke about *Tirconderoga*.

SPANNER

"It was the early seventies then. I went off to UCD and became a vet. *Spanner* came along. He was a very good horse in that he was an ideal two-mile horse by *Orchadist* out of *Prairie Fire* by *Mustang*. A lovely bay gelding. He was a good bumper horse for us initially and was owned by a Mrs Molly Jackson, who was from Northern Ireland originally, but lived in Ryegate in Surrey and had her horses trained here in Ireland by my father. *Spanner* was to become the favourite horse in my life, although it is wrong to have favourites generally. He went on to win the Players Amateur Handicap three times, then the Galway Hurdle. In the Amateur Handicap, we did it pretty much the same each year. In most races in Galway over two miles, I tended to get a nice position on the inside about fifth or sixth and tried to go the shortest way around and sat usually down the far side. Always in Galway the horses pick up rapidly after they pass the stands. Very often they don't go at that great a gallop in the two-mile handicaps. So when they quicken, you need to be in a good position and I'd stay there after they'd quickened and never moved 'till I got to the Castle. At that stage I made my decision, either I stayed on the inner for a run down the hill or if the horses were tiring in front, I'd move out a little bit. If you ever look at that race you'll find some bunching near the Castle where the front horses start coming back. As *Spanner* used to stay well, I tended to take it up with him coming out of the dip as I met the rising ground. I usually went for home on him on the home turn. Same each year. We were lucky enough the third year. We got the first run on Colin Magnier who rode his father's horse *Double Default* and we held on to win by a neck. *Spanner* was tough, stayed well, was a super horse really. He won the Galway Hurdle for me in my first year as a trainer in 1975 ridden by Peter Russell (that same year *Double Default* ridden by Colin Magnier won the second Division of the Hurdle). He won the Amateur Handicap in 1972 with eleven stone and in 1973 with eleven stone three pounds. Then he ran fourth in the Galway Plate in 1974. He wasn't as good over fences as on the flat and over hurdles. His third Amateur Handicap victory was in 1975, the year after his Plate attempt when he also won the Hurdle. He was some horse.

NOT ALL SUNSHINE

"As the Galway Festival developed more as a race meeting it grew in importance for me. The meeting comes at a very good time of year for me, because if you look at the graph of my training of flat horses, I rarely do that well in the Spring of the year as my horses are good action, top of the ground horses — horses that I can sell on to America and other parts of the world. It's the way I train. I tend not to buy round-action horses that want soft ground. My horses usually reach their peak from about July onwards, and fortunately usually maintain that peak from that until the end of the year. We tend to forget what is happening in Europe and even world racing nowadays. The main races of the world, with the exception of the Derby and the Guineas, are all run in the second half of the year, whether it be the Breeders, Melbourne or Japan Cups or the Arc de Triomphe. Nine times out of ten we have a wet Spring. So if you are really going to get stuck into your horses in the months of March, April and May, you'll have nothing left when the main races come along later. I have always followed that theory so that by the months of June and July especially, my horses are coming on song and Galway happens to come at the right time for me. Usually we have had good weather here in the latter part of July. Soft ground never goes well for me.

GALWAY MEMORIES

"Winning both Galway Plates with *Kiitchi* and *General Idea* in the recent past is one outstanding memory. *Kiitchi* won the Galway Plate as a five-year-old. That gave me great pleasure as only one horse ever before did that. He was a horse I trained from the start. Had been a good three-year-old for me. In fact he won in Galway as a two-year-old. That was unique. He was a good horse and very sadly we lost him in Cheltenham the following year. The triumph and the tragedy of racing again. *General Idea*'s winning the Galway Plate with twelve stone on his back was a great performance. Not many horses did it and he did it so impressively with Adrian Maguire. I won the Galway Hurdle with *Strathline,* and also the Thomas McDonogh a number of times — always great finishes to a fine Handicap — and the two-year-old race on the first evening on a Monday fourteen times, twelve times in a row. I did it again in 1994 with *Union Decree* and was second in 1993. *Go and Go* won in Galway too. It takes a good horse to win in Galway. Galway reflects certain qualities a good horse must have. Courage is one. If you have any doubts about a horse they don't usually win in Galway because up that hill finds them out. So it sorts out the men from the boys. *Go and Go* was a very tough horse. An ideal horse for Galway. That is where he started. He went on to be the first European horse ever to win a Stakes race on the dirt in the USA, when he won the Laurel Futurity as a two-year-old. He came back the following year to win the Belmont Stakes to become the first European horse to win an American classic. And he began it all in Galway.

SUCCESS OF GALWAY

"Galway has a mystique all its own. The Kerry Festival meetings have their own charm but as Festival meetings go, Galway, in my opinion, will always remain supreme. It has a wonderful tradition of sportsmanship, good horses and it has moved with the times. It has excellent management and people like John Moloney and his secretary Mrs Gillen and the Race Committee generally will ensure that Galway will go from strength to strength.

"The track itself has improved no end. The track management is superb. I was looking at it again in the 1994 September meeting. Especially its mat of grass. It's an example to other tracks the way the Galway grassland management has improved the track. How well they have improved what was a limited track and was always inclined to get wet down in the dip because of the natural contours! A superb drainage job has been done there. They have done the maximum for what they have got. Anyone who walks on that mat of grass has to be impressed.

"Galway has been good to me. In 1993 I trained five winners out of six races in one day. That has to be one of my better training feats. Won ten races in the Festival in 1994, ten in 1993. Had my hundredth Festival winner in Galway in 1994.

"I'm often asked if there is any such thing as a sure thing in racing and there definitely isn't. You just need a little bit of luck. You can have a horse fairly well, think everything is right and you need luck for everything to go right. I have had horses that I thought were near certainties. Yet little things went wrong and they got beaten.

MY MOST GENUINE HORSE

"The most dependable horse at the very highest level has to be *Vintage Crop*. He never lets you down. With fourteen stitches in his leg he didn't get the luck of running in the Melbourne Cup in 1994 or he'd have been in the first three. I'd have to mention a horse like *Spanner*, who was at his level, a super horse. By the way *Spanner* was kept here in honourable retirement until 1993, when he was put down the same day as *Vintage Crop* won the Melbourne Cup. It was sad for me but he lived a happy and honourable retirement, as any of my old horses do. I may be ruthless for success but there is a soft side to me too and I have kept horses like *Spanner, Pillar Brae* and *Midsummer Gamble,* who had been good to me, here with me to the end.

"Do I prefer Flat or Hunt racing? A lot of people say to me why do you bother training National Hunt horses. All the top trainers in the world concentrate on the flat. I have been sixteen times leading trainer in numbers of winners and seven times champion trainer in prize money in Ireland and the reason I train National Hunt horses is because I enjoy it.

VINCENT O'BRIEN AND OTHER TRAINERS

"Vincent has been an inspiration. In the late seventies and early eighties I was runner up to Vincent on numerous occasions for the Trainers' Championship and Prize money and he was a truly great trainer. He was always helpful to me and we have mutual respect and admiration for each other. As to other trainers like Jim Bolger, Noel Meade and Aidan O'Brien, it's a changing scene. Records are there to be broken. I hope I'm friendly with everybody, be it competition or opposition whatever you'd call it. I've been very fortunate, I've always been treated very well by the people I've met in racing.

"As a trainer, watching races is a great thrill. Riding the horse is a more instantaneous thrill, especially if you win. But as a trainer you put so many hours more effort into the winning. You've overcome many obstacles such as leg problems to produce him fit on that given day to win that specific race. That's what it's all about. As to the whole thing becoming tedious at times, an awful lot of work goes into it. People fail to realise the long hours I work at it, especially in the Summertime when it's not only a seven-day week but it is from morning 'till dark. Your physical and mental fitness is very much in demand.

RETIREMENT PLANS

"I don't know but it will be sooner rather than later and that may surprise a lot of people. I don't wish to go on too long. I've been at it from a very young age and I've achieved a lot of the things I've wanted to achieve in this country. I don't know what the future holds. Obviously there are races I still want to win. Races around the world. I will see how Irish racing is developing. I hope the new Authority is a great success. I think it is very important for Irish racing and that it comes forward as a result. If it does I want to be part of it for another few years. If it doesn't, there are other possibilities. For this book I've concentrated mainly on Galway, my successes there and my great feel for the place, but the biggest thrill I ever got as a trainer was winning the Epsom Oaks with *Blue Wind*. There were reasons for that. She won it in a record time and at that time it gave me a great thrill. Obviously winning the Melbourne Cup with *Vintage Crop* was an indescribable thrill, because of the atmosphere in Melbourne with a hundred thousand people there and doing something nobody had ever done before, the whole occasion. These are the things that motivate and stimulate me. Winning the Belmont Stakes in America — many people still regard *Go and Go*'s triumph on the dirt there as my greatest triumph. I beat the winner of the Kentucky Derby and the Preakness that day named *Unbridled* and it was the seventh fastest time ever recorded for that classic. So we halted a US triple crown effort as it is called. I have fortunately been able to keep the happy knack of having the ambition and will to win a small race in the smallest track in Ireland and equally getting the enjoyment out of winning the Belmont Stakes. I'm fully aware that I'm a professional racehorse trainer, that I owe a duty to all my owners and I try very hard to win races for them all.

BLUE WIND AND JOCKEYS

"*Blue Wind* ran in Galway. I didn't train her then but saw her win in Galway. She was a very good mare. The best filly I've ever trained. Talking of jockeys, I've been very fortunate that very often I may not have had the best horses but I've always had the best personnel. I've built my success on people rather than horses. The three main jockeys who rode for me, Johnny Roe, Wally Swinburn and Mick Kinane have all been champion jockeys. Wally had a hundred winners one of those years and he was a great rider around Galway. Mick Kinane has been ten years with me and we have built up a great rapport and strike rate together. More recently, I've had Adrian Maguire ride for me betimes. I spotted Adrian at a very early age before he ever went to England. He had about seven winners from seven rides for me before he emigrated. I have great admiration for him both as a jockey and as a man and, of course, he won the Galway Plate for me on *General Idea*.

GALWAY 1995

"That's the future. And we always look forward to that. I suppose my operation is changing slightly in that I'm looking more away from Ireland towards Australia. I may bring more horses to Australia to race in the second half of the year. Obviously I'll have a team of horses for Galway. At the moment it is too early to say as the two-year-olds are just being broken. We had some nice two-year-olds in 1994, so I hope to have a strong team of three-year-olds to race in Galway. Unfortunately, *General Idea* injured a hock and is out of training. Talking of the other Galway meetings, I always enjoy the September meeting, especially having a few oysters. It's a good meeting. Needs a little more prize money added to some of the races. There are races that can be developed into better feature races. The Oyster Stakes is a good race. So is the Waterford Glass Handicap and the Northern Telecom and extra money would lift them up a gear. The October meeting is quite successful, too. Finally, I've enjoyed watching Galway develop from strength to strength. It is an example to Irish racing on how to succeed."

Dermot brought me on a short tour of his stables. We talked of Australia, his recent visits there where he has been treated like royalty and of his Galway owners Ray Rooney, Thomas McDonogh, Seán Creaven and Michael Burke. Here's hoping that the Weld name continues to flourish in the Galway he patently loves.

From The Horse's Mouth

The feeling of fellowship

"I have mentioned the feeling of fellowship that pervades the Festival. It is more than just a feeling. Unlike the strict demarcation that pertains on English racecourses, in Ireland — once you have acquired a modicum of status — you become an integral part of the action. You are free to go into the jockeys' changing room, use their loo, buy their sandwiches, weigh yourself on their scales.

Stewards, trainers, jockeys, valets, owners and gatemen are all on first name terms, stand each other cups of tea, pass on duff information, smile."

— *Clement Freud,* **Racing Post,** *Friday July 29 1994.*

6
Riding Long

"Tim and myself travelled by horse-drawn caravan to Galway in the War Years"

— *Martin Molony, legendary jockey.*

*M*artin Molony, now nearing his seventieth birthday, was one of the idols of my youth. His face was to be seen almost daily in the then sparse enough Irish daily newspapers of the forties and the early fifties. He seemed to keep on winning, hunt or flat and to emphasise the name Molony more, his elder brother Tim, strictly a jumps jockey, was for many years champion national hunt jockey in England. Then came Martin's tragic fall in Thurles in September 1951 when in a fall from a horse called *Bursary* he received a fractured skull. The great Martin Molony, legend even then at twenty-six was never to ride in public again. Tim continued to grab the headlines in England until a broken hip from a fall halted his career in 1958. Martin Molony was always going to be a must for this book on his Galway memories especially after he was introduced to the Galway Races attendance on Plate day 1994 and received such a tumultuous ovation. The greatest tribute that can be paid to Adrian Maguire, the Irish star jockey of today is to say his style in some ways resembles the great Martin Molony. A truly lovely man, I spent an entertaining evening with him in his home at Meanus, Croom, County Limerick.

"My father was a farmer. We are here in Rathmore for about six or seven generations. He hunted as indeed did my mother. He was in the First World War and got the Military Cross. My father had the pleasure of training and owning the Galway Plate winner *Hill of Camas* in 1915, ridden by George Harty of Patrickswell. My mother loved hunting too and rode side saddle. She had a wonderful pair of hands and that stood to her.

INTRODUCTION TO RIDING

"I went to England at the age of thirteen, on February 12, 1939, to be an apprentice with Marty Hartigan at Ogbourne in Wiltshire. Gordon Richards served his time with Marty's brother Paddy Hartigan. War broke out in September 1939 and all the apprentices (fourteen in number) in the yard at Hartigan's were sent home just two days after the outbreak. When I got home I kept in touch through George Harris, who had a private stables in Kilmallock. My first ever winner, in November of that year, was through the Hartigans, whose racing options in England were now curtailed, on a mare called *Chitor* in the Curragh. I rode her for my first gallop the Sunday morning war broke out and was due to ride her in a race at Bath or Salisbury some weeks afterwards in an Apprentice race. That was my first winner at the age of fourteen. My next win was for Tim Hyde in Ballinrobe two years later. The winner was owned by a Superintendent Hughes. I upset expectations a bit that day as a horse belonging to Miss Dorothy Paget was heavily gambled on to win.

GAMBLING

"I was never keen on backing horses. Probably had a half crown on the Tote when I was an apprentice. When I got better known later on, I was often asked for tips but I was never a great tipster. These were war years. George Harris was now finding it hard to make ends meet. Very little racing. So I went to Ginger Wellesley in Osborne Lodge, The Curragh, for whom I rode one or two winners. Charlie Smirke rode the winner of the Oaks for him that year. Ginger joined the Army in England and fought in the Second World War. I moved on to Cyril Harty's in Chapelizod at the end of 1942. Cyril, another Limerick man and a friend of Tim's, had a mixed string of two year olds and jumpers. I rode my first hurdle race winner in 1942 in Rathkeale on a little horse called *Prince John* (Rathkeale has closed like so many other racecourses since).

On that day Vincent O'Brien rode a horse of ours trained by Tim called *Knight's Crest* in the bumper though he wasn't successful. Tim was a great friend of the O'Briens before I got so friendly with them. I actually remember minding Phonsie O'Brien and holding him by the hand at Mallow Races around 1936.

FIRST EVER STEEPLECHASE WINNER IN GALWAY 1942

"The horse's name was *Knight of Venosos* by *Knight of Kilcash*. Owned originally by one of the Purcells of The Wilderness, Clonmel, Captain Harty bought him for a Belgian millionaire called Bobby Lowenstein, who was killed during the war. So Cyril fell in for the horses owned by the Belgian. I had ridden him once or twice over fences before then. The first horse I ever rode in a steeplechase. That gave me great pleasure. My first experience of Galway was as a child in 1936. We had two runners there that year trained by my father and Tim rode one of them, *Inverax*, to be third in the Galway Hurdle. The other one ridden by Tim McCarthy fell at the last fence in the Plate with the race sewn up. It rained for the two days non-stop and Harry Ussher trained the winners of both the Plate and Hurdle that year. He was a great man for Galway then. He was Galway. Jack McNeill rode both winners for him. We got drenched of course and I remember the journey home in a 10 horse power car driven by my father (the horses went home by railway) with a slipping clutch that didn't allow us to travel faster than 15 mph. Home early in the morning.

TIM'S DOUBLE IN 1948

"I would have ridden both that year but I was claimed by my retainers to ride their horses as I had ridden both horses before then. My trainer then was the late Joe Osborne. I had ridden *Silent Prayer*, which won the Plate, to win both the Ulster National and the Conyngham Cup beforehand for Paddy Sleator. She was a good mare. The Hurdle winner was trained by Dan Ruttle, son of Jack, who trained the Aintree Grand National winner *Workman* in 1938. We stayed out in Salthill that year. There was a very nice man outside Galway a patron of Jimmy Brogan, a builder named Joe Stewart for whom I rode a winner in Tuam.

"The year I won the Galway Hurdle with *Wye Fly* for Vincent O'Brien, I rode three winners the following day in Tuam, the last time I rode there. Two of them were trained by Jimmy Brogan. The previous year I rode all five on the card in Navan — a day Pat Taaffe rode the bumper winner. So Pat Taaffe and myself shared the spoils. Pat rode the winner for Chally Chute, a brother-in-law of Lord Harrington, who now lives at the Curragh. I got a good run. Someone was praying for me. The Lord gave me great talents and he helped me to make the most of them."

In between 1943 and Martin's first chase success and Martin's Galway Hurdle victory in 1951, the Molonys had become famous as jockeys.

FEARS AND THRILLS

"When you're young you'll do a lot of things that you won't do when you grow older. To be a jockey is a young man's game. When you enjoy doing something that you like it is not hard work. I did a lot of travelling back and forth to England for the last four years of my riding career. That was tough going at times because travelling was more difficult then. It's wonderful when you enjoy yourself, when you give a horse encouragement and he responds to it. There is a wonderful thrill going over a jump. When you're playing golf and you hit a good shot you get a good thrill out of it. It's so much better when you're dealing with a live animal. There is a great rapport between the jockey and the horse. Every horse is different. You ride no two horses the same. Some horses don't respond to your encouragement like others. Hands, legs, the whole body, you're together. Everything is changed now with the media and television. The camera captures everything. Watching television I can see a horse ten strides from a fence or hurdle and know whether he is going to meet it right or not. The Lord gave me the grace of never trying to shorten the horse's stride. This I see some jockeys doing today which is fatal. You should never shorten the horse's stride. It's a gift you have or you haven't.

"You never see danger coming. If you think that, you should not be riding. You should hang up your boots then. My late brother, Tim, always said, 'Ride him to the ground and you won't get injured'. Always stick to the horse. When you have your leg in the right place you can squeeze him with the calf and the knee, something most jockeys can't do today because they are riding too short. Riding styles have changed, of course. Lester Piggott started it in this part of the world. It came from America originally. There it is completely different because they ride on very level tracks. They ride 'acey deucy', one leg a little shorter than the other because their turns are so sharp. I rode very long. Lester Piggott developed the unique style as I said. He is a very brainy man. The greatest flat jockey of them all. Both a good judge and a good jockey. Piggott was a great judge of the performance of a horse. Gordon Richards was a great jockey but nobody could judge a horse like Lester.

GREAT JOCKEYS OF TODAY

"Mick Kinane is a grand rider. He sits into a horse well, doesn't ride too short and makes very few mistakes. I made many mistakes in my own day. He rides with success anywhere in the world yet like myself stays at home in Ireland where he obviously appreciates his home with his wife and family.

"I was blessed and enjoyed my time and wouldn't change one iota of my life. Your heart has to be in the right place to give the horse the proper encouragement and to give the owner and trainer good value for money. Losing a horse can be very hard on everybody. You'd be affected but when you're young and riding every day it is part of your job.

"You don't tend to remember the falls at the last fence! One day in Dundalk I had a race won by lengths on a horse of Joe Osborne's called *Desdar* and between the last fence and the winning post he broke his leg and turned over. A nicer thing happened to me at Liverpool on *Cloncarrig* at the November meeting around the Grand National fences. I won twice on him there in the Molyneaux Chase. He did the same, crossed his legs and turned over after passing the post but he got up and there was nothing wrong, thank God.

AINTREE AND CHELTENHAM

"I rode in three Nationals and never got round. Fell at the first fence the first year on *EP*. I rode him the following year and got to Beecher's the second time around. The last year I rode the favourite *Shining Flame* but was brought down at Beecher's first time round. That particular day was most enjoyable for me. I rode *Sugar Palm* to victory in a six-furlong flat race just prior to riding in the National. The horse was English trained by the late Frank Hartigan. *Silver Fame* actually won the Gold Cup in Cheltenham for me the following year 1951 but I was second the two previous years on *Happy Home* and *Finnure*, the first for Miss D Paget, the second for Lord Bicester, both times to Vincent O'Brien's *Cottage Rake* ridden by Aubrey Brabazon. Aubrey and myself were always the best of friends. We were all friends then in the jockey's room. No jealousies. Money has taken too much control now.

RECORDS

"One year I had twenty-one winners on the flat and one hundred and nineteen winners *en toto* all in Ireland. In the same year I had sixty-five winners in England, all obtained between November and March. Tim headed the list of winners in England that same year and my total was second to him. The year was 1948 or 1949. When Tim and myself were riding in the same race, either in Ireland or in England we always talked to each other during the race. 'How are you jumping?' or words to that effect. 'How are you going sonny boy?' was my usual salutation as we passed each other. Or he would say it to me. We were in opposition once we got on horseback. One day at Lingfield in a hurdle race my horse, trained by Ger Wilson, went lame on landing over the last hurdle and I knew after a few strides that he was shortening his stride. So I eased him up and Tim grabbed the opportunity to pass me on the line. Somewhat like when *Arkle* got injured and got passed on the post.

HORSE-DRAWN CARAVAN

"After my first success in Galway in 1942, I rode every year in Galway afterwards and on the Friday in Tuam. Had more success in Tuam than in Galway. Tuam was a lovely little course. A good straight finish. In the war years we travelled to Galway by horse-drawn caravan, Tim, myself and a few neighbours. We stayed in the caravan park in Salthill, near the strand there. We swam in the mornings before racing and often again after racing. No cars at all. It took us two days to get there. We travelled

43

the Tulla road from Limerick and stopped the first night in Kilsheelan and the second night in Gort or Galway.

"I never managed to win the Plate, but was placed a couple of times in it. Rode the favourite a few times too. *Knight's Crest* and *Cloncarrig* were both favourites. *Wye Fly*'s Hurdle victory in 1951 was my only major success in Galway. Vincent O'Brien was really hitting the headlines then in National Hunt spheres.

"As to celebration, I never did much of that. Never drank or smoked in my life. Through discipline I kept as light as possible, always close to nine stone. In fact I rode *Abadan,* the winner of the Phoenix Park '1500', a very prestigious flat race, with a weight of 8-12. The lighter you are the more opportunities you get on the flat.

"I rode three times in the Epsom Derby, getting third once, sixth another year. I was second in the Irish Derby.

GREATEST THRILLS

"*Sugar Palm*'s six-furlong success in Aintree looms high. My first flat race success in England, in fact, one of my first flat races in England. *Silver Fame* and *Golden View* (on whom I won the Irish National with 12-7 for Dan Moore) were the best chasers. As far as jockeys are concerned, Tim was a great horseman. Horsemanship means a lot in jumping races. Very few people combine the two — a horseman and a jockey. And he did. John Francome and Fred Winter were two good jockeys and good horsemen. Richard Dunwoody and Adrian Maguire of today.

"Adrian has great affinity with the horse and is a great trier. My secret of success was to persevere from beginning to end. I was always trying. I'd give the horse the best encouragement I could. I never remember beating the ground with disgust after I fell like some of them do now. I'd get disappointed later in the evening for mistakes I made earlier in the day. I was booed and jeered at times, too. It was always money talking and money speaks all languages. It never bothered me.

THE END OF THE ROAD

"I won three Irish Nationals on my mother's horses *Knight's Crest* (1944), *Golden View* (1946) and *Dominick's Bar* (1948). The end came for me in Thurles on September 18, 1951. I got a fall from *Bursary* whom I had ridden to success in Tralee a fortnight previously, trained by Martin Quirke for the Queen's Racing Manager Major Moore. I fractured my skull. I was in a Nursing Home in Thurles for a week afterwards and stayed in bed for six weeks. Tim got married a second time shortly afterwards (his first wife had died) and while in London a doctor advised me to give up for a year. I came home, started farming and never returned to the saddle. It was a blessing in disguise, because to do the horse justice and to do your owners and trainers honour you have to have the whole of your nerve and your health. I was only twenty-six. Tim stayed on riding until 1958. Another fall which resulted for him in a broken hip. I always looked up to Tim, who was six years older than me. He was a second father to me when I was in England, where I wasn't familiar with the form, etc. But Tim would always advise me about spare rides. Still I never refused a ride in my life.

"There was no such thing as a difficult horse to ride for me. I got on with horses and won with them, horses that Tim hated to ride when he rode them afterwards. I was often asked if a horse ever ran away on me and I would have to say that I was only a passenger on a number of horses. I wouldn't be able to hold them back to stay in the middle of the field. They just made the running. A lot of them won. Because you were often able to give a horse a breather in a race. As a jockey gets experience he knows when to give the horse a breather and when to keep pushing on.

NOWADAYS

"I breed horses here in Rathmore. The horse is a wonderful animal — has great intelligence. They have a great interest in life. One thing the Lord has told me is you must keep interest in life or you're dead. You keep persevering to the end. When I rode I had great energy to push a horse — a big advantage. I still have that. It's wonderful to be occupied. Julia, my wife, is a great lady and my son Peter continues the horse tradition. He hunts. He is a very tall young man and manages a stud a few miles from here. We have three daughters as well, Jan in India, Mary in Los Angeles and Sue in London. I hadn't been to Galway for thirty years before being introduced to the crowds last year. The crowds are too big.

We have the box now. Television brings Galway right into your home. There is a marvellous buzz to Galway. Similarly with Cheltenham. It gave me great pleasure in Galway last year to think people hadn't forgotten me. There was a man with us that day, Paddy Brady a cattle dealer from Gort, who came with a friend and me. He hadn't much interest in racing and he was really surprised that people had such an interest in me. I met an elderly man in the Stand that day and he said, 'You gave my daughter great pleasure today when you signed your autograph for her'. Lovely.

"My favourite tracks were Leopardstown in Ireland and Sandown in England. Things went right for me in both places. You get attached and I liked riding there.

GALWAY FEATURES

"The two Moneen fences are easily the most difficult ones. They are so close to each other. If a horse meets the first wrong, he usually makes a mistake at the second one. It's hard to right yourself between the two. I worked with Mickey Tully of Galway, who won the 1946 Galway Hurdle. He was a great character and we worked together in Captain Harty's yard in Chapelizod. Always laughing. I rode his horse *Fair Pearl* a few times, a good handicapper."

At this stage I showed Martin the photograph which appears later in this book of the finish to the 1946 Hurdle with Mickey Tully about to pass Danny Morgan on *King of the Jungle* and he had these comments on it.

"Danny Morgan was another to include in the category horseman and rider. Rode an amount of winners in England for the Anthonys and rode for three different Kings. I rode for Danny afterwards when he joined the training ranks. Just observe the length Danny rode. *King of the Jungle* was a full horse and a sire afterwards, same as *Monksfield* later. Barney Nugent, a very nice man, trained the horse. I'd like to see jockeys riding longer and I'm sure the owners and trainers would get more value for money. I send my best wishes to Mickey Tully. I have really enjoyed talking to you and going back on the old days. I wish Galway well in 1995. One final point about my father's Plate winner in 1915. *Hill of Camas* is a farm that is a landmark up near Bruff. Wonderful farmland and still in our family, now farmed by Peter."

"Among the jumping jockeys, there has never been a rider to equal Martin Molony."

— Tony Sweeney, from *The Horse in Ireland* by Noel Phillips Browne (Pelham Books 1967)

 From The Horse's Mouth

The origin of the Galway Plate

"At the start of the 1860s, there were seventeen royal plates in Ireland worth one thousand six hundred and seventy-five pounds. Their distribution reflected the dominance of the Curragh where thirteen were run for including the Lord Lieutenant's Plate and the Royal Whip. Down Royal Corporation enjoyed three, one of which had belonged to Londonderry (Derry) until 1836 and which was restored to it in 1861. The seventeenth royal plate was run at Bellewstown every July.

In 1868 when racing reform was at an uncharacteristic peak, new rules regarding the royal plates were introduced. Henceforth, no meeting would enjoy possession of the plate where its added money failed to reach one hundred and fifty pounds. In 1877 the year before Londonderry (Derry) was to fall foul of the Turf Club and lose its royal plate to Galway, its added money had fallen below the required minimum to one hundred and forty pounds."

Horses, Lords and Racing Men *(Published by the Turf Club)*

So the Derry Plate became the Galway Plate in 1878.

7
Week-long Party

"After Punchestown, you think of Galway."
— *Noel Meade, Trainer*

*N*oel Meade is a very tall man. Approaching his mid-forties, Noel trains in Castletown, County Meath, just about ten miles from Navan. In recent times, he, like Dermot Weld, became the darling of Ballybrit, producing a steady stream of winners over the years. His name has become synonymous with the Galway Races. When I visited him at his home and stables, I found a man, as I expected, fond of horses, Galway, sport, and life generally. Being a Meathman, he is a staunch Gaelic football fan, friend of Meath footballers past and present and likes nothing better than to watch an inter-county game involving Meath in the company of friend and former star, Martin Quinn. But then interest in horses and Gaelic football is woven into the fabric of Meath society. Was the interest in horses in his blood?

"A lot of people are bred to be in racing. I was one that wasn't because nobody in our family had any connection with racing whatsoever. My father was quite anti-horses, in fact, and thought that anyone that had anything to do with race horses went broke. From childhood, I was always racing mad. We had our own ponies when we were kids and I loved them. The first pony was a Connemara pony which Dad bought at the Spring Show. There were quite a few fellows around at the same time who were interested in ponies. One of them was John Burke, the jockey, whom we sadly lost this year, the same John who went on to ride the winner of both the National and the Gold Cup.

"It wasn't the Connemara pony which started my love affair with Galway, whatever about horses. That credit I'd give to my uncle, Tom Halpin. Tom brought his son James and myself to the Galway Races, where we stayed in a caravan. Early memories include Bill McLernon winning the Players Amateur Handicap on *Musty Penny* and Jimmy Tormey winning a big race on *Evilo*. From then on it was a religion, every year, just to go to Galway for the Races. We stayed in various places.

"When I came home from school in Multyfarnham at the age of sixteen to run the farm for my father who was very sick, a pal of mine Michael Condra and myself bought a horse between us. We had a couple of horses here and there after that. Then we bought a very cheap horse called *Tu Va* which we called this place after eventually. He was my first winner. I rode him myself early on, very badly I must admit. He was beaten in Galway in the Amateur Handicap Hurdle. He was a bit of a rogue because when he got to the front, he didn't like it. I rode him that day in Galway and I took it up jumping the last passing 'Mouse' Morris on a horse called *Wild Buck*, then sort of looked around to my left and by the time I looked back again Mouse was after getting back up on the inside to beat me by a neck on the line. I was sick. That was *Tu Va*. At that time I was training under permit and the following year was the first year I had a trainer's licence. We had four horses in training and the first horse I ran in Galway was a horse called *Lark's Venture* and he won the very first race in Galway at the Festival meeting. I'm not great on dates but it was 1972, I think. It was a maiden hurdle and Tommy Carmody rode him. That was a good introduction but then things went very poorly and for years after that we didn't have another winner in Galway. Not until the start of the great *Pinch Hitter* era in 1978 or 1979.

PINCH HITTER AND STEEL DUKE

"Then it all began to happen. We just happened to come across some particularly good fast ground horses at that time, and fast ground hand-icappers as well, like *Pinch Hitter* and *Steel Duke*, two amazing horses because both of them loved fast ground and were at sea on any other type of ground. Both were geldings and had no breeding value as such and they were both very good flat horses. *Steel Duke* in particular seemed to handle Galway better than he did anywhere else. In those particular years the ground in Galway always rode very fast. The owners of *Steel Duke* were two very nice men named Jim McKeown and Noel Kavanagh, both from Readypenny, just outside Ardee. Jim was a publican and Noel is still in business.

"*Pinch Hitter* was a very difficult horse to train. From his three-year-old days he had a leg problem which caused us endless headaches. He spent most of his life after that standing getting his legs hosed. He ran in three McDonogh Handicaps, winning two of them, beaten by a neck in the third and then won two Galway Hurdles in succession 1982-1983. Unfortunately the leg gave way and we couldn't train him after that. It is very difficult to compare himself and *Steel Duke*. François Doumen, the great French trainer says it is not fair to compare horses. They are like children and it isn't fair to compare children. Both those horses are very dear to me. We just put *Pinch Hitter* down this year. *Steel Duke* was put down a year ago. Gillian's mother used him as a hack up until then. *Pinch Hitter* just started to fade away this year and we thought it was fairer to put him down. They were totally different individuals. When Pinch Hitter won his first race in Gowran Park as a two-year-old, I was loosening the girths as he was walking back in and he absolutely split me with a kick. That's the kind of horse he was all his life. He was very quick footed. Jonjo O'Neill rode him in the two Hurdle wins and Stephen Craine was his jockey in the flat races.

"I'm looking at a photograph that you're using in the book showing *Pinch Hitter* leading *Steel Duke* in the Galway Hurdle at the last first time round. That photograph is in the Owner's and Trainer's Bar at Galway and is a great photo. If you want to show an aspiring youngster the right way to sit on a horse then a study of Jonjo on *Pinch Hitter* in that photo is a must. Tommy Carmody is on *Steel Duke* and Tommy is sitting just as near to perfection. Two great jockeys and two very stylish riders. Altogether I had four runners in the race that day. I wouldn't be drawn on which horse I fancied most. My other two runners were *Chammsky*, owned by people from Ballinrobe and *Fane Ranger*, another very good horse who had top weight on that occasion and was also very dear to my heart. I really thought we'd have first second third and fourth as they went out, not knowing which one would be where. Despite the fact that *Pinch Hitter* won and *Steel Duke* was fourth, poor old *Chammsky* fell at the second last and he was positively cruising at the time.

FINBAR CAHILL

"*Pinch Hitter* was owned by Finbar Cahill and Brendan Carolan. I don't think anybody in the history of horse ownership ever got such a kick out of winning as Finbar got out of *Pinch Hitter*. The party just seemed to go on from year to year. It started outside the Owners' and Trainers' Bar after the McDonogh win on the Monday evening and would continue all week. Champagne for the whole week. Finbar is a Dublin solicitor, still a marvellous friend and a great owner to have. In the heel of the hunt, despite all of *Pinch Hitter's* successes, I'm sure he lost money. We used to stay at that time in the Ardilaun Hotel and it was just one continuous party. Brendan was a builder and eventually moved to London. Finbar was the main man even though the horse ran in Brendan's colours. That particular time gave me a great feel for Galway. One year we won the McDonogh on the Monday, the Amateur Handicap on the Tuesday, the big race on the Friday and *Avocan* was second in the Plate. Around those years it was all happening. It seemed to be all sunny days and great crack. We celebrated long and hard.

THE GALWAY HURDLE

"The year *Pinch Hitter* won the Galway Hurdle for the second time, we won the McDonogh, the Hurdle, Niland's on the last day and in all we had six or eight that year. It looked as though everything we ran won. The Galway Hurdle was the one race I had always wanted to win. I don't know why. It was like Jack Berry and the Ayr Gold Cup. The first year he won it *Pinch Hitter* was only a four-year-old and he won it very easily. That was a great sensation. I remember later that evening with Stephen Craine driving my car, we did a lap of honour around the racecourse after racing, at about 60 mph with Finbar Cahill and myself sitting on the roof of the car out through the skylight. We were probably waving bottles of champagne and if Luke Mullins caught us in the act, we'd have been banned from Ballybrit for life. We were so high after the race that night that we carried on in similar fashion on our way home to the

Ardilaun. We wouldn't do it now. We tend to have settled down a bit.

"Galway has developed over the years no end. It just gets bigger and bigger. The hospitality tents have changed the whole thing a lot. I think the special thing about Galway is that there is no high up and low down about it. It isn't at all like the Curragh or Leopardstown or somewhere like that. Everybody is at the same level in Galway. All there for the bit of fun. They are on holidays and in good humour. I hope they never get to the stage of special boxes for that would destroy the atmosphere of Galway. You nearly know where to go in Galway to find the same people all the time. The weather is always a great help too. Many of the people I trained for then and now were true sports people. They went, and go, for the sport. They like to have a bet, have a drink and a bit of crack. To have a horse, to win in Galway, to have a few quid on and to have a party afterwards that's what it was about.

"Dermot Weld has revolutionised Galway in a way. Up until ten or fifteen years ago it was difficult to win the top races but the rest of the cards were not that great. You had upside-down-handicaps. If you had a horse which was reasonably well handicapped and he went on the ground, and you had the right jockey or whatever, then you had a great chance. Nowadays in the two-year-old races we have seen *Committed*, who was a champion in France afterwards, *Go and Go* the Belmont Stakes winner, *Blue Wind* who ran in Galway also. Dermot Weld has brought great horses to Galway and before that it would have been unheard of to bring such quality to Galway. He particularly has made the competition very strong. The flat racing has got very competitive and Jim Bolger brings some of his top horses too. The track has been changed too in that the track has now been conditioned by water. Ten years ago, if it was a dry July then you had fast ground and you had to put up with it. And as a result smaller fields. Nowadays the ground is regularly watered if needs be and doesn't get that fast. The roadways too are better covered than they used to be. So the horses come out of it safer.

"In general racing has become more competitive. There are so many very large strings and some very good trainers about who are prepared to bring horses to Galway and elsewhere. Years ago Vincent O'Brien was the top trainer and he would never dream of going to Galway. Neither would Paddy Prendergast. All has changed.

THE PLATE

"I haven't really had many chances at winning the Galway Plate. *Avocan*, owned by two great characters P J Moran from Lavallyroe near Ballyhaunis and Séamus Fallon from Dunmore, was second one year. As a partnership they were too successful at the beginning. Only for that they would have lasted much longer. The first couple of horses they had won every time we wanted them to win. *Bective Road* was a good horse, won about fifteen races and *Avocan* and *Tobar na gClog*. *Avocan* broke down jumping the last fence in the Plate. It was only her second run over fences ever and she carried eleven stone six pounds. An unbelievable performance. She had won a chase on her first run the previous September and we had high hopes. *Hamer's Flame* won the Plate that year (1983). Then we had *Mubadir* last year, who had been second in the Galway Hurdle in 1993 to a well handicapped horse *Camden Buzz*. *Mubadir* has never been quite as good over fences as he had been on the flat, or over hurdles. He likes the ground very fast. I very much hope that he will be back to try and win it again, because he is a good horse around Galway having won there in 1992. So he might be the one to break my luck in the Plate.

LILY

"Lily from Dublin, one of the ladies who sell the fruit at all race meetings is an old friend. Everybody who goes racing, I mean all the professionals, have one of the fruit ladies that would be theirs. The other ladies tend to know that and leave you alone. I always get my cards off Lily. Lily, God bless her, has been praying for me for years. The year we won the major haul of big races in Galway, as we were coming out on the Monday after a helluva party outside the old Weighroom, who did I meet but Lily who told me of her prayers and how delighted she was at our major win, and as she said herself 'she deserved a few quid'. So I said I'd see her on my way out on the Friday. On the Tuesday we had a good day again and most unlike her, she tackled me on the way out. Once again I told her I'd see her on Friday. We won the Hurdle on the Thursday and were up all night celebrating. Didn't go to bed till the dawn. Went to the races on the Friday and *Steel Duke* was running in the Niland's Handicap and he had 10-6, having incurred a penalty of six pounds for a race he won on the previous Wednesday. I couldn't see him winning and I remember sitting beside Paddy Sleator in the Stand watching the race. Even Paddy thought we were asking too much of the horse. But good old *Steel Duke* won guaranteeing us another celebration. We went straight to the bar after the presentation and I ordered three bottles of champagne off Paddy, who was well known to me, only to find I hadn't a penny in my pocket. Paddy in typical Galway fashion said it would do on the morrow. Then who comes up behind me but the bould Lily and she said, 'Noel it's Friday'. I told her I hadn't a tosser on me and though I expected a lacerating from her all she said was 'Are you stuck?' and when I said, 'Yes,' off she went and was back in a flash with a hundred quid. Good old true blue, Lily.

"Another memory from one of the good years. It was Saturday, the final day of the meeting. As usual we had played long and hard and everything had gone well and we had only one runner on the final day. At about 7 a.m. I got a phone call in the Ardilaun from my travelling head man, Mattie Murphy, to tell me the horse had gone lame. So we took him out of the race at that stage and it meant we had a free day. I hadn't intended to go racing at all and dressed informally in a pair of jeans and a Tee-shirt and got into a celebratory mood early. Then we decided to go racing and Carmel, my wife, was driving. We got to the gate into the Owners' and Trainers' car park which was across the Track. I remember it as a beautiful day and the man on the gate told us we weren't getting in. I told him who I was. He just didn't believe me and said, 'Everybody tells me something like that. Off you go or I'll get the Guards'. I shot up through the sun-roof and said 'I am Noel Meade' but he still would have none of it. 'Listen,' he said, 'I know Noel and his lads and you're not Noel.' Anyway he got the Gardaí and they wouldn't believe me either. At this stage there was a huge back-up of cars and horns blaring and so I left the car with the keys in my hand and one of the Gardaí told me he'd arrest me if I didn't move the car. Then Carmel eventually found my driving license and we all laughed.

THE UPS AND DOWNS

"The worst day I ever had in Galway was the day *Dromod Hill* broke down in the Galway Hurdle. He was after doing a '*Pinch Hitter*' on it, winning the McDonogh on the Tuesday. I firmly believed all he had to do to win was to go around. But whether he put his foot in a hole or whatever he did, he broke down very badly on both front legs jumping the second last hurdle. He was an exceptionally good flat racer and had the potential to win Group races. He was still a colt and is still at stud. I always regretted it afterwards for running him in the Galway Hurdle as there were plenty of flat races still to be won by him. I took that very badly because I shouldn't have run him. The year was 1987. So far I have been concentrating on the highs but we had quite a few downs too.

"There is no such a thing as a certainty in racing. You can have *Nijinsky* or indeed any horse and never be sure of winning. O.K. the better the horse the better the chance but something can always go wrong. Of all the horses I have trained the most genuine were *Pinch Hitter* and *Steel Duke*. They hardly ever ran a bad race. The second year *Pinch Hitter* won the Hurdle as a five-year-old he was beaten by a neck in the McDonogh in which he ran an excellent race. That year he just got pushed wider and wider coming up the straight and just couldn't get out and get a run. He didn't like to be in front for too long but was a very tough genuine horse.

PAUL CARBERRY

"Paul has fantastic flair and fabulous talent. He has the ability to be as good as his father Tommy and as good as there is. He can be another Maguire but he just needs to keep himself steady. He is so full of life. He has tons of natural talent and it is a pity his weight went too high for the flat. But he has settled down now. Talking of jockeys it would be very remiss of me if I didn't pay tribute to Stephen Craine. He was the life and soul of Galway for us. He was with me here for years after he finished his apprenticeship. Along with being a very good jockey he was also good fun. He neither gave nor expected quarter from anyone. I know Mick Kinane is outstanding in the world scene and you can't compare anyone else in Ireland with him today because he has got to such heights and is a thorough professional and a lovely fellow too. But he has the backing of a strong team behind him especially since he started riding for the Arabs as well. Mick is the same fellow I met when himself and Stephen came out of apprenticeship together. He has matured of course. Jonjo O'Neill was a big hero in England when he rode *Pinch Hitter* for me. A very nice fellow but he was basically an English jockey. Based in England, he just arrived in Galway for the day and rode *Pinch Hitter* very well. I remember Stephen Craine giving him instructions on how to ride him before his first Galway Hurdle win. The second year Jonjo told me that even though he won, the horse was never travelling that well through the race because he felt he was feeling his legs, which he was, because we actually poured so much water on his legs through that whole Summer that his feet started to rot. In fact we had to stand him up on a draining board, to keep the water out from under his feet. He was a very difficult horse to train. Mick Kinane is the best flat race jockey I've ever seen. I'd rate him in the same league as Piggott. Through his years he has never got into trouble and he has proved his worth by winning on half chances. He is the most stylish jockey to watch, and as good riding a mile and a half maiden in Clonmel as in winning a big race at Ascot. You get the same value from him in Clonmel as you'd get from him anywhere.

NATIONAL HUNT JOCKEYS

"Of late Charlie Swan has broken all the records and he is a very good jockey but for me, I was always a great fan of Tommy Carberry, Paul's father, who like Paul had great natural flair, great feeling for a horse. When he was riding for you, whatever it was about him, he could ride winners. Even on bad horses there were times he could coax them to win. I had great time too for Tommy Carmody, a thorough professional and a brilliant jump jockey. Some jockeys lose their nerve as they approach the end of their careers. That never happened to Carberry or Carmody. Things have changed in Ireland. Charlie Swan is a thorough professional and he plays a great percentage game. He only rides horses he thinks will win, especially in novice chases for instance. He only rides horses he fancies and he is the perfect diplomat, a great man to talk to a trainer or owner. As soon as he comes into a parade ring, he exudes confidence and this is infectious. He knows the horse he is going to ride because he has looked him up, knows his form, the ground he likes. He has his homework done both on his own mount and on his rivals too. And for a champion jockey he is very young. In England it has become more the norm now that the top jockeys ride the top horses. Maguire,

Dunwoody, Williamson, Osborne, Dwyer all have their agents and they themselves don't have to work so hard to get their rides. They are hardly ever sitting in the weigh room. Before this the top jockeys would ride for their own stables and maybe one other stable. Nowadays the top jockeys would ride in every race. Take Cheltenham, those top jockeys are picked up for practically every race. The duels between Maguire and Dunwoody for leading jockey have generated a lot of hype but have been fed on sensational journalism. Hardly a day goes by but when you pick up the paper it's Adrian this or Richard that. This is pushed at you all the time and it does build up the hype no end. Both are nice lads despite it all. I have the greatest of admiration for Adrian Maguire, another Meathman. It was all thrust on him when he was very young and many a good rider who had the same success as he had at his age went the wrong way. He has only ridden a few times for me but he has impressed me with his ability on these occasions. He has kept his head.

THE FUTURE

"Originally when I started training, my horses were practically all jumpers. Around 1977 we switched towards training flat horses which is kindergarten stuff comparing to training jumpers. Vincent O'Brien was the greatest trainer of all time. I don't think anyone will ever do what he did with jumpers first and then the flat. It was probably as easy for Vincent to be as good as he was with flat horses after being as good as he was with jumpers. The record he had in Cheltenham with twenty-three winners was unbelievable. The ones he didn't win, he was second in. We reached a stage where we were 75% flat 25% jump. In the last few years it has moved back the other way and at the moment it is 50/50, probably more jumpers than flat. When the Aga Khan moved his horses out of England, he sent half of his string to Ireland and the rest to France and he alone caused owners to switch from flat horses back to jumpers, because they couldn't compete with him on the flat. His horses were very well bred and were on tour practically, picking up races in places like Wexford and Sligo. Every year he had fifty maidens coming out to win a total of ninety races which altogether lessened the pool of Irish owners. They couldn't compete. In my stable we generally have fifty to sixty horses.

HOPES FOR GALWAY

"I'd love to win the Plate and the Hurdle again. I've won the Hurdle only twice and been second in it three times. *Rushmoor* beat *Fane Ranger* in 1986 and I was very annoyed because I felt we were unfairly handicapped. *Fane Ranger* carried 12-0 to *Rushmoor's* 10-8 and on a line through *Rushmoor* with the English Champion hurdler of the day namely, *See You Then*, my horse was wrongly handicapped. That was one second. *Natural Ability* was second to *Natalie's Fancy* and *Mubadir* was second to *Camden Buzz*. And as I've said I have been second and third in the Plate. We will be giving both a bash in 1995 and afterwards. Galway gets bigger and bigger every year. You can't compare Galway with Cheltenham because Cheltenham is a National Hunt Group 1 Festival but through the holiday fixtures, which in Ireland have got bigger and bigger in places such as Galway, Tralee, Listowel and Killarney, a great excitement precedes the Galway Festival week especially. Every year you more or less pick out your horses well in advance and prepare for Galway. You need to plan well for both the Plate and the Hurdle. Both are handicaps and if you go up in the weights by winning smaller races your chances are lessened. If you have a horse capable of winning either, you have to start minding them. Usually you look to Galway for the next big prizes after Punchestown in April. The top Galway events are worth a lot of money now. You go from one Festival to another Fairyhouse — Punchestown — Killarney — Galway — Tralee — Listowel — Christmas at Leopardstown. Galway hasn't been as good to me over the last number of years as it was in the years before that. You need the right type of horses for it and perhaps the good days are looming again."

After the interview Noel brought me on a tour of his stable and the gallops. He got on so well with all his horses, *Coq Hardi Affair* who fell the previous weekend at the last fence with the race sewn up getting a special friendly pat, little *Bob Devani*, a great servant, *Heist* and others. His living room walls are covered with framed photos of horses winning at venues everywhere with suitable captions overhead. We talked of his other great love, Gaelic football and his reverence for men like Seán Boylan, Colm O'Rourke, Brian Stafford and the late Noel Keating of Kepak the main sponsors of Meath football.

"I called one of my horses Staff after Brian Stafford but unlike Brian he didn't turn out to be a winner. I called another horse *Rourkey* after Colm, whom I admire very much as one of the great players of all time, but I changed his name when I thought he wasn't going to be a good one. But he has won three races for me! I have great admiration for Seán Boylan who is responsible for the strength of Meath football. We were all devastated when Noel Keating of Kepak died a few years ago. His son owns *Mubadir*, third in last year's Plate. Many of the Meath lads are very fond of racing and I meet them regularly at the Navan meetings, lads like the up and coming Jody Devine, another racing fan."

 From The Horse's Mouth

Killarney Galway Connection

"*The winning strike rate of Killarney horses (horses which earlier in the month of July had run in Killarney) continued to improve over the years and in 1985 eleven Killarney horses won in Galway. An outstanding memory in Ballybrit that year was Pargan's devastating run up the hill under the welter burden of twelve stone seven pounds with Willie Mullins looking casually around him for non-existent dangers. The 'Amateur' had never before been won with this weight. The cheer that greeted him from the packed stands was evidence that his two cantering wins at Killarney two weeks previously, had not gone unnoticed. A whopping nineteen winners in Ballybrit in 1986 proved a real bonanza for punters who followed Killarney form.*"

Horse Racing *by Finbarr Slattery.*

8

Keeping it in the Family

The Collen sisters Ann and Sarah Pioneered Galway Plate History in 1987 and 1989.

*V*ery unusual indeed that two sisters of a family should pioneer Galway Plate history but the Collen sisters Ann and Sarah did just that when Ann became the first lady trainer of a Galway Plate winner — *Randoss* — in 1987 and younger sister Sarah became the first lady jockey of a Galway Plate winner — *Bold Flyer* — in 1989. The latter horse was trained by Jim Dreaper and both horses were owned by the girls' father Standish Collen from Kinsealy near Malahide, County Dublin, a well-known businessman (Contractor) and interested in horses all his life. Ann's achievement first.

"We grew up with horses. My grandfather rode. Every one of us rode from an early age. I wasn't two years old when I joined the hunt on a donkey and I have a photo to prove it. I've never known anything else.

"I used to go to Jim Dreaper's to ride out over there. So watching him in action gave me a hint of what needed to be done. I read every book on the subject that I could lay my hands on. I love to get every bit of information possible on a subject. Jim Dreaper and myself were born on the same day. We were in a pony club together. We were good friends. Here in Kinsealy I had no gallops apart from Portmarnock strand nearby. Jim let me work my horses on his gallops and but for that facility I'd never have got going.

"I had a good horse first called *Larry's Latest* which won seven races for me. He got badly injured and I ended up with no horse to train. Jim had been training *Randoss*. We bought him from Jim as a five-year-old and he had won three or four races including one in Galway. The horse was on his summer holidays on the farm here so Jim said, 'Why don't you take him over and train him next season?', which was very generous and typical of the man. That was 1986 and thus began my training partnership with *Randoss*.

LARRY'S LATEST

"*Larry's Latest* was my very first winner. He used to show jump and hunt as well. I trained another horse called *East Wall*, my first runner in Galway. Not a happy experience for me as the lorry I was driving to Galway came to a grinding halt in Kilbeggan *en route*. So we had to hitch a lift for the horse. Colm Magnier gave a lift to both the horse and my stable lad William Condron and I had to stay in Kilbeggan. The horse ran and got placed.

"*Randoss*'s first race for me was down in Thurles on ground he hated and he ran very well to be third. So we aimed for the Findus Chase at Leopardstown with a nice light weight for a young horse on the way up, a race he won against the odds. He got the three-mile trip and ground he liked. He liked firm ground and that is why we began to think of Galway from an early stage. Ken Morgan, the jockey, was very keen on Galway. He didn't ride him in the Findus because he couldn't do the weight. He was Jim Dreaper's stable jockey at the time and knew the horse well and had ridden for me all along. Martin Lynch rode *Randoss* to victory in the Findus.

"So the preparation for the Galway Plate was hectic. As usual I made use of my kind neighbourly trainers such as Paddy Griffin in Rolestown, situated between Jim Dreaper's stables and mine. I used his ploughed up facilities once a week. I rode him all the time myself and used Donabate and Portmarnock strands a lot. Part of the joy of training a horse is to be able to ride him yourself on gallops. He was in great form all along.

"I'm a pessimistic woman and never really hoped for anything special in Galway that year. I'm usually in a worse state than the horse. No relaxing. A lot of fussing. I hoped and hoped. But with steeplechasing so much can go wrong. Some other horse can fall in front of yours. The horse can trip up on landing. There is so much luck involved. I knew he was in good form because he had run well in Down Royal in preparation.

MARGARET TIMOTHY

"One thing I remember well. Our housekeeper Margaret Timothy, a devout Catholic, when she was ironing the colours to be worn by Ken, she sprinkled holy water on them. It was the first time that was ever done in our house. Ken knew the horse well and I had great faith in him. Then to the Owners' and Trainers' Stand and I remember being right up at the top of it with my father. There was a false start that year which made it even more nerve-wracking. He got a good start. Got near the front and jumped well for the first circuit. Then *Bavamour*, the favourite, fell at the fence after the stands. That was a relief but even then it could have gone all wrong as he was in front of us. Then we were lying second. About five fences out *Randoss* took the lead and my heart started to thump. Would he last out? *Supper Furrow*, the top weight, was catching up going into the dip. *Randoss* had two super jumps at the last two fences. He pinged both and won the race there. He stayed on up the hill on the rail. I raced down to the Parade Ring. It was a fantastic feeling. We had a great crowd of supporters there. William Condron, my right hand man, led him in. Great excitement. My father hugged me. The Bakers, who bred the great *Arkle*, the Leemans from Fermanagh, Paddy Griffin were all there. Being the shy sort, I let my father do the talking. It was a brilliant feeling. I took the horse back to the stables and remember being invited to the Committee Room, where I celebrated with one glass of champagne with Lord Killanin and friends. I was in a daze and we gave the horse a good hour to recover. Gave him some grass and had him out beside the lorry with his rug on, inscribed with Digital Galway Plate Winner 1987. It was a great feeling. I kept looking at him saying, 'Did he really do it?' Then the long drive home.

EVA DODD

"*Randoss* went back to Galway in September without success. The ground wasn't as good as in August. Then he ran once in Tipperary a month after. He broke down getting ready for Galway the following year and never really raced with any success afterwards due to the injured tendon. He lives with us here in Kinsealy. He has been used as a hack off and on and has a lovely temperament. A few days after Galway we had a great party with the breeder Eva Dodd from Ballyboughal. Eva is a great old campaigner.

"Ken Morgan the jockey was thrilled with the success. I'm still training my one or two horses. I thought the Galway Plate win might have attracted some outside owners but it didn't. A bit of a disappointment that, but I don't think I'd have coped with a large string of horses. It is enjoyable when you have just a few. At the moment I'm training *Bold Flyer*, now aged twelve. Jim Dreaper trained him for the Plate in 1989 but I won a couple of races with him in Down Royal. It was the fastest run Galway Plate up to then. Finally, I'd like to thank our neighbour and friend Charlie Haughey for the use of his indoor riding school. It is difficult to get jumping experience on grass during the Summer months on the hard ground. We used to give the horse a few pops around loose to get his eye in, which we found very helpful."

After the interview Ann brought me to see *Randoss, Bold Flyer* and *Kilkilowen,* another former star belonging to the Collens.

SARAH'S SUCCESS IN 1989

Michael O'Farrell (*The Irish Times*) in a tribute to Sarah Collen being the first woman to ride a Galway Plate winner wrote, "Sailing over the last two fences Sarah Collen on princely novice *Bold Flyer* came home, easing down by eight lengths having made all the running in the Galway Plate. The huge crowd rose as much to the winning jockey Sarah Collen as to a young horse with jumping powers reminiscent of the same owner's *Kilkilowen.*" Trainer Jim Dreaper said, "He jumped terrifically under Sarah Collen, riding for the first time over this difficult course. With ten winners to her credit she has now lost her seven pounds claim. This determined young rider, who is married to amateur Ray Jennings, is a daughter of the winning owner Standish Collen, whose other daughter Ann trained another horse owned by him, *Randoss,* to win the Plate two years ago."

BY ACCIDENT

Sarah got into horses more or less by accident. "I never did my Intermediate Certificate. So there was nothing else I was qualified to do except to work with horses. It turned out I wasn't too bad at them. Never really liked them that much to tell you the truth but they have been good to me. That I can't deny.

"As to riding I enjoyed working with the race horses more so than the show jumping. I liked the thrill, the speed of the flat, and the jumping of course. I started off riding in bumpers and point-to-point. I rode *Bold Flyer* in all his races for my father except for one hurdle race when Ken Morgan rode him. The horse was very precious to my father and he wasn't over-keen on my riding him in novice chases, a bit iffy about me in novice events. I insisted because I never liked to have people say all she had to do was step aboard a 'made' horse and on she goes. He was in his novice season, a six-year-old, when he won in Galway.

"I won a bumper on *Bold Flyer* in 1988 and a few chases before the Galway event. We won a three-mile-chase at Roscommon. That day he made every yard of the running, surprising Jim Dreaper, and won by about twenty lengths. He also won at Gowran. So he was well prepared for Galway.

GALWAY

"Galway is a great place. I had been to Galway before often. Galway isn't a place I'd go to to ride and spend a few days there. You'd need to be a fit man or woman to take in Galway. It is a twenty hour a day place — special. That year my father kept me out of trouble! We stayed in Sweeney's Hotel in Oughterard. A lovely place. Quiet.

"I never quite realised the Galway Plate was such a big event. Not till afterwards. The day after the success. Making the front page of *The Irish Times*. Blimey, that's not bad. The six o'clock and nine o'clock news. But I'm going ahead. The atmosphere beforehand was electric."

I was shown a video of the race and some special photographic albums kept by the owner as very proud exhibits to complement the Galway Plate replicas holding pride of place in two rooms of the house. What gave Sarah her greatest thrills during the race?

Mickey Tully (right) winning the 1946 Galway Hurdle clad in the Corinthians jersey, on board his own Fair Pearl, getting the better of the 1945 winner, King of the Jungle, ridden by Danny Morgan. Note the riding styles in vogue then. Mickey later lost the race on a technicality.

Alberoni, farthest from the camera, trained by Vincent O'Brien, gets his nose past Lucky Dome to win the 1952 Galway Plate to the obvious delight of spectators surrounding the winning post.

Vincent O'Brien won the Galway Plate in 1952 with Alberoni. Here he is photographed behind the Main Stand with the winning horse held by his owner Mr H.H.M. Stanley. Alberoni earlier that year won the Irish Grand National.

Arthur Helliwell, *(right) on his tour of Ballybrit before writing a column for "The People"on the Galway Races, meets up with well-known Tuam King of the Infield, Tom McNally. Tom is still alive and well in Tuam.*

1952 Galway Hurdle: Warrenscourt Lad ridden out by T.P.Burns takes first place from Cloncaw (2nd) and Cool Water (3rd) to the cheers of spectators on the rails.

Mrs D.J. Duggan (wife of owner) leads in Warrenscourt Lad, the winner of the 1952 Galway Hurdle, ridden by T.P.Burns.

A crowd scene from the Stand at the Galway Races of 1957. Were you there?

The 1957 Galway Hurdle winner Tymon Castle with Willie Robinson on board, being led in by owner Mrs P. Meehan.

The great Paddy Sleator, a Galway maestro, checking the Galway fences with W. D. Kelly (Committee) and former Course Foreman Mick Connolly.

1957 Plate Finish: Knight Errant (ridden by Bobby Beasley) easily wins the Galway Plate from New Hope and Nickleby. This was one of Paddy Sleator's many Galway Festival successes.

Galway Plate Presentation 1957: Mr Joe Young (Chairman) presents the Galway Plate to Mrs B. Biddle after her horse Knight Errant, ridden by Bobby Beasley, had won it. Also in the picture are Galway Committee members, Alderman Michael O'Flaherty and Mr G.D.Naughton (extreme right).

Full of tents, activities and people,
this is what the infield free area used to look like in Ballybrit.

A closer look at another tented scene from the free infield area.

Parading before the start of the Galway Plate in the 1950s.
The crowds were huge then, too.

Another parade scene before the Galway Plate of a later date.

Papal visit to Ballybrit on 30 Sept. 1979: His Holiness the Pope blesses the assembled youth of Ireland in Ballybrit to the obvious joy of Capt Luke Mullins, Bishop Magee of Cloyne and Canon Leslie Forrest among others. That day saw Ballybrit's greatest ever assembly of people.

The Hunt: The Galway Blazers led by T. McDermott-Kelly (Former Chairman of the Galway Race Committee) and including near rear of photo, Lord Killanin (also a former Chairman).

The visit of Seán T. Ó Ceallaigh as President of Ireland to Ballybrit is recorded here with (from left) Alderman Joe Costelloe, Mr Joe Young (Chairman) and on the extreme right, Lord and Lady Killanin.

Galway Races 1977, President's visit: Front: G.D.Naughton, President Hillery, Lord Killanin (Chairman), Brigadier E.R.Mahoney. Back: W.D.Kelly (Manager), J. Brennan, P. O'Flaherty, R. Kelly, R. Rooney, J.D.Coyle, Lord Hemphill, G.V. Malcomson,Capt. L. Mullins (Sec) and P.D.Ryan.

The 1980s: Another crowd scene showing the Betting Ring (with the Terry Rogers umbrella) and in the distance the Parade Ring, the office, the Weighroom and the ancillary buildings including the stables.

Galway Plate Presentation 1986: Mrs Charmain D.Hill, owner of winner, Boro Quarter, being presented with the Galway Plate by Derek McHugh, Digital, with Paddy Ryan presiding. Mrs Hill was better known as the owner of Dawn Run.

Phil Cahill and her sister, Brid McMahon, were much photographed on Ladies' Day in the past. This photograph was taken in 1979.

Most Elegant Lady 1989
Ms Arlene Capot (France).

Most Elegant Lady 1992
Ms Gillian Bagnall,
Tullamore, Co. Offaly.

Former Taoiseach Albert Reynolds with John Moloney (Racecourse Manager) who was being presented with The Racecourse of the Year Award for 1991.

Simon Kelly, the course architect, observing the construction of the new stand at Ballybrit.

Tom Broderick, the man in charge of course upkeep, surveys the scene at Ballybrit.

Mícheál O' Hehir who helped to make the Galway Races so popular.

Lord Hemphill, Chairman of the Galway Race Committee, escorting President Mary Robinson, on her visit to the Galway Races in 1994. Also in the photograph is Mrs Breda Ryan, wife of Paddy Ryan.

Charlie Swan receiving a presentation from Ms C Byrne owner of Camden Buzz.

Faces from the 1993 Festival

Faces from the 1994 Festival

"The second last fence the last time round. I must have been up in the air for a few seconds. It felt a long time. A super jump. He was a brilliant jumper. There was just one fence he didn't jump as well as the rest. He just pecked a little on landing over the last. He could hear the loose horse behind him and had his eye on the wing of the fence. I had one or two beads of perspiration, yes, but we survived and then we were coming up the hill. I took a look behind and knew we were away in a hack at that stage. I had a job pulling him up after the post. He'd have gone round again. The horse he was in those days, he'd stay alright and he had a turn of foot. Looking back on it all now I wasn't really worried.

THE RECEPTION AFTERWARDS

"Amazing. The crowd was terrific. The Parade Ring. The Weighroom. Jim Dreaper was chatting to me about the race. Then Ted Walsh grabbed me by the hand saying, 'Come on, come on, come on'. I wasn't expecting to be interviewed on television. 'Let me brush my hair and put a bit of lipstick on,' I said. 'No, no, no,' said Ted, and then I was on television. From there, it was radio straight afterwards. All buzz. The other jockeys were all great. All delighted for me. All the National Hunt lads are so generous. They are real sportsmen, more than their flat counterparts anyway! I remember meeting the French Ambassador. And there was loads of drink. I wasn't too bad because I'm a fair woman! I'm able to go a gallop. It was only about eight hours later I got a bit overcome. My father bought me a lobster that night out in Sweeney's. Great place. It was packed to the doors. The owner Pat Higgins had fifty pounds on me and he's not a betting man at all. Great sing song. Don't remember when I went to bed, four or five in the morning. Then all the papers and a bottle of champagne were delivered to my room. I drank champagne in the bath reading the papers. God, this is it. On top of the world.

AFTER GALWAY

"Five days after that I rode a 20/1 winner in the Phoenix Park. On the flat. Both the flat and the jumping had their own attractions. I find them quite different. I rode at nine stone. I'm expecting my second child now but I keep myself fit walking five or six miles a day. I'm not good on dates but I was married and had a two-year-old child when I won in

Galway. Claire is with me here today and is out riding her own pony at the moment. Afterwards I rode winners for the Aga Khan, for Sheik Mohammed and I rode a winner around Galway afterwards for Robert Sangster. The greatest thrill of all was winning the Galway Plate and Galway is special to me. I just rode there three times and won twice, the Plate and a flat race for Robert Sangster in his famous colours. Wow! No wonder Galway is special to me. I'll be in Japan when the book is launched. Please bring me back again to Galway.

THE PHOTO

"I'm looking at the photo you intend using of *Bold Flyer* jumping the first fence in the Plate. Over at the far side of the fence you'll see a jockey in conversation with a bystander. That was the late David Parnell, son of Buster, who died in a traffic accident afterwards. I remember David coming up to me before the race and wishing me well as he chatted to me. It is obvious he had his fingers crossed cheering me on. David was first jockey for Kevin Prendergast and a good friend."

STANDISH COLLEN, THE OWNER

Standish Collen is over eighty now and lives next door to former Taoiseach Charlie Haughey, with whom he rides out many mornings on Portmarnock strand. He too loves Galway.

"I have gone to the Galway Races for over sixty years. Went there with my father as a boy and I can very well remember it as a two-day event, Plate Day and Hurdle Day and I've seen it develop from two days right up to six days. The atmosphere in those days was as it is now, special. The Plate always appealed to me. The bigger fences, the greater thrill. For that reason the Plate and the Irish Grand National were my great aims once I started to own race horses in the fifties. I never won the Grand National, getting third and seventh in it. *Randoss* ran well in it. I had other good horses like *Kilkilowen* and *Feltrim Hill Lad* whom I owned jointly with Patricia Leeman. *Kilkilowen* was the best horse I ever owned and was the making of my daughter Sarah. He was a big horse and one of the best horses on the circuit at the time winning a good few races, running in Ascot, Aintree and Cheltenham.

GALWAY

"Galway, despite going to six days since my day, has kept its flavour. One of my first memories is of sitting in the jockey's room and hearing my father giving instructions to a jockey on behalf of an owner, whom he represented. That was in the late twenties about 1926. In latter years I have made Sweeney's Hotel in Oughterard my stamping ground. We had two rare old nights there in 1987 and 1989. Nights and days, round the clock. I had recommended *Randoss* to friends in Galway in 1987, and to the people in Oughterard I said *Bold Flyer* with nine stone seven pounds would win. I'm not a punter myself but I gave my judgment and they accepted it. So the success was sweet for many in Oughterard. Sweeney's was packed and there was a sing-song which went on in 1989 long after I went to bed. Pat Higgins had a very late night."

From The Horse's Mouth

Plate Day 1960 spoilt by rain. Sleator's fifth win.

"*It was a most miserable day at Galway yesterday when rain spoilt Galway Plate day. The Plate was won for the fifth time by Paddy Sleator who trained the first two horses home Sparkling Flame (first) and Clipador (second).*"

— *Irish Independent.*

9

Following your own Instinct

"Dawn Run won her third bumper in Galway ridden by my brother Tom"

— *Willie Mullins, Trainer.*

*P*addy Mullins from Goresbridge, County Kilkenny next door to Gowran Park is regarded as the Grand Old Man of National Hunt Racing in Ireland. A very quiet man he has no intention just yet of handing over the reins, so to speak, though his two sons Willie and Tony have set up their own training stables close-by. The Mullins name is legendary in Ballybrit over the years between Galway Plate, Hurdle and Amateur Handicap victories. I visited the stables of Willie Mullins on a bright April day this year to assess this Mullins thing and Galway. Was it inevitable that Willie would travel along the same road as his legendary father?

"I don't think so. I went to school in Mount Saint Joseph's, Roscrea, did my Leaving Certificate there and didn't think horses would be my life anymore than any of the other options held in front of me then. It wasn't until I got much older that I decided what I was going to do. In Goresbridge, in my youth, I suppose we had horses for breakfast, dinner and tea. We all played different games at school but amongst ourselves we very seldom talked about football, hurling or anything like that. It was horses mostly. There were five of us, George, Tony, Tom the youngest, Sandra our lone sister and myself and we were all totally interested in horses. You'd get fond of certain horses, build up a kind of relationship with them, but you wouldn't get fond of all of them.

GALWAY

"Galway was always a tremendous high point in the Mullins household. Something we looked forward to annually. It is a tremendous meeting. My Dad had, and still has, a great affection for Galway. It is a great place to have winners. Everyone loves to have a winner there. It is just a great Festival and it has been built up steadily over the years from two to six days. Everyone is on holiday and usually the weather is good and people are just in a real good mood. One of my first memories of Galway was the wet Festival meeting of 1974 when *Bunclody Tiger* won the Plate on a Friday, when the two fences in the dip were left out. We used to stay with Mrs Kennedy in Loyola Park close to the Dog Track. She used to fix all of us up year after year. Usually we drive up and down nowadays. You want to get home and see your own horses in the morning. I know that road very well now.

"The other high points of the year began with having a good horse for Fairyhouse at Easter, then Punchestown, the Christmas meetings of course, if you can for Cheltenham or Aintree and Listowel is another great Festival meeting. If you have a horse you might fancy for some of the big races in Galway your whole Summer is geared towards having the horse right. The three weeks or so beforehand, you are wondering what the ground is going to be like not so much what the opposition is going to be as you have a fair idea of that and all your plans hinge on whether it is a wet or dry Galway.

GALWAY SUCCESSES

"Of all the great Galway successes we had over the years the winner that gave me the greatest pleasure was *Pargan* winning the Amateur Handicap in 1985. He carried 12-7, a record weight for that race. He won it so easily. He was bred by my father owned by my mother, ridden by myself. A whole family thing and he wasn't a particularly big horse either. Just about sixteen hands but a very strong horse and built like a tank. That was a good thrill but I've had others along the way. *Boro Quarter*'s Galway Plate win was special because we had waited so long to win the Plate. It was one race my father always wanted to win and this had eluded him for years. Especially after winning so many other Galway races. He ran in the *Dawn Run* colours. She (*Dawn Run*) won her third bumper in Galway ridden by my brother Tom. She won easily enough that day. Winning the Gold Cup in 1986 and the three Champion Hurdles in the same year two years before that (Irish, English and French) in such a short space of time was some achievement. She is a real favourite still in Cheltenham and the memorial in her honour much admired.

"Galway has been good to me, too. I was leading jockey there one year. Some of my earlier riding successes were on *Victor's Barge* and *Billy's Cottage*. In one year I rode ten winners between all the Galway meetings and got disqualified on another one. *Dessie's Gift* was one that won the last race on the last day for me. Ken Morgan thought he had won the Jockey's Award and had stayed over to collect the prize. My horse hadn't been fancied and came in at 10/1. So Ken and myself had a laugh over that.

TRAINER

"Two or three years after I left school, at about the age of twenty-one, I made up my mind to become a trainer. I'm here at Closutton, Leighlinbridge, County Carlow for about nine years and have been training about seven of those years. We have forty boxes here, mostly NH horses and about ten flat horses for the Summer months. *Tourist Attraction*'s Cheltenham success this year has been my greatest training achievement and I also rode *Skehanagh Bridge* to get third this year in the Festival Bumper. I rode two winners in Cheltenham, the first on *Hazy Dawn* in 1982 and *Mac's Friendly* a few years later. Cheltenham is another great place to ride a winner in. Comparing Cheltenham and Galway, it's a great feeling to ride a winner in both. You certainly hear the crowd, especially if you arrive in either place at the bottom of the hill and with a chance of winning. If you happen to hit the front, the roar that goes up can stop horses, certainly if they are a bit timid. You can hear the roar but you're too busy at your job to be affected by it.

COMPARISON

"Galway in comparison with other tracks is very tight, more so on fast Summer ground. You either have to be up there out of trouble or you come around on the outside. If you get caught in, in Galway, you're finished. Races in Galway are usually fast and well run in the Summer and invariably horses go too fast. Getting up that hill takes some effort but if you can come with a sweeping run without getting into any trouble you have a great chance of winning in Galway. It's hard to compare the two hills, Cheltenham and Galway and you can only appreciate both if you walk the courses and stand in the dip in either place. Television tends to flatten the scene out a lot. It's usually twice as steep as people imagine it when they walk it for the first time. They're both very tough. My own ambition for Galway is to win a Galway Plate most of all. There is a great tradition about it and it is a very old race.

LUKE MULLINS AND GALWAY

"Having my uncle Luke as Secretary/Manager of Galway gave an added dimension to Galway for the Mullins family. He did a tremendous job on the Track with the aid of a good Committee behind him. While he was there, the Track was really transformed into a top Racetrack. He levelled out a lot of the bumps, cambered bends, put in proper rails and the work he did on the fences was appreciated by all, especially jockeys. He constructed good Summer chasing fences as distinct from Winter fences and it was a pleasure to ride around these fences. His input into the Track is something many people wouldn't realise but which jockeys and trainers certainly did.

"As to how the three Mullins trainers, father and two sons, cope with each other, there are no problems really. Tony tended to ride from the front, me from the back. We often discuss different horses and training methods and we would share a lot of our experiences across the board. If we had a problem, we would go to Dad with it but we have seen so much over the years ourselves, we probably know the answer before we go. The experience of being brought up with him is a great help, his advice is good but nearly always is to follow your own instinct. My wife Jackie rides and so does Tony's wife. In fact the three Mullins ladies often ride in the same race, Jackie, Tony's wife and Sandra my sister. We always wish each other the best all the time and there is great friendship between all of us. My father has no intention of handing on the reins in the foreseeable future.

"Sometimes punters wonder what kind of advice is proffered by trainers and owners to jockeys in the Parade Ring. A lot of the time if you have your own stable jockey, the trainer knows that he has to trust the jockey. If the horse is one he hasn't ridden before you might say to him that the horse prefers to be up there or maybe not. I'd rather give the jockey a free hand and let him be confident going out that he can do what he wants to do. There's the difference between a good and a bad jockey. The good fellow will disregard your instructions sometimes and go and do what's in his own head. Sometimes he'd be wrong and you just have to take that. That's part of the sport. I have given out to a jockey betimes — ask Frank Woods! Human nature ordains that you have to be critical of the man you're paying if you think he/she was at fault. It doesn't mean I'd fall out with the jockey. Just that I'd be annoyed about a certain thing on a certain day. If he gives the horse what I think is a bad ride I have to let him know that if he is to continue riding the horse. He'll look at the race again on replay and assess what I thought and I do the same as well. There are some great highs in racing and so many lows. It is really a life of disappointments but when you get that one good horse to win, that one good winner wipes the whole thing clear. If you had just two horses you'd never have the two right on the same day. That sums it up. The day everything comes right, comes so seldom. Everything went right for *Tourist Attraction* at Cheltenham this year. She hit the last hurdle the only thing she did wrong but she still had enough in the tank to come up the hill and win.

GALWAY MEMORIES

"I was about twelve or thirteen the first time I went to Galway with a schoolfriend of mine Barry McIntyre and I think we had a fiver each coming out of the Races. We ran into a three-card-trick man on our way out and pushed our way through to the front of a milling crowd. It was my first time ever seeing the three-card-trick and we couldn't get over how easy it was to find the lady. It was a cinch. Barry proffered his fiver and found the lady. Someone grabbed us and pulled us out. Obviously we had been used as bait to grab other punters who would be duly fleeced. So Galway started off lucky for us. Winning money off both the horses and the three-card-trick man. Hopefully, I'll win the Plate yet!

CENTRE

"Where I train is a great centre for training horses. Tom Foley who trains *Danoli* is just on the other side of Bagenalstown. Jim Bolger's Coolcullen is just up the hill, four miles from here as the crow flies. Pat Fahy, who trains *Nuaffe,* stables at Leighlinbridge. Then Dad is only five miles away and Tony is beside the racetrack in Gowran. Pat Hughes trains close by too. There is great employment from the industry in this area. We have ten working here including ourselves. My father and Jim Bolger would employ much more. We tend to help each other if needs be. We meet a lot at meetings. Peter Curling and Philip Myerscough who owned *Ventana Canyon,* and got second to us in the Sun Alliance Novice Hurdle at Cheltenham were the first people over to us to say well done. People don't mind being beaten by a friend.

BUMPER

"I mentioned *Pargan* as a great thrill in Galway. There was another. It was a two-mile and five bumper and it was the last race of the Festival. I was on *Bucko Reef* and he was favourite or near to it. I jumped off in front and there was a huge gamble on Mick O'Toole's horse ridden by Homer Scott. Homer got instructions to wait behind and I just went and I must have been a furlong clear by the time we passed the Stands first time. I remember Buster Parnell telling me he thought we were only on our way to the start I was so far in front. This couldn't possibly be a race he thought. The last circuit going out everyone was leaving the track and lined along the rails the whole way around, people shouted me on. I was so far in front they wanted to see me hold on. The cheering and the whole atmosphere was brilliant. It was like as if there was someone painted along the rails. And then when it seemed as if we'd hold on coming up the hill the place went mad. A lot of people from this area of Carlow-Kilkenny go to Galway. This place must close down during Galway Race Week. And it seemed as if every one of them was on the rails that day. The way it was done and the way the people reacted to my win is a great memory and a perfect finale to the week. We won by twenty-five to thirty lengths. Racecards were being waved. Youngsters leaned out over the rails. It was precious. Now there are double rails and people cannot get that close.

JOCKEYS

"My father thought Martin Molony the best he'd ever seen in his life-time. I never saw him but I've never heard anyone criticise him so he must have been fantastic. I always liked Tommy Carberry's style. He had a tremendous pair of hands and he would settle horses so well. He just sat up the neck and had horses settled. He rode quite short, much shorter than the present day riders. It was a style in those days. He rode with a great brain as well. He clicked into a horse the minute he sat up on one. He had great natural ability. Of present day riders, Charlie Swan also has that same natural ability. He'd get on a horse and be able to assess him/her immediately. Charlie has ridden a few winners for me. There is such demand for him it is hard to get him.

"A lot of our present day jockeys are very good and the standard gets better all the time. Riders are much more self-critical now and use video-tapes a lot to help improve. Riders are learning through a lot more schooling, getting tuition for their jumping. Race riding over jumps is evolving over the last five years or so. It is the way forward I think. The horses are as fit as they will ever be. Training seems to have gone as far as it is going to go, but the standard of jockeys across the board can rise tremendously. The top fellows have it and there are more people gaining their level. Many of them are learning the riding at a young age because there is so much more racing nowadays and the burn-out rate is high. Especially in England where jockeys are racing up and down the country day after day. Here a jockey has a much easier lifestyle with more days off for family life. In the US they race for five days and have the weekend off. You can see the benefits of it when people like Charlie Swan and Mick Kinane don't opt for what would be perceived to be better jobs in England but rather opting for a far better lifestyle in Ireland and yet take in the top races in England and abroad as it suits them. Family life gets more important to you as you get older. I can foresee the top English jockeys becoming much more choosy in the future. It has tended to go that way in the States where the top money spinners don't ride the most winners.

TONY AND TOM

"Tony and Tom had some good escapades in Galway in their younger days. When they were about six and seven years respectively they were brought to Galway and between hopping and trotting in and out of the Tote window they made a cool £20 or £30 on a Tote double for half a crown. When they came home my father sat them down, told them a few tales of gamblers going broke and not to look at it as being the be all and end all of racing and finished up saying 'I'm at horses years and years and I never made any money out of gambling'. Then Tom piped up quite seriously, 'Daddy you'll come to Galway with us the next time and we'll show you how'.

"Another time when they were a wee bit older and after the Races they had gone to Salthill to make their money in Claude Toft's Arcade at the roulette wheels. Tony did well the first night but next night Tom who wouldn't be quite as brave a gambler as Tony, gave all his money to Tony for the wheel. But Tony's luck ran out and they lost all their money. With ne'er a tosser to get a taxi back to Mrs Kennedy's place in Loyola Park, the lads bided their time, met one of their Dad's owners Eddie Morrissey told him their 'sgéal' and Eddie gave them a fiver to get a taxi. Tony grabbed the fiver, shot straight back to Claude's, slapped it all on, lost it again. Tom's face wasn't at all amused, being always more serious. Tony giggled away but Tom said quite sincerely 'Don't make me laugh because I don't want to laugh'. So they had to leg it home in silence, Tom with smoke coming out his ears! We often talk of these little escapades when Galway starts to come round every year."

10

"The Better Bettor"

"You begin to look towards Winter once the Racing Festival is over."
— *John Mulholland, former Mayor of Galway, owner of a chain of Bookie shops in Galway.*

John is better known in Galway as "The Better Bettor" as his advertising slogan proclaims. Son of former Galway All-Ireland football star Ned, a bookmaker himself, he also inherits a great musical tradition and as a talented pianist is the life and soul of many post-racing celebratory social events. He was an excellent Mayor of the City of the Tribes and is also a very useful golfer, counting Christy O'Connor Junior among his closest friends. He got a love of the Galway Races early in life.

"My first memory of Galway Races was of *Carraroe* winning the Galway Plate in 1962. I remember Fred Winter came over from England to ride her and I can still see myself running down afterwards to the winner's enclosure and I managed to get Fred Winter's autograph with the saddle still in his hands. I just walked in and got Fred's signature. The same day I had five bob on the winner at 4/1 and I had the Tote double up with a horse called *Four Aces*. So that was a big thrill.

EARLY SCHOOLDAYS

"After that I was boarding in Saint Mary's College and sometimes we'd get up in the middle of the night and have a smoke in the top dormitory and during the day I remember being able to see the Stand in Ballybrit from the toilet windows upstairs where we'd be smoking and pining for the Summer and the Races. At that time there was only two days racing,

Wednesday and Thursday but it was absolutely magic. The mystique of those two days was next door to the Christmas feeling. My father used to run a book at the races but he was finished with his Course activities when I started going. He then had bookmaker's shops in Galway and Athlone. I didn't always intend to be a bookie, but when I was in UCG doing a BA degree, I often whiled away the time during boring lectures working out new ways of making up bets quickly. The bookie business is nerve wracking and can be disheartening. If you don't try to get rich quickly, in the long run the odds are in your favour because bookmakers make the odds. If you can tread out the time when things are going badly for you, inevitably you'll finish on top. As long as you can keep the turnover that is the important thing. That is why during the Galway Races everybody looks at what the Tote Turnover was and how it compared with the previous year's turnover. My Dad came over to me in London where I'd moved shortly after leaving college, and told me he was getting fed up of the betting game and showed me the figures of the two shops and offered me one of them if I was interested to carry on the family tradition. He was closing them down if I didn't show interest. That was 1970. So I came back and started in Williams Street West with old Pat Frieze an ex-captain in the Army. He taught me the technical part of the whole scene even though I had a general idea of it.

GROUP FROM SPIDDAL

"Pat was a great Irish speaker having been interned in the Curragh in the thirties. They started their own Irish classes in the Curragh and that's where Máirtín Standún from An Spidéal, who died recently, got his love of Gaeilge. Some of the men from Spiddal were great clients — men like Máirtín Folan, Tommy Hughes, Máirtín Standún and Pat Frieze — and Dad had great rapport with them. They had their own Irish speaking circle. Máirtín Thornton as well. In fact Máirtín was one of the first people to start betting on gaelic football and hurling games in a big way.

"I now have a chain of eight shops in Galway. Every betting shop in Galway is packed at Galway Races time. I turn over six times my normal during race week. And you have Goodwood on that week too. Bigger by far than my returns for Cheltenham. The Aintree Grand National meeting would be next especially since it became a three-day Festival and with the extra TV coverage and the advent of the SIS who supply the live pictures of all races where every race is televised in the shops. People are much more inclined to have a bet when they can be present to see what is going on before their eyes. Modern technology does help.

ON-COURSE BETTING

"I help a bookmaker named Paddy Lynam out because I love the atmosphere of the betting ring in Galway. I generally do it as it helps me to monitor the market for my shops. It is better for me to be on the course because I can back them quicker on the course, quicker than I can if I'm sitting in my head office and I can get a better price because I can see all the different prices that are there. Though it is very busy I enjoy it immensely. I meet fellows who return home just for the Races. Sometimes you might not have met them for ten years. Guys that don't even return home for Christmas. The weather is better, the crack is too and there are more people around. Most of them share the same interest as you, racing, football and hurling too. It's a huge sporting occasion. The height of the provincial finals and the All-Irelands to come. You meet Cyril Farrell, Johnny Clifford, Paddy Kehoe of Wexford, Fr Breen the great racing priest, the man who says next to God his greatest love is racing, and those great men from New York's Rosie O'Grady's Restaurants Austin Delaney and Tom Clarke. The latter pair cause a stir in the ring when they arrive. The Boiler White, a former Kildare star, is a great judge of horses. The Long Fellow Prendergast, Paddy Prendergast Junior and, of course, Seán Purcell. I tend not to socialise too much during the Races nowadays. The Hilltop was a real mecca for Dad's old football and hurling and racing friends from everywhere. I got to know a lot of them through the O'Malleys, Tony, Myles and Frank and Tommy Godwin.

"Paddy Prendergast Junior was the first man to train for the O'Malleys and they had some good winners in Galway. When I was young I used to stand in with the great Ginger Murphy, who had a bookie shop in Eyre Square and was one of the best dog men I ever met. He had a horse called *Red Hanrahan* which won in Galway and Ginger set up a great coup that year. He backed the horse from 10/1 down to 4/1. He was trained locally in Athenry by John Daly and duly won.

"I play golf a lot with Mick Kinane, whom I got to know through Christy Junior. Christy and Mick are old friends. As a jockey he is the best in the world today. Sheik Mohammed has the choice of all jockeys in the world and yet he comes to Ireland for Mick. He must be the first man ever to refuse the Sheik's offer. The Sheik wanted him three years ago to ride full-time for him and Mick didn't go. He made him an offer that only he could refuse!

MEMORIES

"The Players/Wills Amateur Handicap, as we used to know it, was a fine race. Dermot Weld won it a few times, so did Bunny Cox and it was hard to beat Mr W McLernon. I remember *Winning Fair* running in it. Galway is a very stiff track and if horses win there, they invariably come back and win again. Truly horses for courses applies here.

"For a lot of people the end of Festival week is the end of the year. It signals the end of the Summer in Galway. You begin to look towards Winter once the races are over. Everything in Galway revolves around them. It definitely affects tourism especially in Salthill. If you have any sort of guesthouse or a small hotel or a shop or like myself are in the betting business, this is your busiest week in the year, the week that will pay the rates for you, and when you pay off long standing bills. Without the Galway Races, Galway would be a far lesser city and would not have progressed to what it is today. Not only the Festival itself but the talk it engenders, the advertising it brings, the live television coverage for a full four days now and the fame it brings, makes Festival week the place to be in Ireland at that time.

COUPS

"The most recent coup was *King Wah Glory* last year. Prices went from 14 or 16/1 in the morning in the shops down to 4/1. The money on the course was huge. Trained by P Burke and rumoured to be owned by Christy Roche. They backed him like he was never going to be beaten and he won that way too. He won by a distance. Other coups have been brought off by feared gamblers like Noel Furlong or J P McManus. I cannot remember the specifics but they took a lot of money out of the ring and generated a lot of excitement among the bookmaking fraternity. It's the buzz a gambler gets and equally so for a bookmaker when they see something going on and you try to beat the price. I remember being stung very badly once. A fellow I knew, Tony Gleeson, a builder in London, whom I met first at a Pro-Am in Ealing, used to run a book on that tournament, which Tim Colleran, Brian Lavin and myself used to patronise in the good old days. Tim was a great racing man too. Well Tony had a horse about five years ago called *Rotherfield Greys* and he ran him in the Stewards' Cup in Goodwood. I remember in the shop in Salthill, it seemed everybody had him. I phoned Dublin and England and nobody would take any money off me as they were up to their necks with him too. I got some off but like everybody else I was caught. And he duly hacked up. I could see him for the last furlong coming and winning by a length and a half.

"Galway is really the Cheltenham of Ireland. It is everyman's festival not your top hat and tails like Ascot. The prince and the pauper are all there. Hospitality tents are there alright but there is plenty of room for everybody. Another new Stand is in the offing. The Race Committee is a very progressive one and we owe them a debt of gratitude. They always keep ahead of the posse. An often debated topic here in Galway is whether the track is used enough. Overkill is another factor. Take snooker for instance. Too much of it on telly. There is probably too much racing in Ireland as it is. Galway has just the right balance. Let's consolidate what we have not put on other days which may not live up to the hype of Festival week.

"Finally regarding the *Rotherfield Greys* coup. It was the biggest ever and you'll never have one like it again. It was the last of the major coups pulled S P. Tony had major Irish wealthy connections and they were all on the horse. The winnings went into millions. Since then and the development of telecommunications to such a sophisticated degree it is so easy to ring up now. We were stung all over the place. You can talk of the *Gay Future* stroke which was highly publicised and contained a lot of codology but Tony Gleeson's one was sorer. If you can't get the money away you're in trouble. On the course you see it all happening. The bookmakers start scrubbing. There is panic in the ring. A lot of people running. It's time to watch out."

They Make it Work

From The Horse's Mouth

The First ever Stewards of 1869.

They were:

The Marquis of Clanrickard

Viscount Bourke MP

Sir Roland Blennerhasset MP

Lord Clanmorris

Marcus Lynch

Captain Valentine Blake

Harry S. Persse

Pierce Joyce

George Morris

Captain Blake Foster

The officials were:

Manager — Mr T Waters

Hon. Sec. — Mr J Reddington, Dalysfort

Judge and Handicapper — Mr R Hunter

Junior Clerk of the Course — Mr Thomas Flynn

*Source: Rambler's Column, **Connacht Sentinel**, June 17 1958.*

11
The Chairman

"The Moneen fences are very unusual for a Steeplechase."
— Lord Hemphill.

Lord Hemphill, current Chairman of the Galway Race Committee grew up at Tulira Castle near Ardrahan and became interested in horses from early childhood.

"We always had horses there and we were very interested in the County Galway Hunt. I subsequently became Master of the Hunt in 1957 and remained so for nearly thirty years. I'm still interested in it, no longer Master, sort of Trustee of it now. In the old days, it was a very colourful scene, more of the red coats and that sort of aspect of hunting, whereas today there are a lot more people hunting and a lot of people now can't afford the fancy part of it which has got very expensive. Today, hunting is something which was a good fabric of the rural economy, and is now catering for more people who are actually in the business of both producing and hiring horses, and is very much part of the tourist industry."

He became interested in the Galway Races specifically as a boy, being brought along by his parents in the pre-World War II era.

"I'm hopeless for remembering names of the first Galway Plate or Hurdle winners but I do remember people like Harry Ussher being there then. He was one of the great trainers who himself was a Galwayman. He had an owner then, a Michael Shaw-Taylor, of Castle Taylor and they had a great horse called *The Gripper*.

TRADITION

"When I'm asked what makes Galway Races so special, I suppose it's a tradition. The Plate from a long way back has been very big. The Galway Races started near Kiltulla, where we now live, and it was one of the earliest Irish race meetings in the early days of the Irish Turf Club and National Hunt Committee. Then when it was transferred to Ballybrit over one hundred years ago, they built this double fence in the Moneen which is still famous today. That had an effect on the Galway Plate. In some extraordinary way it became almost an 'in and out' fence. It's a very unusual fence for a steeplechase and then the run-in uphill is a very long run-in which is also very unusual for a chase. Most chasing people would tell you it is too long and we saw how last year it proved too long for Eddie O'Grady's horse *Minister for Fun* and for many other horses before him. It's very often produced some strange results, with horses coming from nowhere like *Feathered Gale* last year, and nearly always great finishes. It's a handicap anyway and should produce good finishes.

"From the very early days too, Galway was given this great holiday fixture. For years and years back it has been a great holiday period in Galway. One of the reasons for its success is that we had so much emigration from the West coast since the days of the Famine and much of it was to the New World, particularly America, many to England and Australia. The Galway Races became a sort of Festival where the home folk would entertain the members of their family who had emigrated. It became a great meeting place for all and sundry. And it is still today a great meeting place for all types and kinds from Ministers of the Government down to farmers, labourers, tradesmen, professionals, and all on a level basis.

POPULARITY

"There is more movement, more tourism, there are more people taking holidays today than there were long ago. But the same principle applies. In the old days it was just two days, Plate day and Hurdle day. In fact when I joined the Race Committee in the fifties it was still a two-day fixture. Since then it has developed to a six-day Summer Festival, plus a three-day September and two-day October Bank Holiday programme of racing. You'll get a situation eventually where trainers will take their horses and move to the West for a fortnight of racing in this holiday period where they will have the crowds and they will have a lovely holiday, everybody together. It takes time for these things to evolve but I would see it happening here as it has happened in other countries like France where they often go down to the South of France to race or to Deauville where they incorporate horse sales as well.

GALWAY 2000

"I don't see extra meetings in Galway because funnily enough they are not such a great success. It took us years to get the September meeting off the ground at all. October we got it off the ground with the coming of the Bank Holiday, which again pulls back to the idea of the holiday spirit. We can provide a service to the racing community, provide a place for horses to run. We tried a January fixture once but the course was too wet and the horses got bogged down. After about November time it is virtually impossible to race in Galway. After the Christmas there has always been a great clamour mostly from the business people of Galway for a Spring meeting in Galway. I don't think it will ever happen because it interferes with the whole management of the course. When racing is over in Galway, sheep are turned on to the course and they play a great part in the management of the grassland and of the track by the action of their feet and the way they eat and deal with grass itself. They make a very good turf. If we were to race in the Spring we wouldn't be able to put any sheep on at all. It would interfere very much with grass growth."

Lord Hemphill is a member of the Turf Club and the Irish National Hunt Committee. These were the totally governing bodies of Irish Racing but as of this year there is a big change with the new Racing Authority which has just come in. That takes over the financial control of Irish Racing and takes the Tote over from what was the Racing Board. Before this the Turf Club and Irish National Hunt Committee were in total control of all the fixtures etc.

"Being a member meant I did a lot of stewarding of all the Racecourses. Irish Racing works on a system of voluntary stewards as opposed to statutory ones or paid officials. You make the rules, of course, for racing and keep them up to date. The main body meets about four times yearly. I was Senior Steward of the National Hunt Committee for two stints of three years. Later I became a Steward of the Turf Club and Senior Steward of that body. The Turf Club was in complete control so being Senior Steward was a great honour. The Turf Club was based in the Curragh. Earlier it had its base in Hume Street, then moved to Merrion Square before moving to the Curragh. Being Chairman of the Galway Race Committee is in itself a great honour. I felt a very honoured person the first day I was elected to the Race Committee under the then Chairmanship of Joe Costelloe, father of Dr Joe. Joe Young had preceded him in that office, which very much operated by seniority then. I came in about 1957. The Race Committee meets monthly and there are various sub-committees which meet from time to time so as Chairman you'd have total involvement and be in touch the whole time.

NEW ZEALAND STALLS

"The introduction of New Zealand stalls to Irish Racing happened when I was Senior Steward of the Turf Club. I was very keen on finding out how racing worked elsewhere. I didn't think that we were that good. Our amenities, I thought, were hopeless. We used to think the amenities in England were that much better and I'd seen that amenities in France were way better. And in the States they were better still. So England was out in the cold there. I wanted to travel. So as Senior Steward I got an invitation to travel to Japan, Tokyo specifically, for an Asian Racing Conference. During that trip we went on to Australia and New Zealand and met a lot of racing people from all parts of the world. We were on a quest for these stalls. We looked for them in Japan at the beginning. The gates in Japan were far too big and expensive for use in Ireland. We went to Australia and observed their gate system which wasn't suitable either. We received great hospitality in Australia, were guests of all the Racing Clubs saw their stewarding system in action and even had a race in Randwick (Sydney) run in our honour. They called it the Irish Turf Club Handicap and I had to do the honours by presenting the prizes afterwards. We were shown all their equipment and taken all round their courses. Then on to New Zealand. At this stage we knew them all because we had met them in Tokyo at the conference. The stalls in New Zealand which were mobile and could be taken apart and transported, impressed me immediately. We got the rights of those and had them manufactured here in Ireland. That's the story behind the stalls which came to Ireland in the latter half of the eighties. There was a dreadful start to one of the top flat races in Galway before that and that had a big influence on me. It was the McDonogh Handicap. There were several bad starts. We operated a Newmarket Gate system then using a tape. That was a total failure and took somebody by the neck. It was particularly bad one year — something like the 1993 start at Aintree. So we had to improve on that system. The new stalls and the Budweiser Irish Derby would be the greatest innovations attributed to my Senior Stewardship. The arranging and bringing in of Budweiser as sponsor of the Irish Derby was possibly my greatest achievement. Guinness have been associated with Galway for years and now sponsor two days.

EARLY IMPRESSIONS

"My family was keen on racing. My father was a Director of Mullingar and I took on his share-holding in Mullingar when he died. I was sad to see Mullingar close as a Racecourse because it was the first place I ever stewarded. From there I stewarded at all the western courses, like Sligo, Roscommon, Ballinrobe and Galway. One of my early Galway memories was of the earlier days of Captain Luke Mullins as Manager and Secretary. We had done a big drainage job on the Racecourse and on the straight down at the Moneen we had dug a drain that went straight across the flat course. It was quite wide and carried a big drainage thing. It had all been put back and nothing was apparently wrong. It was half way down the hill from the corner and all was well until the skies opened. The ground was so hard that the water ran along the surface of the track until it found a place which wasn't so hard — the replaced trench. This coincided with the start of a two-year-old race just after the downpour and the two leading horses fell over flat on their noses and one had to be destroyed. We went down just after the race to examine the track and on sticking a pole into it, found it came up all liquid, almost like a pool. That was the end of racing for that day. We emptied it all out and filled it up with sand and were able to race next day.

1994

"Certainly one of the best ever Festival meetings. The sponsorship in Galway has grown tremendously and with that we entertain the sponsors, particularly since we got the new building in the course. The sponsor of the day is occasionally entertained along with many of its top people and their clients. And we would also invite Ministers of the Government, the Taoiseach, the President, TDs along also. This year was the first time President Robinson has come but our former Taoiseach Albert Reynolds was a regular at Galway long before he became Taoiseach. In the past Dr Hillery came and I remember Sean T O'Kelly coming too. I remember we had to get this special whiskey for Sean T. I think it was the Mitchell's Green Spot Whiskey we had to have. President Robinson is a woman of tremendously wide interests and experience. A delightful person who enjoyed her visit and created a great impression. Very entertaining. Regarding corporate entertainment we have tried to do something completely different from other courses here in Galway. It happened accidentally for us at the start. We set up tented space and sold off tables for eight, ten, twelve at such a price and it worked. That still persists. A great cross-fertilisation took place with people enjoying themselves and moving from one table to another. This only happens in Galway. Private parties within an open space seemed to suit in Galway. A good contact place. This past year we had a Fianna Fail tent and some other bigger corporate units like the Doyle Hotel Group, for instance. These were different from the open plan and will I feel be repeated.

RECENT DEVELOPMENT

"We were very lucky with the developments this year past because really they were a tidying up operation prior to maybe getting on with a new stand which must come in the next few years. The Parade Ring needed a lift and I had seen Cheltenham where a huge amount of money was spent on the Parade Ring. We designed these steps and things thinking it would be much better than what was there before, increasing capacity, etc. To our surprise when we had it all done we found it looked very well and wasn't at all ugly and when filled with people, it was fabulous. In fact it changed the whole atmosphere of the Parade Ring and we were able to use it to very good effect for presentations and so on and the introduction of the President. It was lovely to hear the spontaneous ovation she got when she walked into the ring. I was delighted with the interviews of personalities introduced also in 1994. The PA system we use is for the entire racecourse and you wouldn't want it to be too loud in the ring in case it would upset the horses. I understand there was some difficulty in hearing the interviews last year but we will work on that. I didn't hear the interviews because they took place while I was engaged in the entertaining of guests prior to or during lunch but I'm told the spontaneous applause for Martin Molony and Aubrey Brabazon was brilliant. I spoke to Aubrey before he went out and he was terrified. Afterwards he was delighted with it all.

FUTURE WISHES

"I would like to see it as the first Festival of racing certainly in Ireland. It got great reviews in England this year. Clement Freud has come now for the past few years and he has come to like the Festival. This past year we had an even more difficult man in John McCririck and he got a great reception from the crowd when he walked into the ring. We treated him well. He loved it all and when he went back he put the whole thing on Channel Four at no cost to us. My wife who judges the best turned out horse for each race was present when he received the warm welcome from the crowd. Every place he went people sought his autograph, somewhat like when Jack Charlton came for the October meeting some years back. Ladies' Day is very much associated with the late Fergus Foley. It goes back a long way and it's always Galway Hurdle Day. Then we started with sponsorship seriously and we now have one hundred percent sponsorship of races. Not alone have we got the races sponsored but we have got a jockeys' championship (flat and hunt), a trainers' championship, a best turned out horse in every race, prizes for stables, etc., and of course, the best dressed lady plus prizes on the racecards everyday. Last year Jury's Hotel weekends were offered. There was a great feedback from that. At the October meeting last year, the main sponsor, Bank of Ireland, drew for a car at that meeting. A fortnight of racing may not be in my lifetime but it's not so far away either. The success of the meeting is due to the Committee and the management. Galway is very lucky in both. When I joined the Committee first we had little or no management as such. No stables, no amenities of any kind for owners, trainers etc. That's gradually grown up. With the advent of Captain Mullins we got a more or less professional type of management that carried on right through the year. He did a lot of great work with the track itself. He transformed it all. Then on to John Moloney — probably even more professional still, in that he has grown up in racing completely. John has a great love of the sport and his first job was with the Racing Board in Tipperary Racecourse (Limerick Junction). He is so efficient and dedicated. As well as that we have, as I said, a committee of very high calibre and very representative of the Galway Community as a whole with some very high-powered people on it. I can tell you as Chairman they are not an easy lot. You couldn't count any of the twelve as a yes-man!"

From The Horse's Mouth

The Cost of the Catering Franchise in 1944.

Letter to Mrs Lawlor of Naas June 16, 1944.

"Dear Mrs Lawlor,

Your letter received, for which I thank you. I placed the matter before my Committee on Wednesday last and they decided that in view of the difficulty in travelling etc., they would accept seventy pounds for the catering this year. This price however is an emergency measure not to affect future years.

Yours faithfully, Joe Gavin Secretary."

This was the year before the end of World War II. Travel restrictions were at their worst and the Galway Race Committee, as always, had their priorities right.

12
The Manager

"It's magic to hear them cheering home the winner of the Plate every year."

— John Moloney, Race Committee Secretary/Manager

*J*ohn came to take over in Galway to replace Captain Luke Mullins in February 1989. Luke had been the man in charge before that for eighteen years. John took me through his career in racing before then.

"I was involved in the breeding of horses with my father, all my life at Riverside Stud, Knocklong, County Limerick, where we farmed and bred yearlings for sale and my first visit to Newmarket was way back in 1965 when I was only fifteen. I'd been hunting and riding ponies since I was eight or nine. I always had a great love for the horse. That led on to farming and then the position of Assistant Manager came up at Limerick Junction Racecourse (now named Tipperary). I was there for three years as assistant to Tom Burke and Tony Corcoran. Then in the Summer of 1989 the position of Galway Secretary/Manager was advertised in the *Irish Field*. I applied and was interviewed by a Mr Cuthbertson from Dublin. I was shortlisted and came to Galway on a very wet afternoon to be interviewed by Mr Paddy Ryan, the then Chairman, Lord Hemphill, Ray Rooney and Tim Naughton. That interview lasted about one and a half hours. I went away happy and was notified in November that I was successful. Paddy Ryan the Chairman was there to greet me the first day I came to work. We met in the office, Paddy, Luke Mullins and myself. Paddy, an absolute gentleman, has been a great friend of mine ever since. We moved into this house where you are interviewing me right beside the Racecourse in April after Luke Mullins had moved out. Noreen, my wife, and our two boys, Eamonn and Michael, moved to Galway in April. Paddy Ryan was an excellent Chairman, had great command of his Committee and had a very keen interest in the racing and on the preparation for the Races. You'd think you'd have everything covered but Paddy would see some little thing that needed to be done. He had a lovely way of getting you to do things, no ordering, making it seem as if it was your own idea. I never heard a cross word from him. All he used do was look at you out over the glasses and you knew he was not in agreement with what you were saying. He had a great sense of humour.

COMMITTEE MEETINGS

"These take place once a month in the Stewards' Room in the office building. They meet on the Sunday before all meetings, walk the Course and inspect the enclosure before a formal meeting just to give the all-clear that they are happy with preparations. I think it is great that they show such an interest in the Races. And they all value their positions on that Committee very much, which is a great help. They're all men of great calibre, brains and initiative, and are very successful businessmen in their own right. They apply that to the Races and their efforts have been responsible for a lot of the success of Galway Races. At the moment Lord Hemphill is Chairman, Thomas McDonogh is vice-Chairman, the rest of the Committee are Lord Killanin, Paddy Ryan, Derry Kelly, John Coyle, Ray Rooney, Tim Naughton, Brendan Allen, Jerome Mahony, Terry Cunningham and Colm Gavin. All Galwegians with a great love for Galway. They know how much the Races mean to Galway. "

Danno Heaslip, owner of Champion Hurdle winner *For Auction* among other horses once told me he always visits the Course on the Sunday before the Festival to capture the mood and it is a sort of festive picnic day for many.

"An awful lot of people come and walk the course themselves to see that everything is OK. Galway people rightly feel they own the Galway Racecourse and are very proud of it and are happy to see it looking well. They will always tell you that too.

FIRST VISIT

"Back around 1972, I remember we had sold cattle at the time to Michael Purcell (Thurles) and I remember him saying Clem Magnier would win the Galway Hurdle on Thursday and to be sure to back him. I came and remember backing the winner *Dictora* at eight to one, ridden by Tommy Murphy. You still get tips like that today. Every fellow I meet here during Race Week, is going to win either the first, third or fifth race on that day. The next guy you meet is going to win the same race. But that is what racing is all about. The Bookmakers' Ring is one place I'm rarely in. But I might have a flutter on the last race of the day on something I'd fancy. When I'm in the Ring, I'm usually chasing Bookmakers' assistants trying to keep the place tidy.

LORD HEMPHILL

"Lord Hemphill is a fine Chairman for a few years now, with a great knowledge of racing from a lifetime's association. He has a terrific interest in the place and has set up various sub-committees, a Sponsorship Committee, a Building Committee, a Finance Committee and he chairs them all. So he could be at meetings on the Course three or four times a month. Like Paddy Ryan, he's very nice to work for. He has a nice flow of words and a fine voice that comes across very well on the PA when he welcomes patrons daily. He believes that the public are always first and should be made happy. He looks after the punter. Sponsorship is a big interest with him too. Tom Broderick is our Foreman and has been here for over forty years. He started working during the Races at the age of fifteen or so and has been Foreman for a good number of years. Another member is Michael Flaherty. Michael's art is that he looks after the fences. They are the envy of every Racecourse both here in Ireland and in Britain. How well the fences are prepared is all due to Michael. He uses a toe-clippers and cuts every twig individually. He gets his mould out and has them in beautiful condition. Michael observes the racecourses here in Ireland but Tom has been to more racecourses than myself, even as far away as America and all over England. Tom Connors retired from here after the 1993 October meeting. He gave a lifetime of service to Galway Racecourse. A terrific character, Tom was always in good humour, whether the sun shone or not, always ready to have the crack. In the office Mrs Gillen is the Secretary. She has a huge input into the Races. She has been here since 1974 with Luke, has a marvellous knowledge of it all and is a great asset. She runs her own side of it, all the organisation. That's the regular staff. We take on one or two extra in May annually and then around mid-June an extra twelve or fourteen students for all the painting, cleaning, cutting grass — you name it. Coming up to the Festival you could have anything up to forty working here. There'd be plumbers in checking out everything, electricians, Western Pleasure erecting tents, Lydon House and all their catering staff. During Race Week itself we'd have anything up to two hundred employed. The caterers would have even more. The Tote staff will have two hundred and fifty. The Bookmakers about one hundred and ninety. All of these earn a living that week out of the Racecourse. So it is big business. Almost one thousand people.

GEARING UP

"Today we meet one of the sponsors. I met Lord Hemphill beforehand to discuss strategy. We have been involved in selling hospitality. We have increased it this year to service an extra one thousand three hundred people. We have a niche in the market which is not as expensive as happens at other meetings. A day at the Races including lunch and champagne and afternoon tea costs around seventy pounds. At other courses like Fairyhouse, Punchestown, or the Curragh, or at Rugby Internationals or GAA Finals you could add another one hundred pounds on to that price. Cheltenham would be so much more expensive. During January we prepared our accounts for auditing before our Finance Meeting, so we are ready now to really prepare for the 1995 Festival meeting. Last year we carried out some development work. We did a good job on the Parade Ring. Concrete steps instead of the grassy mounds. Better viewing facilities. We repaired a roof where the Quick Snack and County Club buildings are. It is one of the old buildings. Maintenance on the Course is a huge cost."

In the course of my research for this book I visited the course fairly regularly between March 1994 and 1995. Saw the Parade Ring viewing facilities being constructed. Observed the greater activity on the Course as Festival week approached. Went there on the Saturday before the big week when I knew I was in the way. All last minute hitches were being seen to. The increased corporate hospitality facility was very evident during Festival week.

SUCCESS OF GALWAY

"It's hard for me to answer why Galway is so successful, being here such a short time. It's going on for so long. The first Galway Plate took place in 1869. First a two-day festival and they say forty thousand attended the first one. It was a holiday time and became very popular. The Committee had the foresight to build it along step by step from two to three and three to four days. Then Tuam went on the Friday and they took in Friday to make it five days. And then they went on to include Saturday. What was the point of going back to the Metropolitan area to race on the Saturday with everybody down in Galway? Saturday has become a very popular day in its own right. A lot of new faces come starting the Bank Holiday weekend in style. It has come on a lot even the short while I'm here. I don't envisage seven days on the trot. Even the Lord rested on the seventh day. I think everybody has enough after six days. All the workers need a day's rest.

"Here in Galway people say the horses are always doing their level best to win. The Festival is the same to any trainer as Cheltenham, Liverpool or on the flat, Ascot for instance. He or she won't take the horse here unless they believe they have a chance of winning. At other meetings you might hear people say, 'We are minding him for Galway' or 'We are putting one away for Galway'. They really are getting them ready for Galway. Ninety-five per cent of them coming here think they are going to win. There is never a slow run race here. Coming out of the gates, they go a good gallop. The way the course is structured with the steep downhill run into the Moneen helps. A lot of the good trainers have said to me that if you haven't a good position coming down the hill, you won't have it coming up the hill to the finish.

AROUND THE TRACK

"The Galway Plate course is the one to follow. They start just a furlong from the winning post, at the West side of the Lower Stand and we stand there on the Stewards' Stand out on the Course and when they are approaching the first fence just at the turnstiles, it is amazing to watch the fellows jockeying for position, shouting and screaming as they go along, because the entrance to the first fence at the weighroom which is the widest fence we have, is on a slight bend and if they aren't right for that they are on the ground afterwards. Then around the turn and they face what we call the Lisheen Fence because it is beside the Lisheen cemetery. That one causes very few problems. On from that to the Pen Fence, the reason it is so called because long ago when the sheep were left on the Track for the Races they used to pen the sheep there. That's another straight and ordinary fence. Then across the road (where the traffic comes into the Course) and they jump the Regulation Fence. That one is a fine fence. It's at a slight angle and can catch one out. On then to Paddy's Jump, one of the trickier plain fences, called because it is beside Paddy McDermott's house. Then the long run down into the Moneen. They say if you meet the first one right you'll meet the second one right too. The opposite is true too. There was an article done in the *Racing Post* recently where an English amateur jockey who had ridden here measured the distance between the two fences as seventy yards. A very short distance between two fences in a steeplechase. After that comes the very steep climb up the hill to the finish. Anybody who ever backs a horse in Galway and blames the horse for not being able to come up the hill should walk up that hill sometime. There is a huge incline from the last fence up to the winning post and you're climbing the whole way. It's a terrific test of a horse. The horses that have won in Galway over the years have included some very good chasers but some of the flat horses who ran here *Cairn Rouge* and *Go and Go* went on to bigger things in Belmont Park and elsewhere. Comparing us with Cheltenham, there is a nice gradient up-hill in Cheltenham but ours is much stiffer. They don't have as steep a hill to come down either.

FLAT HUNT MIX

"Tradition has it that we have always had a mix of handicaps and the flat. Generally two hurdle races per day or a hurdle race and a chase plus a few flat races daily. A lot of people lose sight of the flat races here. We have zero to seventy-five handicaps here which is as low as we run and they still generate plenty of betting. We have betting figures for all the individual races and sometimes the feature race is not the biggest betting race. I'd always keep an eye out as to what is happening at other tracks. You can't really compare one track with another because you go to Leopardstown and they have five times our width on their straight. Or you go to the Curragh or Fairyhouse which have huge widths too. We are very confined with the amount of ground available for our straight and, because of our design, we cannot improve on this. We can run twenty horses in the Galway Plate and seventeen in a flat race daily which is as much as there is demand for. You'll see some innovations elsewhere and you'll copy them. Cheltenham is a great pointer. They have terrific facilities, cater for huge numbers and manage their track very efficiently. They market things well. It is easy enough to market Galway but you have to be ahead of the posse always. Newspapers only carry current news but you have to generate stories like the participation of top English jockeys and horses a week ahead of time, or a horse backed down quickly in the offices beforehand. In 1993 and 1994 we had Adrian Maguire, Richard Dunwoody, Mark Dwyer, Norman Williamson, Graham Bradley and Brendan Powell all here from England. It's in their off season, although that has changed this year. They know the prize-money is here and they are glad to have a go. The top flat English jockeys don't come because Goodwood is always on at the same time. The flat races run here would not merit English jockeys.

HECTIC MONTHS

"June and July are hectic here. It's from seven o'clock in the morning to ten o'clock at night. No matter what you're doing or how hard you're going, there is always somebody looking for you. The biggest problem here is that everybody wants to be in number one position for the Races. You have to get them around to your way of thinking. Hectic yes, but I enjoy it. The worst feeling is to get up here on Sunday morning after the Races and the whole thing is gone. Just gone. You look out. Maybe there might be one or two cars in the fields. One year, one of the Directors rang me on the Tuesday morning afterwards to give bad news. Some fellow had his car stolen at the Races. I asked for details. A Renault etc. Oh, that's here. It seems the owner looked for it in the wrong field! Last year again on the Tuesday night about ten thirty p.m. two fellows who'd had 'one too many' couldn't find their car and it took them nearly an hour to do so.

"During Race Week you're on a high. Bad-tempered at times. Keeping cool is the main thing. The house is always full of friends and visitors. My wife, Noreen, is always a great help to me at Races time. A typical Race day for me is as follows: Up early to go out and look at the Course. That would be seven a.m. and I'd meet Tom Broderick and we would decide on what changes we'd make from the previous day. Then back into the office. Mrs Gillen would have everything covered but I'd like to keep in touch and there would be little things that would have to be done. The Racecards come then. You'd check them out for any major error. They'd be here from where they are printed in Drogheda at nine a.m. We'd be in charge of the sale. We'd order twenty-three thousand for Plate Day and we'd have only about six hundred left over. Hurdle Day is just as good. Monday is the worst day. Everything goes wrong on Monday. Everybody is dragging out of you. You're trying to get new staff into position. Tuesday runs itself really. All hell breaks loose on Wednesday morning. Usually on these days I ramble up to the house about ten a.m., change my clothes and get ready for the day's racing, have a cup of tea. I'd be back down again by eleven and all the gates would close then and the turnstiles would open. It's magic to hear the first clicks of those stiles, slowly at first, then they click faster and you know the work has all been worthwhile and the people are coming and you know you're going to have a good crowd. It's a lovely feeling. A lovely class of people come to the Galway Races. Everybody comes in good humour. Maybe at times there are little problems at the turnstiles but we always try to explain things if there is a problem. Myself and the Directors are always in close proximity to the turnstiles and we attend to any problems. It's always very easy to defuse any situations here. They don't mind queuing. It's the popularity of the place.

GREATEST JOY

"It happens every year. It is to stand in the Stewards' Stand and then hear the crowd roaring for the finish of the Plate. It's magic to hear them cheering home the winner. It has to be experienced. And when the favourite wins like *General Idea* in 1993 you'd want to hear that roar. There is a sort of pride in having organised all this and that roar is what it's all about really. The joy it brings to so many. Funny things happen too. One fellow rang after twelve months looking for his false teeth and we still had them kept in a glass for him in the Owners' and Trainers' Bar. Sometimes an overweight person gets stuck in the turnstiles and there is panic for a few seconds.

"Mick Kinane has to be the favourite here. He is magic around here. No one can compare with him. They haven't really run for Charlie Swan around here. He rode the winner of the Galway Hurdle in 1993 but he is nothing like Kinane here. Mick has a terrific knowledge of the place and he seems to be always in the right place at the right time. Dermot Weld is a terrific trainer and has a marvellous Galway record. I know Dermot for a long time. I met him first in Newmarket when he had just finished secondary school. He was looking at yearlings that year with two great judges of horses, Paddy Prendergast and George Blackwell, the latter an agent and great friend of the Welds. Dermot rode *Spanner* and numerous winners in Galway as an amateur jockey. Then he became a very successful trainer. A highlight was his training of ten winners here in 1993 and 1994. After that the Melbourne Cup with *Vintage Crop*. Every trainer in Ireland supports Galway. They all like it. You have to have things right for them. They are all professionals and perfectionists in their own right. The ground has to be right for them all and that can be difficult because they have horses with good legs and bad legs. And they all look for different ground. A good medium keeps them happy.

ANTI-CLIMAX

"The anti-climax after it is over is huge. We stay around for a week getting the place cleaned up. As a family we move away for a week, then back for the September and October meets. It's a lovely Racecourse to manage in the sense that you have no racing till July and if you just compare that with Fairyhouse. They have the Grand National at Easter, and many other meetings. We have plenty of time to prepare. And good weather to have everything spick and span. Living on the Course is an advantage. Sometimes a disadvantage. You can be out at seven a.m. Come back in anytime and can work until ten p.m. if you like when the days are long.

THE MEDIA

"Wonderful. We have a great relationship with the media. I'd have a quick glance at the papers every day during Festival week and usually keep them to read fully the following week. They all love Galway too. We get terrific coverage from the English media as well. We had three television crews in 1993, two from America and one from England doing documentaries on the Races. At a Rugby international recently, Pat Cataldo the Managing Director of Digital here in Ireland told me he saw me on American Television the previous week in a documentary on the Races here. John Comyn, Michael O'Farrell, Pat Keane, Tom Cashman, Damien McElroy, Michael Clower, Cliff Noone, to name but a few, are always here. Dave Baker usually toddles in for a day, Clement Freud came the last two years. I can't say Bórd Fáilte kill themselves doing anything for us. But, of course, Galway Races caters for itself. You can't get a bed in Galway at Festival time. So there isn't any need to promote the Races really. We look after the Press and they all go away very happy from us. We treat them fairly. If you have something to tell them, good or bad, you tell them. That is my motto and they appreciate it. We had a robbery here a few years ago and though some people didn't want to inform the press, I did so immediately and they already knew!

TELEVISION

"RTE do a terrific job. Ted Walsh, Robert Hall, Tracy Piggott and Tony O'Hehir do a great job. Four days of great coverage. Tony Sweeney does the betting. Chris Darby and Tim O'Connor (Head of RTE Sport) are always here too. In recent years Galway Races got into the first ten in the TAM ratings for the week for the first time. That was the Monday evening of the Festival week. Colm Murray is usually here on a few missions. He does the presentations among other things. Thelma Mansfield did a fine job here in the past too. We have a terrific team of sponsors. We ran forty-two races here in 1993 during Race week, all sponsored, as they were in 1994, and the same with the September and October meetings. The main sponsors like Jimmy Hughes (GPT — Amateur Handicap), McDonogh's, Digital (The Plate — now gone from forty thousand pounds to fifty thousand in 1994), Guinness (The Hurdle — associated for over twenty-five years) who are now sponsoring on the

Friday and Dawn Dairies on the Saturday and the Tony O'Malley Chase. In the September meeting the main race would be the Ardilaun House Hotel Oyster Stakes, the winner of this was trained by Jim Bolger in 1993 and 1994. This is the only Stakes race we have and it is a very good race. The Waterford Crystal Handicap and the Northern Telecom Chase are others. October is Bank of Ireland Family Race day and that has been a huge success because it caters for the family and tries to provide something for everybody.

"Finally it's great to see a Galway owned horse coming into the ring. There is a great buzz in the place. Even if it's a Galway owner who is now in exile. In 1993 *Dancing Cinderella* did it here for the Murrays of Salthill Hotel and Ray Rooney, a Director of the Track won the feature event on the Friday with *Garboni*. Last year there was great excitement when Herb Stanley's *Cable Beach*, trained by Michael Cunningham and ridden by Richard Dunwoody won the opener on Plate Day, followed in the second race by Seán Creaven's *Open Market*, ridden by Adrian Maguire and trained by Dermot Weld. I remember *Natalie's Fancy* (Pat Kelly) and Kevin McDonagh's *I'm Confident* both winning the Hurdle. Many others too. There is always a bit of a gamble and great excitement. Sometimes people who have got a tip forget to place the bet as happened with a very fancied horse here a few years ago and a local banker, who shall be nameless, forget to obey instructions from the Galway based owner! Nuff said."

From The Horse's Mouth

The First World War

In 1915 government pressure caused the cessation of all racing in England except at Newmarket. In Ireland after much debate they decided to continue racing as before. The Galway Plate of 1915 was won by Hill of Camas, owned by Mr W Molony and ridden by Mr G Harty.

— **Irish Horse-racing** *by J Welcome (Gill and MacMillan).*

13
Paddy Ryan

"The thing to do after the Races in the War Years was to go to Toft's in Eyre Square."

— *Paddy Ryan, Chairman before Lord Hemphill*

*P*addy Ryan, well-known Galway businessman, the proprietor of Anthony Ryan's Drapery, Shop Street, owner of the fashionable Ardilaun Hotel, in which his wife Breda takes such a huge interest, former Mayor of Galway and in so many other ways a contributor to Galway city's community life, served as Chairman of the Galway Race Committee prior to the present incumbent. Paddy himself takes us through his involvement with the Galway Races.

"I was elected to the Committee in 1958. Myself and Lord Hemphill, Thomas McDonogh and the late Dr Michael O'Malley were all elected together. Four new members was a lot at one time. The Race Committee then as now is a mix of members of the Galway Hunt and business people from the town. All through my membership, I have been more interested in the actual running of the races and the development of the enclosure and the track than in the Races themselves."

Prior to this interview in his lovely home in Forster Street, Galway, Paddy, who has always been a keen cine-camera man, showed me reels he took of the Races of 1969 — the Centenary year of the Galway Races — and of 1972 which showed the New Stand and New Weighroom and the Stewards' Stand just in use for that year. These old reels are priceless pearls of social history now. Galway was crowded then too. Heaps of parked cars and plenty of excitement as always.

"When I joined, the Committee met just four or five times a year. At the time the Race Office was in Irwin's Yard, upstairs in a small little room, about one hundred square feet in area. Captain Pat Canavan was in charge then and Mr Joe Costelloe was Chairman. He was succeeded by Mr Tommy Kelly who lived in Athenry and was a Veterinary Surgeon. After him came Lord Killanin who served in the Chair from 1970-1985. I served as Chairman for six years from 1985. At that stage it was decided the Chairman would serve for a three year term and could be re-elected for one more term only.

SINCE 1950

"The one we call the old Stand now, the bigger of the two, the one nearest the parade ring, was erected about 1950. That was built by the McNally family. The top part I think was an afterthought. There is a marvellous view from there. The next big development was in 1972 when the old stand, the Lower Stand nearer to Galway was taken down and replaced by what we call the New Stand now. At that stage we also built the weigh-room to replace the old weigh-room which used to be where the Owners' and Trainers' Bar is now. In those days, the placed horses had to come up through the crowd to a little paddock known as the Winner's enclosure and this was extremely dangerous. You couldn't envisage that nowadays when we have become so conscious of public liability. Simon Kelly was the architect of all the development then and since. The new Stewards' Stand went up then but it isn't that easy to see all the track from it. So we may see further developments in this area. All that cost in the region of three hundred thousand pounds, a big investment at that time. The next development I remember concerned the saddling enclosure which we changed from behind the Tote to a completely new set of stalls between the weigh-room and the track which meant that now the horses go from the stables to the saddling stalls thence to the Parade Ring, thence to the Track without ever coming in contact with the public. That also gave us extra room within the enclosure. That took place in 1985. Around the same time we got the opportunity to buy the land between the Track and the Tuam Road and the acquisition of that gave us easier access. With the coming of the new bridge over the Corrib, traffic to and from the Course is not the hazard it used to be. It was about thirty acres in all but John Brennan, one of our Committee members, took half of the acquisition which suited him too. The main improvement after that was the development of the new Restaurant inside the main gate entrance. We actually pushed back the wall forty feet to the road to give us more space behind the Main Stand. That new development included new toilets, new kitchens, the new Stewards' Room including bar and restaurant and the Owners' and Trainers' Bar. We do a lot of entertaining in the Committee Rooms. That new development was opened in 1991 just as I left office as Chairman. I was very proud of that particular development. That and the acquisition of the extra fifteen acres, which as well as generating easy access, safeguarded the parking problems for years to come. There was, of course, the recent development of the area around the parade ring which has created such a fine impression and got rid of the old dangerous grassy slopes. The 1991 official opening was performed by the then Minister for Finance, Albert Reynolds, always a keen follower of the Galway Races. We could easily have had a Cabinet meeting any day of the Summer meeting for the past few years! The Racing Board gave us a great loan for all of our developments and Albert Reynolds was very favourably disposed to the Board. I'm always glad to see the people coming in on the first day and then on Plate Day there is a massive pride to see the huge crowd present and to feel that one has been associated with the development of it all over the years. It is so worthwhile now. It is a marvellous financial boon to Galway and its environs. At least one hundred thousand people come to the Races in the Summer and just imagine what they spend. Racing people are lovely and they come back year after year. It's like a reunion every year.

EARLIEST MEMORIES

"My first memory is as a child sitting on the gate outside and watching the horses walking up from the Station. That was in the thirties. In 1930 the Race Committee bought a strip of land at the end of the Sportsground for three hundred pounds and most of the horses used to be stabled there until around 1960, when we built seventy or eighty extra stables out at Ballybrit. We sold the Sportsground Stables then. I hear people saying at times that the boom has reached its zenith. I don't think the popularity is going to slip. It is very professionally run and the tradition is there of what I would call re-union. The mix of flat and hunt racing appeals too. The Track has been improved over the years. It may not be the best track in Ireland but it is pretty good. Over the years there have been what I would call Galway-orientated trainers and jockeys. Noel Meade, Dermot Weld, Arthur Moore and Michael Cunningham would be the main ones, with Dessie McDonagh and Jim Bolger. In the old days you had Harry Ussher, Phonsie O'Brien, Paddy Sleator and Pat Taaffe.

THE WAR YEARS

"The cars were off the road then and a lot of sidecars operated from out-side the Great Southern Hotel. Five bob a head and they'd carry four. We used to cycle out then but they really gave the horses a hard time of it, doing as many journeys as possible. Fifteen or twenty sidecars at least and I remember seeing a few horses on the Tuam Road who died in the process from absolute exhaustion. Bertie Donoghue's father from Loughrea, an old friend, used to stay with us for the Races and he told me how he came in from Loughrea on a sidecar and one of the boys with him sang the ballad 'The Boys of Lios na Cranchy' all forty-two verses of it. It started in Loughrea and finished in Ballybrit. It was about a foot-ball match and began somewhat like this:

'The boys of Lios na Cranchy
Tooraloorel, tooraloo,
I never travelled with such a crew
'Tis they could drink the honey dew
The boys of Lios na Cranchy
McCarthy with the golden hair
He'd score a goal I do declare
Then you'd see him in the air
For the sake of Lios na Cranchy'

"One of the passengers declared it to be the longest and worst song he had ever heard but it passed the journey. Toft's in Eyre Square used to be there for three weeks altogether. The first week — the week before the Races — was always in aid of the Saint Vincent de Paul. Then Race week and the week after was for themselves. They used to leave Eyre Square in an awful mess especially if the weather was anyway wet. But they had a great show in those days, chairoplanes, dodgems, swinging boats. The thing to do after the Races then was to go to Toft's. I went there regularly then. There was a marquee at the top level of Eyre Square where Kennedy Park is now, and there were three dancing sessions in the marquee run efficiently by John Allen of the Imperial Hotel. First session was 9.00 - 11.00 p.m., the second from 11.30 - 1.30 a.m. and the last one 2.00 - 4.30 a.m. It was a hard week and you were going night and day. My brother-in-law used to boast he left three different girls home on the one night. During the war years trains operated from Dublin to Galway only on two days, Monday and Thursday. So the races moved back to the Tuesday and Wednesday for the war years as a result.

PRESENT INTERESTS

"My wife, Breda and I always had an interest in getting a horse of our own sometime. With partners like Brendan Allen and our own relations we have had a few horses, and we won a few races over the years. We had some good fun with a horse called *Salado* trained by John Murphy in the Curragh. Our present one is with Paddy Osborne, who has always trained for our partner Tom Gavigan and is appropriately named *Ballybrit Boy*. He won in Galway in 1993. It was great to win in Galway. We were hopeful but were afraid to appear confident. He won by a nose and paid handsome dividends. Tom is from Kells and Breda's brother Paddy Fitzsimons, is another partner. The horse is out of action at the moment but may run and win in Galway again."

As I left Ryan's after a most entertaining evening I could not but admire the Ryans who have given so much of themselves to the Galway they love. Paddy was honoured with an Honourary Doctorate in Laws by UCG in 1994, a well deserved and popular recognition for this humble man, who is always the essence of good humour and joy. Breda makes up the perfect team and in her own way contributes so much to Galway life in her work for charity and social organisations. Long may they continue to work for Galway.

14
Lord Killanin

"I met my wife Sheila at the Galway Races."
— *Former Chairman Lord Killanin*

$\mathcal{V}$isiting Lord Killanin at his home near Rathmines Church was a great privilege for me. Though in his eighty-first year, he remembers clearly all his early associations with the Galway Races and was reluctant to talk of his own contribution which many people I interviewed told me was immense. "The big expansion of the Galway Races took off under Lord Killanin", was how Tom McDonogh the present Vice-Chairman put it to me. A noted scholar and writer, Lord Killanin's study is full of books, photos of the former Chairman of the Olympic Games movement taken with heads of state like De Valera, Brezhnev, Jimmy Carter, Tito, the Queen of England, to name a few, and medals and distinctions galore decorating the walls. Lord Killanin is undoubtedly the most honoured Irish sports official ever. I found him a warm and humble man.

"When we came here first it was a much smaller home than our previous one at Lansdowne Road and I had to dispose of five thousand books and about one hundred pictures. Prior to that I lived in Spiddal where I still have a Summer house, the old Protestant Church there. My grandfather, who like myself had a mixed marriage, used to say they couldn't both be wrong because he went to Mass on a sidecar and his wife went to Church in a carriage. My first memory of the Galway Races must have been either 1917 or 1918. I went there as a boy after the First World War and I celebrated my eightieth birthday at the 1994 Galway Festival. My uncle took me to my first Races. I remember thinking that the RIC were all German prisoners of war for they were covered with grey from the dust. We travelled in my uncle's car IM 50, one of the first cars in the West. Very few cars then. I love Galway. I am a Galwegian at heart, as a member of the Tribes of Galway. We have been in Spiddal since we married into an estate there in the seventeenth century, which belonged to the MacGiolla Phádraics of Aran. A great-great-grand-mother was a cousin of Roderick O'Flaherty who wrote the book *Iar Chonnacht*. My grandfather was the first Catholic Attorney General.

"The next time I went to the Galway races was after the Second World War and there I met my wife. My father also met my mother at the Galway Races. We had both been demobilised from the British Army. I took part in D-Day landing at Juno beach. She was a cryptographer at Bletchley Park's Foreign Office and knew much more that was going on in the war than me. We were married in 1945. We've been together for forty-nine years. Around that time I became a member of the Galway Race Committee and I've been a member since. Other members of the Committee then were Joe Young, Chairman, Joe Costelloe and Tommy Kelly whom I knew from the hunting scene. Comdt. Canavan was Secretary then. Tommy Kelly's nephew Mr R Kelly is now a member of the Committee. In those days it was the elder or senior member of the Committee who became Chairman. It was during Tommy Kelly's time in the Chair that we changed the rules and I was elected Chairman after Tommy in 1965 and remained so until 1985.

"Times were very simple then. Just two days and both very successful ones. Tuam traded on Galway then. I saw Tuam going down. I acted as a Steward in Tuam and was later elected a member of the Turf Club. The Stewards' Room in Tuam was the Stewards' Bar and we had to put all the drink under the table. There is still a link, we were able to buy the Tuam railings which are now on top of the Weigh-room in Galway.

MY DAYS IN ENGLAND

"I came over to Ireland as often as I could when I was working as a news-paper man before the war and often covered stories in Ireland for the *Daily Mail* and the *Sunday Dispatch*. I can remember when Sean T whipped John Bull during election time. I never covered the Races but went to them during my Summer leave, which I took to coincide with the Races. So I was there in between 1918 and 1944. The person I remember best from around that time was Máirtín Mór McDonogh. He was a very big man and loved the Galway Races. He lived for the Races as much as I love Galway. The great strength of Galway now is that over a period we extended the Festival from two to six days. I remember receiving a deputation from the Galway Hoteliers asking could we change the date of the Races because they were full at that time of the year. I'm glad I said no because when things slackened afterwards they were glad to have the Races at that time of year. Christy Kerin from Oranmore was another one closely associated. He was a Guinness agent and very active on the Committee. Himself and Tommy Kelly were very active in the founding of the Connemara Pony Society over which I presided as well from 1952 to 1970.

"I don't remember the horses as well as the trainers and jockeys. You see I was more interested in the sport. I pride myself on what I'd call helping to keep classless racing in Galway. We didn't have Grand Stands. We didn't have two-tier racing. We now have seats which you pay for. Lord Hemphill, the present Chairman, suggested moving the weigh-room down to where it is now. That was a major stroke. The old weigh-room was in the Stewards' Bar and a very small space. I insisted there must be a full-time manager living on the spot. Luke Mullins was our first and we built a house for him. It is the only asset the Race Committee has. We always put the people's comfort first. To that end we toured and saw many English tracks. Went to both France and Germany. Simon Kelly, the architect and most of the members travelled. We went to Newcastle where the Parade Ring is in front of the Stands as was the case at the Phoenix Park. But we decided against that but to move the weigh-room sideways so to speak and concentrate on that. Galway is one of the few racetracks where the horses do not pass through the crowd.

THE INFIELD

"Corporate hospitality has come in. The infield is still pretty hectic. The Racing Board couldn't afford to buy it out and you can still race in Galway for a pound. If you're walking it will cost you nothing. Plenty of swings and roundabouts. My memory is fading but there are others I remember like Barney Nugent, Charlie Weld, Paddy Sleator, Phonsie

O'Brien and Clem Magnier, who was a faithful supporter of Galway. Clem had some horses killed in a trailer crash on his way to the Galway Races and it still didn't dampen his enthusiasm for Galway. I remember well the first helicopter to come to Ballybrit. It was used by Raymond Guest round about the sixties. The field was absolutely crowded and the only free space was the Moneen — we were digging him out for days!

IMPORTANT GUESTS

"Practically every President came to the Races at some time or other. I'm very proud that Galway is the only track which makes money for the Racing Board. The gambling is very heavy in Galway always. Listowel and the Holiday meetings generally do well, but they have got the least return from the Racing Board. It has been pretty one way. As to my greatest memories, meeting my wife, of course, for the first time, has to be number one. The Turf Club have done a tremendous amount for Galway. The Stewarding has improved. Jack Duggan of Gowran Park was the first Turf Club National Hunt honourary member of the Galway Stewards. Racing in Ireland is probably as honest and as well disciplined as any in the world and the Turf Club deserves credit for this. John Moloney's father is the Turf Club member now. Originally the Committee members provided the Stewards in Galway. Lord Hemphill and myself became members of the Turf Club and that was very important. Lord Hemphill was there before me. As a result we raced a lot. Dan Comyn from Loughrea was also a Senior Steward of the Irish National Hunt Steeplechase Committee.

MICHAEL "MOUSE" MORRIS

"Michael, my son, has my father's build and is also involved in horse racing. I don't really know where the "Mouse" came from. I imagine it is Mickey Mouse! I loved horse riding and hunting. I wrote the rules of the Galway Blazers. I like organisation and administration. Of the committees I have chaired, Galway Racing Committee is my favourite, even the International Olympic Committee over which I presided from 1972 to 1980 including being President of the Olympic Council of Ireland from 1950 to 1973. My advice to Galway Race Committee is not to be over-ambitious. To have good food and good drink."

Before I parted with Lord Killanin he took me on a tour of his study which, as I described earlier, included many famous names. Lord Killanin photographed with Jabolenski of Poland, Empress Farah of Teheran, Ceaucescu of Bucharest, the King of Sweden who married an Olympic hostess, Princess Beatrix of Holland taken in Papendal, Karemandis Prime Minister of Greece, Lester Piggott, Queen Elizabeth II of England, de Valera who awarded him one of the last Honourary Degrees he conferred. Lord Killanin graduated from Cambridge with a BA in 1935 and an MA in 1939. He also got an Honourary Degree in the University of Ulster. He is photographed also with the first man ever in space, Gagarin, a recent one with Bertie Aherne, and also with some of the Popes, his favourite being Pope John.

"I met him first when I was a reporter in the Irish Newsagency with Conor Cruise O'Brien. He was a Nuncio in Paris then and I travelled with Monsignor Kissane to Luxeuil, a Columban Foundation Monsignor Kissane and myself drank a bottle of Irish each on that occasion. Tito impressed me very much because we had so much in common through the war. It is awful what is happening there now.

FAMILY

"I'm the third member of the Morris family associated with the Galway Races. My great uncle Sir George Morris was an MP for Galway one hundred and twenty years ago. He was associated in the early days of Ballybrit. The second one was my uncle who was Lord Killanin before me. He was the last Her Majesty's Lieutenant for Galway. "

Other photos on the walls showed "Mouse" Morris riding over Beecher's Brook at Aintree in 1973 on *Green Plover* and riding *Prolan* in another race. As I left I had to admire some stained glass sketch work of Evie Hone and Sarah Purcell's Stations of the Cross and two very special medallions, from Spain and Sarajevo. Finally he told me a David Guiney anecdote.

"Galway Races coincided with the Olympic Games when held in the Northern Hemisphere. Once I said to him during the games, 'Dave, do you know you're missing the Galway Races', and he was astonished that in the height of the Olympic Games excitement I'd still be thinking of Galway."

15

Secretary

"It's about meeting someone who is unhappy and putting them at ease."
— *Mrs Dolores Gillen — Secretary*

*M*rs Dolores Gillen succeeded Nora Carroll as Secretary in reply to an advertisement in the *Connacht Tribune* and started on July 1 1974. Dolores hails from Belfast, still has a wee Northern accent and came to Galway via North America, where she spent eight years. Her husband, Tom, started work in Galway RTC the year it opened, September, 1972. With only a very peripheral interest in racing prior to taking the appointment, she walked into the job knowing very little difference between the front and back of a horse. To say the Race Committee got a treasure of a secretary is an understatement. Dolores now loves to see the way it all works, has developed an interest in racing to the extent of going to see racing at other venues like Killarney and Listowel and the Curragh. The biggest kick she gets is out of racing in Galway.

"Watching us doing all the bits and pieces that have to be done here before and during the month of July and then on the final Saturday night after everyone is gone home after the six days of racing, the sense of pride to know that everything worked. I worked three hours a day for ten months of the year and full-time for the time before the festival when I came here first. Now it has reversed. Now it is ten months full-time and two months part-time, such is the increase in the job. I now have a helper in the office from May to December annually. Development has been on-going all the time. Every year there is always something. I think the punter when he arrives on the Monday of Race Week looks around to see what improvements are in Galway from the year before. The very first year I started, in 1974, racing had to be abandoned half way through the card on the Tuesday night due to incessant rain beforehand. Jockeys actually came in and said it was too dangerous to ride any more. We did much drainage work after that. Wednesday was postponed, we had a batch of tickets printed if you like for a rainy day and we gave all punters a ticket which gave them admission for another day's racing at the venue to be used within that year. A store of tickets has been kept for such an eventuality. The Friday card was abandoned and the Galway Plate was run on a Friday that year, the year *Bunclody Tiger* won the Plate. It was a baptism of fire for me and things were so chaotic, I felt I'd never stick this job. John Mulqueen of Teagasc was asked to come in and give advice on the drainage of the grounds. In tandem with Captain Mullins, a huge amount of work was done and there has never been a problem since.

RUN-OF-THE-MILL WORK

"I am present at and minute all meetings of the Race Committee, roughly ten meetings annually. But since Lord Hemphill became Chairman, he formed a Finance Sub-Committee which meets a week before every Race Committee meeting here. They are in charge of all financial matters. We have a sponsorship Sub-Committee and a Building Sub-Committee and I act as Secretary for them all unless any of them are held outside the Racecourse. The Ladies' Committee advise on decor and other matters. In January you start letting people know what your dates are for that year. You'd write to all people affiliated with racing such as the AA, the Hospitals, Doctors, Vets, CIE, anyone however peripheral just to acquaint them for their own calendars. We also produce a brochure fairly early in the year with general information and this is a nice colourful production. The Turf Club handles trainers, owners, etc., and we will eventually be told by them the number of entries per race. They handle declarations too. December is the end of our financial year and we have our AGM in late February. So you have January and February to get the books ready for audit. The Galway Races is dependent on how good the six-day Festival has gone the previous year. The Racing Board is very happy with the way things go here. In March and

April we prepare figures for our annual budget. Mr Moloney always insists we keep to the budget. I'd be on half-time in March and April. We'd be getting busier in May and hotting up in June with interest developing, and much more mail. Telephone calls would be very constant and growing. Phone calls more than letters because of instant reply. People saying they're planning holidays in Galway to include the races. April is the end of the financial year generally and there is a huge amount of work here too in the PAYE sector — making returns for all our staff permanent and temporary, and that is for over two hundred people. That takes over two weeks of solid work, preparing P60s etc. There is always something to keep us busy. People sometimes ask me what I do and I remember saying to someone once that I looked after everything from toilet rolls to income tax. You have to be sure particularly during racing that you don't run out of anything. The nitty gritty.

THE FESTIVAL

"The month of July is absolutely hectic here. We are going from 9 a.m. to 6 p.m. every day. The phone is hopping. People are standing outside waiting to talk to you. Some people are inside too and three phones going at the same time. You can't afford to lose your cool, and if you get excited, you'll slow yourself down. A heap of letters daily. You list your priorities and get them done. I have a book for July, September and October and every job that needs to be done is listed in that book. We don't have much to do with Owners and Trainers really. I'd meet them as they come into the public office, if they wanted something. I'd have got to know most of them over the years. They are always very, very pleasant, very nice people. The best known are the most unassuming, Dermot Weld for instance, and Jim Bolger — always very courteous, never demanding or impatient. It's the same with the jockeys. But I'd be dealing even less with them.

STORIES FROM RACE WEEK

"We had a letter last year from a lady from Ennistymon, County Clare. She was over ninety and she wrote to say when she was young, she always came to the Galway Races and would like to enter for the Best Dressed Lady Competition and how would she go about it. We wrote back to her and told her you had to be invited to enter for it but told her to contact the organiser Fergus Foley. We sent her tickets for Ladies' Day and we asked her to drop in and see us. This she did and we took her up to Fergus and he treated her very well. Her photo appeared in the papers later. She was a real lady and it seems was the best dressed lady many years ago.

"If the work isn't done before Race Week it will not get done. We are very hectic during Race Week dealing with people, arranging for wages which are now paid by cheque. Keeping people happy no matter what the complaint. It involves a multitude of things from trophies to wages. Mr Moloney is almost like a clone. He is all over the place and knows everything that is happening. I never see what is happening outside. Take the October meeting, I'll never see Macnas or the children's playing area.

BEST MOMENTS

"I suppose to meet someone who is unhappy and to put them at ease. People come in very upset about the most trivial things but to them it is very important. PR is very much part of this job. An old man came in last year after having his pocket picked. He was very upset. 'I know you always warn us but you never think it will happen to yourself,' was more or less what he said. I gave him time and because I felt sorry for him I gave him two tea tickets to comfort him and he went away happy. Last year also a man came in and asked me had a glasses case been handed in. I asked him had he lost his spectacles but he said no. Unfortunately, he had six hundred pounds in it and had left it on the counter of the Owners' and Trainers' Bar and walked away. When he went back it was gone. I've heard people come in here and tell us they have had their pockets picked when they had the money pinned on to them, but to leave it in a spectacle case!

"I don't get involved in the social whirl at all. I'm usually here from 9 a.m. to 11 p.m. on the Monday and the Tuesday. I'd finish at 8 p.m. on Wednesday and Thursday and you're so tired that all you'd want to do is go home, take a wee walk maybe and go to bed. Over the years I have developed a keen interest in racing. I go to race meetings now in Ballinrobe, Tralee, Listowel. It's inevitable to compare notes. During the

Summer I called to see Killarney Racecourse on a non-race day. Listowel is terrific. It has got the type of atmosphere we have here though on a slightly smaller scale. They have huge crowds too and the Totes are fabulous, but Galway is special. A man from Orange County, California was buying seats last year. He comes to Galway Races every year. We are getting queries now for this year's dates.

"The media people are always very pleasant. The racing journalists have a very hard job to do, keeping deadlines, sending in stories. We have a whole series of phones installed for them now. They all love Galway. The presence of the top people from across the water generates tremendous interest. It is nice to see them coming and nice to see the home horses take them on.

SOUTH AFRICA

"One year we had a letter from a doctor in South Africa who had actually raced in Galway about fifty years ago. He was just reminiscing and we wrote back to him. He noticed that Mr T McDonogh was listed as being a member of the Race Committee and wondered was he the son of the Mr McDonogh the great merchant of Merchant's Road. The same man enquired if Mr Paddy O'Flaherty was the son the Mr Michael O'Flaherty. We sent him on a brief history and a brochure. We also sent him some photographs. We reply to all letters, to people who collect racing souvenirs, etc. I'm delighted that you have decided on a book on the Galway Races.

"Anything that boosts Galway Races will be a help. Racing is a huge industry. The amount of people the Galway Races bring to Galway is huge. There were years in the late seventies when we had huge crowds. Even bigger than now. Although we are coming close to those figures again. The new steps around the parade ring in 1994 provided a great boon. The introduction of so many racing personalities from the Ring on the two big days in 1994 was all Mr Moloney's idea. Finally, I hope we keep going the way we are. Give people what they want and hope they keep coming back. I love the September meeting too. It is very quiet by comparison. The October one appeals too and the children make that meeting. The job suits me in that it has become more demanding as I had more time to give it and I have grown very much into the job. Also I have a very supportive husband, he is chief cook and bottle washer for the whole month of July and doesn't complain."

16
Head Groundsman

"Seeing them come to the first fence in the Plate puts the heart crossways in me."

— *Tom Broderick, Foreman of the Course (Head Groundsman)*

Tom Broderick is a hurling son of Castlegar, a staunch back who won six County Senior Hurling Championship medals and played full-back for Galway in the 1955 All-Ireland minor hurling final. When did he start working in Ballybrit?

"I started temporary in about 1954 first, just after leaving school at the age of fifteen, and have worked there permanently since about 1958. The lads with me at the time were the late Mick McDermott and the late Dan Feerick also known as John. Paddy McDermott was in charge. He lived beside the track in a house where the factories are now built. I got a fondness for the place from an early stage and was keen on racing from the word go. Seeing horses racing was always a thrill for me. And building up for the annual Racing Festival was always satisfying. I lived within a mile and a half of the course as the crow flies. As a kid of five or six we used to hear the amplifiers blaring out and that was a huge drawing card. My grand-aunt, Mrs Ward, first brought me to the Races. I was about seven or eight then. Later on I used to go with my father. We used to go to the fair of Turloughmore as he was very interested in horses too. I remember being at the fair on the morning of the Races and there were horse dealers there from Limerick named Sheridan. One of them, named Danny, and my Dad fell out over the sale of a horse but despite that

Danny told him to back *Saint Kathleen II* in the Plate and she won. The year was 1951. About 1983, I took over as Foreman from Mick Connolly. Mick was in charge from about 1974 and I learnt it all from him. He was a great character and we really missed him when he left. There was never a dull day with him. He had a great outlook on life. If it wasn't hurling it was fairs or cattle or horses.

BUILD-UP

"It starts to get hectic the few months before the Festival. Fences have to be right, the hurdles too. But above all the ground must be A1. When the October meeting ends, it really starts there. You put the ground back as good as you can and let it settle for the Winter. The grass from Springtime on has to be cut to a level of about three to four inches and has to be cut and maintained two or three times a week as it needs it. There are four of us working here now and rain or shine there is always something to do. Hurdles to be fixed, some painting and general repairs. The four with me now are Michael Flaherty, the man who cuts the fences and shapes them, Johnny Coyne, Paddy Long and Paddy Keary, all locals, not all full-time. Michael Flaherty does an expert job on all fences and it is most important. I've seen fences in courses both in Ireland and England and ours are as good if not better than most. In all there are seven fences. The first one past the Stands is called the Weigh-room fence and it is the one that puts the heart crossways in me especially in the Galway Plate, which starts about two furlongs away. When you have over twenty horses in it and you see them all coming, it's a great sight to see but you're always worried that a few of them will fall. One year four fell at that fence. Val O'Brien's *Tubs* came down there in 1994. Another worry is that so many people want to see the action at that fence and it is so difficult to keep them away from it. After that is the Lisheen fence, then the Pen jump, the Regulation, then Paddy's fence and of course the two in the Moneen which are legendary because of their closeness.

SUCCESS OF RACES

"We have a top class Committee and good management. John Moloney keeps on top of it all. We'd have ten to fifteen working here in the weeks before the Festival and a whole lot of local Castlegar men work temporarily at the jumps, hurdles and elsewhere during the Races. We move back the rails every second day. We'd have three different tracks that way. The length of the track is a mile and two furlongs. We usually take up the rails on the Tuesday evening after racing. New ground for the flat and hurdles for Wednesday and Thursday. Another change then for Friday and Saturday. Too dry conditions present problems. We have two water tankers for watering the track. Three years ago we had to do a lot of watering. Our facilities are second to none and we get very few complaints. The last thing I want to see is a horse being put down. Some break down first before being put down. There is always much grief. Some are family pets. I hate to see it. I've seen many people devastated over a horse being put down.

FUN

"In the very early days I saw some great fights out in the free area. Mostly between the people running the hurdy gurdies or the three-card-trick men. I still go out there for a while during races. One fellow from Limerick named Harte, a great character, has been coming for years and our own Galwegian Paddy Dodd. The three-card-trick men are banned from the Stand area but they still manage to get in. I enjoy seeing people enjoying themselves. There is great satisfaction for about a week afterwards. But it is back to work straight away cleaning up the place. But it's more relaxed, less excitement, the rush of adrenalin is gone. It's easy enough to prepare for September and October. Things fall into place for those two meetings. The Plate of course is the highlight of the Festival. I usually watch it from the Stewards' Stand and when you get a close finish like we got in 1994 it is the greatest feeling in the world. The place is alive. I've been to a lot of race meetings across Ireland, and Ascot and Goodwood are lovely also, but in Galway the atmosphere is superior to all of them. In any other place it's an ordinary day's racing. In Galway it is different but perhaps I'm biased.

EXCITEMENT

"The excitement, the crowds, the atmosphere. The roar of the crowd in the Stand is immense, even in a minor race if there is a close finish. And the Hurdle generates as much interest almost as the Plate. Very good horses come to Galway. The first one I think of would have to be *Dawn Run*, although we didn't realise how good she was at the time. Dermot Weld's *Go and Go* is another. Tom Dreaper used to have some great jumpers. *Leap Frog* was one of the great jumpers. Paddy Sleator, Clem Magnier and Phonsie O'Brien great trainers from the past. Noel Meade like Dermot Weld so successful in recent times in Galway. And then there is young Aidan O'Brien, who may become the best of them all. He is such a modest young fellow.

"As for jockeys, Kinane is the daddy of them all. When you see him coming up on the outside in Galway watch out. He moves at the furlong pole and that's it. Johnny Roe was good. Kinane has such determination. He knows what he has under him when he comes round that corner.

"We have been very lucky with everything here over the years. Regarding the free area, the crowds have diminished and I'd hate to see that area go altogether. The atmosphere out there twenty years ago was marvellous. You could see monkeys there then. I saw a man lying on a bed of nails and another man break a stone on his chest with a sledge. A helluva spot then. The track is improving all the time. It is hard to please everybody but we do our best. It was a great thrill to have the Pope come to Ballybrit. Seeing the helicopter landing near the winning post and watching our Pontiff walk along the track. I thought I'd never see that day. All my family were on the Stand. It is possibly my greatest ever memory. The September and October meetings are panning out into very good meetings. The October meeting is better supported. The Bank of Ireland do a good sponsorship job and then you have Macnas and lots of things happening for the kids."

Punters' Paradise

From The Horse's Mouth

Charley McCreevey's first Galway Visit

"I have been coming to Galway for years. When I was younger I was able for the whole Festival. Nowadays just one or two days is nearly too much. The first time I came with two teenage pals, Eddie Shanley, now a shopkeeper in Sallins and Ian Blanchfield. We pitched our tent in a field alongside the steep hill going to Ballybrit. Being more of a gambler than the lads, I went to the Dogs after the Races one night while they went to the 'Sound of Music' in the Estoria. I lost everything at the Dogs. So they bailed me out for next day. Between all of us we lost everything next day. So we hitched to Leopardstown for the Saturday because we knew we'd get a lift home from there. But we still had to negotiate getting in free there. I remember taking advantage of an ambulance gaining entry. So that was my first Galway Races."

17
Jackpot Seekers All

*O*ver the years, many people from all walks of life and all corners of Ireland and elsewhere travel to Ballybrit to enjoy the 'craic', lay their bets, hit the jackpot and make their fortunes. Some are lucky, some aren't. Let me introduce some of them to you.

J B DONOHOE ALIAS BERTIE OF LOUGHREA

Bertie Donohoe or JBD as he has been known for years in the *Connacht Tribune* is one of the great lovers of sport to be found anywhere. Seventy-seven years young the night I interviewed him for this book, he had just returned from a Galway against Cork National Hurling League game in Ballinasloe on a damp November Sunday. On the same day his beloved Loughrea won the Galway Junior Football title, the first such adult gaelic football title for this well-known hurling stronghold for years.

"I'm delighted for the Loughrea lads. I was on four Loughrea teams beaten in East Galway Junior Football finals, once by Kilconnell who had the famous Kerry footballer Paul Russell playing for them. Rugby was my major sport and in all I played thirteen times for Connacht, once as a college player against Leinster at out-half, when I actually scored a try, and twelve times as hooker and prop-forward for the senior team succeeding Amby Roche in the position and succeeded by Eoin O'Malley, son of Surgeon Michael O'Malley."

His weekly sports column covering all sports entitled '*World of Sport*' began over thirty years ago but he is a *Connacht Tribune* journalist for fifty-four years. Racing has always been one of his favourite sports. It was Paddy Ryan who sent me in search of Bertie (see Paddy's interview) and the story of 'The Boys of Lios na Cranchy'. Bertie was quick to elaborate on that story.

"Christopher Griffin was the driver of the sidecar or trap and Paddy Leahy the other passenger with my father Michael. They were travelling home from the races and my father began the poem in Ballybrit and finished it at the Railway Bridge in Craughwell and Paddy Leahy turned to him and said, 'I never listened to anything longer nor worse'. I only remember one other verse which centred around my father himself:

> *Mick Donohoe our captain Bold*
> *He searched Loughrea for cars to hold*
> *The famous team who never sold*
> *The name of Lios na Cranchy*

all this to the air of 'The Boys of Killiecrankie' which commemorated a famous massacre in the Highlands close to scenic Pitlochry.

"I went to the races first in 1930. Harry Ussher's horse *East Galway* won the Plate. That year I went to Garbally College in Ballinasloe at the age of thirteen. I remember going to the Roscommon Races in Lenabane and my first ever successful bet there on a horse called *Hakimon*. The horse won at 3/1 and I had a half crown on it, a brave sum then. A mare called *Heartbreak* ran that day in Roscommon and got third in the Aintree Grand National the following year.

"The best bet I ever had was in the Hurdle in 1972. I was at the Phoenix Park Races shortly beforehand and my good friend John Dillon O'Farrell, who succeeded me as President of the Garbally PPU gave me a strong tip for the Galway Hurdle for a horse named *Hardboy* trained by Dick McCormack. His cousin had given him the whisper even though the horse had never raced over hurdles before and was to be ridden by flat jockey Tommy Murphy. I was sceptical but in the first race that day I had a winner and cheered him home. Beside me stood former Galway footballer Bosco McDermott and his brother-in-law John Maguire and when they asked had I anything else I gave them *Hardboy*. My bet was thirty pounds and twenty pounds place on the Tote and I won eight hundred pounds. When the race ended, with *Hardboy* winning of course, John Maguire lifted me off the ground with glee. His bet was bigger still and we celebrated on champagne and brandy in the Owners' and Trainers' Bar afterwards.

"Seeing Mickey Tully, a fellow student with me in Garbally College and a good friend, waving his cap in the air as he stood in the stirrups before reaching the winning post on *Fair Pearl* in the Galway Hurdle in 1946 is a great memory. I remember four of us cycling to Ballybrit during the war years on a beautifully sunny day in 1942, Paddy Ryan, Paddy Kelly, Tommy Lally and myself. We stopped for a drink in Glynn's of Oranmore. A friend of ours Jack Hannafin had just joined Dr Dan Comyn as an apprentice. Dan, an LLD and captain of the Irish cricket team in his time, was a Steward and former Chairman of the Galway Race Committee. Dan Moore (father of Arthur) and Georgie Wells had set out from Rathoath for the Races on the previous day in a horse-drawn spring car, a more fashionable kind of sidecar, but it broke down at Glasson near Athlone, site of a recently developed golf course. Anyhow Dr Comyn got our friend Jack and Paddy Grace to drive up and collect the two racing greats at that time. They got them to mark their card for Plate day, noting every tip and passed on the word from 'the horse's mouth'. All six won. *Golden Jack* ridden by Dan won the Plate. *Mountbrown* trained by Tom McDermott-Kelly won the first race that day at 20/1. I placed all the bets for the lads and I always remember what the poor bookie said to me as we raced to pick up the winnings, 'Why the hell did ye all pick on me?' We stayed overnight, a rare luxury. I'm still going to Galway and I wouldn't miss the Races for anything."

MICHAEL GILLEN, BARBER, BOXER AND RACONTEUR

He is known as "Chick". A man of many parts, Chick is the quint-essential Galwegian. Has the accent to go with it and the twinkle in the eye to go with his trade. His barbershop in Dominick Street is a great meeting place. The day I interviewed Chick for this book, who walked in with his little dog on a leash only the oft remembered Mickey Tully who rode his own *Fair Pearl* to victory in the Galway Hurdle of 1946. Chick has a great love of the Connemara pony and horses generally and one of his sons now owns a racehorse.

"I have been going every year since I was seven years old, about 1940. The first time I went was with Sam Cunniss and his sidecar. He let me sit on the axle underneath. Sam loved horses himself and was very kind to them. *Red Shaft* was a winner that first day. I'll never forget the day Mickey Tully's horse won the Hurdle in 1946. I was right at the winning post standing alongside Jimmy Duggan the hurler, who had a bob on *Fair Pearl*. We were outside, of course, where all the action was then. Mickey used to stable the horse in Raleigh Row with his pet goat Billy. I remember he had two rubbers covering the goats horns in case he'd puck *Fair Pearl*. That day long ago Mick rode the winner in Josie Owens's Corinthians jersey and he was the first jockey I ever saw to raise his hands in salute as he passed the winning post. He was waving to us inside in the gods as it were. You had to have money to be in the stands.

"I have great memories of the Galway Races. In those days it was huge outside. Great free crack and entertainment. You had plenty of musicians, men balancing cartwheels on their chins, lying on beds of nails, swallowing razor blades and lumps of glass, every kind of trick of the loop. And you had three-card-trick men everywhere. The best man I ever saw at that was the late Paddy Dodd. I never saw him lose money. He'd let you win for a while using his own cronies and then after building your confidence he'd clean you out. He always gave back some luck money to those he cleaned. You'd get a good feed that time in Lawlor's Tent for three and six pence. Fine place and spotlessly clean. All the waitresses with white aprons. You wouldn't see a surgeon dressed better! Another tent missed from the outer area these days is the Old Malt Tent run so well by the Walsh family for years. I never ever miss the races. They are part of me. If I was crippled I'd crawl out, I think."

COLM HANNELLY, TARMON, CASTLEREA

Colm who recently retired from Telecom Eireann in Galway, is a sports fanatic and super statistician. Once selected as the GAA Brain of Connacht, steeplechasing is another great interest, his special Galway feature being the Galway Plate.

"I first came to the Races in the sixties but had an interest much earlier. Just listening to the commentaries first from Mick Byrne and then Mícheál O'Hehir. My brother Father Pádhraic used to say it was the latter who made me interested because he used to ring off the names of the jockeys like you'd ring off the names of the footballers, fellows like Tim Molony, Aubrey Brabazon, Martin Molony and Tim Hyde. I remember *Swindon Glory* winning for J M Mangan twice in the Plate (1943 and 1944) and *Grecian Victory* for Harry Ussher in 1945. That time we used to be working at the hay. The late Father Pádhraic was in Saint Patrick's College, Kiltegan at that time and he'd be out hay-making too. No matter what the weather was like we all downed tools and trooped in to hear the radio commentaries of the Plate and the Hurdle from Mícheál O'Hehir. It was a two-day event then (Wednesday and Thursday) with the Friday in Tuam. Pádhraic brought off a great double in 1946 on *Keep Faith* in the Plate ridden by Tim Hyde and trained by Tom Dreaper and on *Fair Pearl* in the Hurdle (ridden, owned and trained by Mickey Tully). The latter lost the race twenty-four hours later to Dick McIlhagga's *King of the Jungle* on a technicality. We placed our bet in the local bookie's in Castlerea, John Keenan's, the father of Donal, later to become President of the GAA.

"I started coming on a regular basis in 1962 when I started to work in Galway. Dermot Weld was a young fellow riding in those days for his father Charlie. My first winner was in 1952 when I started working in Claremorris with the Post Office Engineering Branch. Vincent O'Brien was a big name in racing then with all his Cheltenham successes with *Cottage Rake* and *Hatton's Grace*. So I decided to follow his horse *Alberoni* which had also won the Irish Grand National that year. We were working at the time outside Canon Curley's house in the town and I remember him coming out of his house and asking us who would win the Plate. I gave him *Alberoni* and we all had a successful flutter.

"I always go on Plate day as I love chasing. The great trainers were Vincent O'Brien, Tom Dreaper, Charlie Weld, and Phonsie O'Brien who was a good jockey before that. Phonsie won four Plates in succession on *Carraroe*, *Ross Sea* (twice) and *Blunt's Cross* all under top class jockeys Fred Winter, Bobby Beasley, and Stan Mellor. Paddy Sleator too. I can't forget *Hindhope* winning for Eddie O'Grady in 1979 under Jonjo O'Neill, the great jockey of the time. I used to work near Eyre Square and at the time Jonjo stayed in the Great Southern Hotel and Tommy Carberry, another brilliant jockey stayed in the Skeffington Arms. Great to see those fellows passing by. The Great Southern Hotel on Race nights would always be packed to the doors. Same with the Skeffington. You could bump into anyone on race days.

"1974 was the year the Plate was postponed to the Friday. I backed the winner *Bunclody Tiger* but that was a stroke of luck really. I met Tom Joyce, an Army man who was then stationed in the Curragh and hailed from Cornamóna, on the Thursday in the Great Southern and he put me on Kevin Bell's horse which duly won. Last year I got a tip from a Wexford man on the Sunday night of the Connacht final in the Corrib Great Southern to back the Wexford horse *Feathered Gale*. He was up for the week but his real interest was a neighbour's horse which got up in a fantastic finish, as good as I've seen in the Plate. Other memories are of *O'Leary* winning in 1976 and *Firion's Law* in 1991. I was on my way to see my brother Father Pádhraic who was very ill in Kiltegan and that one is a sad memory. I saw the race in Quinn's of Baltinglass. They actually owned the horse and were all in Galway. The place went mad that day. Later on that year Pádhraic went to his reward but he enjoyed that story. The *O'Leary* victory I remember for a different reason. I missed it because my daughter Olivia, just a year old then, stuck her finger in my eye and I had to get medical treatment that day in hospital. So I watched it on telly with one eye!

"The Galway Plate is a chase out of season. Most of the top Cheltenham horses are out on grass at that time of year. *Leap Frog* was an exception when he won for Jim Dreaper and Tommy Carberry. The easiest winners were *Sarajay Day* and *Chow Mein*. The former seemed just to run away and win the race. The best piece of jockeyship I've seen in Galway was the year Jonjo O'Neill brought off the double with *Hard Tarquin* in the Hurdle. I watched him closely and he really lifted the horse over the line.

"I love the inside area and always go out there after the main feature race. I remember a very funny three-card-trick incident there. Three or four fellows were standing together and watching the three-card-trick man. They were obviously mates. One of them threw on twenty pounds and won. This other fellow obviously not one of the gang came along and put on twenty pounds and won. Next he put on forty pounds and lost. Then another twenty and lost again. A final twenty pounds and he lost that too. Well, he drew a left footed kick and sent the table flying. The guards then came along and the three-card-trick men ran. They had the money!"

Steel Duke and Stephen Craine winning in Galway in 1982.

Dawn Run and Tom Mullins winning the bumper at Galway.

Committed and Wally Swinburn winning at Galway in 1982.

Pinch Hitter and jockey Jonjo O'Neill jumping in front of stablemate Steel Duke before going on to win the 1983 Galway Hurdle.

The Kings, Charlie and Mary with the Galway Plate in 1988.

I'm Confident and Fran Flood winning the Galway Hurdle on the line in 1989.

Bold Flyer and Sarah Collen take the first fence before winning the Galway Plate in 1989.

1990 Winners of Fashion
From left: Ms Audrey Power, Limerick (Racing Miss), the late Fergus Foley of the Blue Cloak, Ms Ann Bourke, Toronto (Most Elegant Lady), Ms Orla Cahill (Most Elegant Hat), and Ms Barbara McMahon presenter of Head to Toe, RTE.

Natalie's Fancy and Jason Titley are just behind Natural Ability and Charlie Swan at the last before going on to win the Galway Hurdle in 1992.

Adrian Maguire (left) and Richard Dunwoody with the clock presented by the Committee to record their great duel for the Jockey's title in 1994.

The Gooser and Adrian Maguire being led in by owner Margaret O'Leary after winning the Galway Plate of 1992.

The Parade Ring in Galway before a race in Festival week.

John Moloney,
Galway Racecourse Manager.

Mick Kinane,
leading flat jockey.

Mrs Mary Burke presemts the Channelle Top Trainer's Award to Dermot Weld with (left) Lord Hemphill and (right) Michael Burke.

Martine McDonagh photographed at the Tote building in Ballybrit.

The Lady from Ennistymon. Mrs Josephine Curran, seventy years going to the Races.

The finish of the 1994 Galway Plate. Feathered Gale gets up close home to pip Minister for Fun (inside) and Mubadir (Number 6).

Oh So Grumpy, with trainer Jessica Harrington and jockey Mark Dwyer in the winner's enclosure after winning the 1994 Galway Hurdle.

JOHN AND MACKIE RUSHE, DUNMORE, CO. GALWAY

John, the elder by two years and his brother Mackie, two bachelor farmers from High Street in that well-known Gaelic football stronghold, Dunmore, my native place, have been racing *aficionados* since their national school days. When did they start going to Galway?

"We were both brought, in our father's hands literally, the first time in 1945."

Mackie, the younger, got lost regularly early on because he used to ramble in among the horses but he always found his way back. The Plate winners they remembers best in those early days were *Swindon Glory*, *Grecian Victory* and *Silent Prayer*. John remembers the latter for a reason.

"At class in Saint Jarlath's College, Tuam, Mr O'Sullivan, one of our teachers, always said a silent prayer before every class and that lovely custom put me on to *Silent Prayer* for the Plate in 1948 and he delivered. We never missed a year since. We try and arrange it for the stock. At Summertime there isn't much of a problem with feeding them. If there was a problem with stock one of us might have to miss a day but we'd do that in turns. That seldom happens. Never for the Plate or Hurdle. We go to all Meets in the West of Ireland, about twenty-five meetings a year. Roscommon, Sligo, Ballinrobe and all the days in Galway. Galway is number one. It is the glamour spot. Once I couldn't get up into the Stand with the crowds, and just as the race was over this Frenchman in his late twenties beside me also looking up into the Stands said 'Paris is supposed to be the spot for glamour but here I've seen glamour to beat anything I have ever seen in France. And at my age I like to watch the girls'.

"We always do the jackpot together. I'm sure we have won it in Galway about ten times but we have never landed a real big one. Some of the trainers recognise us and give us the odd nod of recognition whatever about tips. Des McDonagh, the trainer of the great *Monksfield* of Dunmore connections (the Mangans) is a friend. We always wore two blue hats at the Races and were able to identify ourselves in the Stands easily enough if we needed to swap tips. Michael Anthony Greaney, a former Dunmore man who worked in Dublin, told us they were Australian cricket hats. Dessie McDonagh tackled us one day for not wearing the blue hat claiming that Mackie's blue hat seemed to bring him luck!

"Of late Mick Kinane is superb on the flat. We saw Martin Molony and his brother Tim. Also Eddie Newman. Paddy Sleator a great trainer from Grangecon. Bobby Coonan another great jock. And we backed Wally Swinburn dozens of times. *Leap Frog's* win in 1973 under twelve stone was a great achievement. In that race for a second Tommy Carberry, the jockey, almost brought him the wrong side of the bollard separating the jump and hurdle courses but he switched him just in time to win brilliantly. In the old days horses carried up to thirteen stone on their backs.

"In the fifties we used to go to Galway only. Afterwards we got the bug and followed racing as a sport. If we pass on up in that Track, certainly if we have to go suddenly, we hope it is at the Races and while we can move we'll be there le cúnamh Dé. When it was a two-day affair, the Thursday evening saw us always depressed when we came home. Summer was ending and Winter was nigh. Our local postman Paddy O'Hagan used to say, 'When the Galway Races are over, the Summer is over'.

"In the early days my father used to hire a car in the post war years. An old V-8 belonging to Jimmy Moran, an old Dunmore family, was the car and I'll never forget the number IM 6074. We used to go up to Moran's house and wait patiently outside their little shop in Barrack Street and eventually sat in the car. The sister Kathleen would always come out and spray us with holy water for the expedition, for that it was then. Jimmy wouldn't drive too fast. In fact he had a little block under the accelerator in case it would go down too far! He was dead afraid of traffic and parked it in a quarry on the Galway road about a mile from the track and we'd all have to leg it there, but we got used to it. Our uncle Jim used to come on Plate Day. We always stopped in Reilly's Pub in Tuam for a drink. Jimmy the driver would have a glass of Bass with a little drop of raspberry. Funny the things you remember. If we ever got separated then, we met under the number board which carried the names of the jockeys. We won the jackpot once on a very famous horse *Dawn Run*. We did a combination, which often cost us forty pounds and we had three up going into the last leg. *Dawn Run* was one of them. It was a four or five horse race and to make it worse we got a tip for one of the others so we laid off one hundred pounds on the tip to cover us. *Dawn Run* won and we got about five hundred and sixty pounds. So we really threw one hundred pounds away being careful. We tended to trust her after that!"

JOHN GARRY, DROGHEDA, COUNTY LOUTH

Originally from Athboy, County Meath, John went to the Galway Races many a time and had the great thrill of owning a winner at one Festival meeting.

"I always liked the atmosphere of the event. The people in general make it. I remember it first as a four-day event and the last few times it was a six-day event. Quite different from all other meetings I have attended you could still enjoy it after six days. In Listowel or Killarney or even in Cheltenham you'd have enough after three days racing, not so with Galway. It's a mixture of racing (a nice blend of flat and hunt). I actually had a horse which won in Galway in 1979 called *Princely Ray* which I owned in partnership with Oliver Finnegan of Navan, trained by Arthur Moore. We won eight times in three years with the horse before he broke his leg in Leopardstown. When I started racing originally, I always hoped to have a runner in Galway not to mind owning a winner. On that particular day he was beaten in a photo finish by a horse called *Nobody Knows* owned by a Parish Priest, but we won the race on a Stewards' enquiry. The race was a two-mile flat race, the Barna Handicap and Pat Gilson rode our horse. Joe Byrne, the rider of the winner was known to me and he asked me not to object even though our connections favoured an objection as they felt the other horse had crossed our line. We didn't object but got the race after the Stewards' enquiry, twenty minutes after the race ended. We celebrated the win afterwards in the Great Southern Hotel."

MATT CONNOLLY OF SHANTALLA, GALWAY

Matt Connolly now lives at Conaire Road, Shantalla, Galway and can be seen walking the Salthill Promenade on a daily basis, walking generally 'on his ownio' always bedecked in peak cap, and has been a racing *aficionado* all his life.

"I started going to the Races at the age of four, in or around 1925. An old working mate of my father's, Martin Melia, who had no family himself used to take myself and my brother Mick with him. He worked as a stoker in the Galway Gas Company with my father Paddy. It was a two-day event then. The horses used to stay then down in Irwin's yard in Eyre Street, also in John Cunniss's yard in Eyre Square, and in the Galway Sportsground stables. At that time they used to take the horses up through Bohermore, where we lived, about six in the morning and I remember Martin pointing out a great horse called *Clonsheever* who used to run in England even then. After that we used to get up early ourselves to see the horses pass by. All year we'd be looking forward to the Races. Most times we'd walk up along by the back of Castlegar Church and come out at the Moneen on the course. Máirtín Mór McDonogh owned a horse called *Corofin* and he was a good one. There was another one named *Kyleclare,* and *Easter Hero* was another good one.

"During the war there was no transport and the horses arrived by train then. We used to go down to the Station to see them being unloaded. It was sidecars for most then and they did a roaring business (half a crown one way). We used to walk out as usual. I joined the Army in 1937 and remember being stationed in Bere Island (County Cork) and I missed the Galway Plate one year. It's the only one I remember missing. *Ring of Gold* won the Plate that year on a very wet day but I got home that night in time for the Hurdle. I've never missed the Plate or Hurdle ever since. That was 1940. And I hope to be going 'till the day I die.

"I always went to the Moneen and we had plenty of bookies there too. Horses I remember well were *The Gripper,* who used to carry top weight, *Swindon Glory* who won the Plate twice in a row and our own *Fair Pearl* ridden by Michael Tully of Saint Mary's Road to win the Hurdle in 1946 and beat the great *King of the Jungle.* The great names I would associate with Galway include Aubrey Brabazon, Dan Moore, who rode for Dorothy Paget, Don Butchers from England who won the big double in 1938, Pat Taaffe, Harry Ussher, Tom Dreaper, Phonsie O'Brien, Paddy Sleator. Tommy Burns was a first class flat jockey over one and a half miles, like his son T P after him, and in the jumps it was hard to beat Martin Molony, Jimmy Brogan and Harry Beasley.

"We got involved in horses ourselves later but we never had a winner in Galway. *Crystal Clipper* was beaten by a head by a Dermot Weld trained and Michael Kinane ridden winner. We had another good one named *Le Stelle*, which won first time out as a two-year-old in Navan and did likewise as a three-year-old. In fact it was Dessie Hughes's (the trainer) first ever two-year-old win. One final memory, about 1940 I was at the Races with my wife, Mary, and she asked me to put half a crown on this outsider called *Amor de Cuba*. I thought she was crazy and didn't put on the bet. The horse won at 40/1. She didn't talk to me for about a week and I was mad with myself. Five pound winnings was a lot of money then."

THE McGOWANS OF LOUGHGLYNN — FATHER AND SON

The McGowans owned a bar business in Loughglynn and sold it over a year ago. The father William James is eighty-two years old and when the one hundred pound ticket for a numbered seat in the Stand came up in 1994, the McGowan family purchased one for their Dad and he thoroughly enjoyed his sixtieth year at Galway Races without a break in great comfort for the entire six days. His memory isn't too clear now but:

"I remember we could only travel fifty miles one way in the car once during the war. So we had to park in Claregalway and I sprained an ankle climbing over one of those famous Galway stone walls and had to be carried most of the way to Claregalway afterwards. My best bet was on *Red Hillman* in the Hurdle in the thirties. The same year I think as *Reviewer* won the Plate (that was 1935). A good friend of mine from Thurles, P J O'Meara, Solicitor, who was at Castleknock College with me, met me and told me to back it. Another year the same jockey won the Plate and Hurdle, I wish I could remember his name but I had a pound on the Hurdle winner at 50/1. That was some win."

Liam, the son, who now lives in Ballyhaunis is a real student of form. In 1994 he did very well in Galway. I stood beside him for the Hurdle and he was on the winner *Oh So Grumpy*. He took it all in his stride, but why wouldn't he? He had won the Jackpot earlier that week, a cool three thousand two hundred and sixty-eight pounds and was to do better, much better with another Jackpot win on the Friday. In all he had won three Jackpots in Galway in two years. His first Jackpot ticket in 1994 cost him thirteen pounds and fifty pence. The big one cost him three hundred. He had four horses left in the last race including Joanna Morgan's mount *Lady Blakeney* trained by B V Kelly and she came in at a great price.

"But I'm a lucky devil. Wasn't eighteen months old when I won a car in a raffle. I'd need another one now! I bought a horse out of my Jackpot winnings this year and he is being trained by Bill Lannigan at The Heath, Portlaoise. My biggest thrill in Galway was scooping the Jackpot this year and you're only the sixth person to hear about it. Never told my father. The world will know it now. It was a cold sweat kind of thrill though.

"It hasn't been all sunshine in Galway. In 1992 as one of the Riverside Racing Club which owned *Solar Flash* we entered in Galway and felt we had a great chance. So we all gambled and the price fell from 33/1 to 6/1. Some of our friends laid bets of ten pounds and twenty pounds on the outside and got the best odds, but then the money moved on the horse. He only finished sixth and even though we were skinned we enjoyed seeing the Bookies almost crashing into each other racing to lay off the money.

"In 1973 I had a chance meeting with Mr Scully's son, the connections of Galway Hurdle winner *Lesabelle*. He said his father's horse would win. So I told some of my friends including Dad and they told me I was crazy. So I didn't back the horse. My father put fifty pence each way on the Tote on *Lesabelle* which won against the odds. I was so upset he gave me the winnings and advised me never to be put off a bet by others. I have always heeded that lesson since. As to the Galway Races, they are absolutely special in our house. If any of the McGowans or my in-laws, the Curleys, die during Galway Races, I'm afraid the funeral will have to be held over until after the Races. That's the way it is with us."

PASCHAL SPELMAN, COMEDIAN, INSURANCE BROKER

Paschal Spelman is one of my favourite people. As a comedian, he has been part of Galway life for over forty years. At last year's Oyster Festival, he returned to the boards with his son and brought down the house as usual. He has always had an interest in the nags, has a flutter every so often and as a native Galwegian, who didn't come in the Oranmore Road or any other road, loves the Galway Racing Festival.

"I was one of the guest artists at the Herald Boot Fund Concert in 1959 in the old Capitol Theatre with the great Mícheál O'Hehir as MC. In introducing me, Mícheál told of seeing this familiar face every year at the Galway Races staring up at him and wondering what he was doing. Then years later when Mícheál went down to the Great Southern Hotel in Galway as Guest of Honour for the first ever Galway Sports Star Award Ceremony he realised that what the man was doing was listening and observing his voice delivery so that he could do the perfect impersonation. That night in Galway I came close to mimicking the great O'Hehir with a commentary on the Galway Hurdle involving among others Galway's own Mickey Tully who rode *Fair Pearl* to victory in 1946.

"As to the Summer Festival meeting it means a great occasion for the coming together of hundreds of people. You'd meet old friends walking the streets at Races time. The spirits are high and the atmosphere and goodwill are second only to Christmas time. As to bets the late Mark Scully told me his horse would win next day in Galway and even though I kinda doubted him I had a flutter on *Lesabelle* in the Hurdle in 1973 and she won. I was too young in 1946 to really appreciate Mickey Tully's win on *Fair Pearl*. I do remember him losing the race subsequently on a technicality but that didn't matter. I don't go as often now as I used to but I'd always go for a day or two during the Festival. Mostly I go now to say hello to a whole host of old acquaintances.

"I'll always remember the first time I went with my brother Jackie and a neighbour from Presentation Road around the corner from where we lived called "Dodo" Lydon, one of the best judges of form I ever met. His family ran a famous fishing tackle shop in Presentation Road, Galway. Needless to say we were in the outside enclosure — the free area. On Dodo's advice, Jackie and myself put a shilling on a horse called *Hydrabad* ridden by Joe Canty and he obliged. The odds were low, we got 1/6 back and it was a fortune to win three pence apiece. When I look back and think of it the highlights of the entertainment then, apart from a variety show in the Savoy Cinema, were the hurdy gurdies with Toft's in Eyre Square. My father and mother brought me there once during the Races and I won a golliwog on the Spin the Wheel and it meant a lot. Real innocent fun.

"The best piece of jockeyship I've ever seen in Ballybrit was the year

135

Pat Taaffe rode *Bonne* to victory in the Galway Hurdle. I got a tip for him in the Great Southern Hotel the night before and I knew after seeing them jump the first hurdle that Pat Taaffe and his mount were going to win."

SEAMUS CULLINANE — ATHENRY, COUNTY GALWAY

Séamus Cullinane, Principal of Athenry Vocational School, former Castlegar and Galway hurler, grew up near Ballybrit and got the smell and love of horses at an early age. He now owns a horse or two and never misses the Races.

"Everybody in the West of Ireland identifies with the Galway Races. It is the highlight of the social year. It was the annual holiday for the farming community and that is a tradition that has lived on and grown. It was a source of income for us as youngsters in Castlegar. We used to get thirty bob a day on race days for some small job or other. As we grew up it became a rendezvous for meeting old acquaintances and still is. I sometimes don't meet these people again until the Festival a year or two later and we usually part by saying, 'Meet you here again next year, le cúnamh Dé'. There is always an air of expectancy in the whole area as Races time approaches. Now the whole of Ireland identifies with it and that includes all classes. It has even become one of the biggest race meetings of them all and you can include Cheltenham, Liverpool and Punchestown in that."

SEAN DUGGAN, GALWAY HURLING GOALKEEPER

There is no more respected sports figure in Galway City than one of the greatest of all hurling goalkeepers Sean Duggan. A very fit man for his age, he swims in the sea at Blackrock daily, hail, rain or snow all year, every year. He has been a Ballybrit devotee all his life.

"My earliest recollection is of leaving College Road with my mother and father, walking down to Eyre Square getting the bus there and making our way to the Course. On getting there we would walk into the free area or the outside enclosure. I remember the camera men taking snaps. Their great selling point was of course instant photos and we'd all be delighted to get our photograph taken. We used to hold them dearly until we'd get home to show them off but when we'd get home they would have all faded away. There were several other stall holders selling fruit and sweets but the one I remember most of all was the lady shouting, 'Twelve bars of chocolate for six pence!' We'd rush to get this bargain and we'd find there was twelve squares in the bar. That was the bargain. They were up to every trick.

"There were many other sideshows. The three-card-trick and the man in the barrel. You bought four short sticks and when the head of the man would appear you'd throw the sticks hoping you'd hit the poor unfortunate man. If you struck him you won a prize which I think was a balloon. He had this peephole in the side of the barrel as a lookout but he was good at the bobbing up and down. There was also a very big marquee, operated by the Old Malt House, the Walsh family Ned, Willie and Fursey plus all their neighbours and friends who helped. I even helped collecting bottles myself in those days. They were a fine Irish family with all the traditions of our national way of life.

"Later on as I grew older I used to walk to the Course on my own like many more Galwegians. We took a shortcut through a lane known as Mike Burke's Boreen. I still go that way. The boreen is gone but through the kind offices of Digital this tradition of the area has been maintained. I remember Danny Butchers winning the Plate and Hurdle the same year (1938). Another memory is seeing *Stepaside Lord* breaking a leg going up the dip in a hurdle race. He was destroyed on the spot at that time and it left a marked impression on me.

"The Races for me are full of happy memories but think of the happiness for those who come home from London, Manchester, Coventry and places farther afield to be amongst their own for the week. Today Ballybrit is part of the city. It was deep in rural Galway when I started going. Now like life, time marches on."

SEAN PURCELL, FOOTBALL STAR AND RACING MAN

Seán Purcell is generally recognised as the greatest Gaelic footballer of all time (Mícheál O'Hehir and Mícheál O Muircheartaigh are just two who have held this always). He has always been a keen racing man as well as following the dogs.

"1940 was my first year. It was the last year the cars weren't off the road and our family travelled by taxi or hackney car as we called it then. *Saint Martin* won the Plate that year. For the rest of the war years, my brother, Frank and myself together with Jimmy "Chronix" Nohilly cycled both days from Tuam. The place was black with cyclists then. Other Plate winners then were *Swindon Glory* and *Grecian Victory*. Frank had a good wager on a horse called *Cockasnook* which won. The success of Galway is a combination of the racing and Galway itself as a tourist venue. Friday was always Tuam's day then and placed horses in Galway were looked on as good things for Tuam but it didn't always work out that way. It was a great pity that we lost that fixture in Tuam. I remember getting up early and seeing the horses exercising in Parkmore out through a back room window. The town would be full of Dublin accents, women with white aprons selling race cards. Over the years the horses I remember best were *Saint Martin, Leap Frog, Keep Faith* and *King of the Jungle*. I won't forget the day Mickey Tully came home on *Fair Pearl* or the Gleesons, from Dunmore originally, winning the Hurdle with *Carrantryla*. As for jockeys, Aubrey Brabazon and Martin Molony were great. In recent times the top hunt jockeys in England, Jonjo O'Neill, Peter Scudamore, Richard Dunwoody and Adrian Maguire have added to the scene. Our own Charlie Swan is as good as any of them."

TOM BOURKE, PHARMACIST, MERVUE AND CASTLEBAR

Tom Bourke, a Galway Races *aficionado*, has always wanted to write a book on it and started it off once. He can rattle off the names of winners of Plate and Hurdle any year. What is it in his opinion makes Galway Races so popular?

"It's our great love of national hunt racing. The West is the home of the stone wall and stories are legion of the deeds of great horses and great riders in this part of the world which are now part of our folklore.

"Galway, especially during the war years has many happy memories for me. From an early age I loved to hear of the feats of our great, steeplechasers at home and abroad and to be in Galway for the two-day Festival then was heaven. There was an air of expectancy everywhere coming up to the races. The hay was made with unnatural haste and prayers were said for fine days for the Races. I went to the Races for the first time with my mother in the forties and I had the pleasure of seeing Aubrey Brabazon steer home Miss M O'Mathieson's *Saint Martin* in 1941. Aubrey was a household name then belonging to an élite band of men including Danny Morgan, Willie O'Grady, Tim Hyde, Jimmy Brogan, Dan Moore, T McNeill and the Molony brothers Martin and Tim. The city during those years was a veritable child's paradise. Eyre Square had Toft's amusements inside its imposing railings, and sidecars and traps plied their way to and from the Racecourse by day and Salthill by night where the Hangar Ballroom catered for the midnight revellers under the baton of Johnny Cox whose signature song was:

'Dancing feet near the foreshore neat
In Salthill by the sea
Come and join the happy throng
Where joy and laughter is free
Life will be gay while on your way
To Salthill by the sea'.

"The Square had its Hunt Balls. Pubs, guest houses and hotels were full and there was a sound of revelry everywhere until the small hours. Nobody seemed interested in sleep and there was always the third day in Tuam on the Friday on your way home.

"On the first morning of the races the atmosphere was electric. Tips were always plentiful. No better place to suss them out than at the barber shop or in the baths in Salthill, where some of the jockeys would be wasting away some pounds. It was a simple time, money went a long way and if you had a few pounds in your pocket going to Ballybrit you had riches beyond compare. Ballybrit even then was a blaze of colour. Huge tents sprawled in the free enclosure right up from Ballyhack Castle to the railings. All the fun of the fair was there and it wasn't unusual to hear a booming male voice, shouting over the crowd, 'I'm robbed, I'm robbed' and approaching the scene you'd see a vast crowd gathered round a man who having words at will would convince you that if you invested in one of his lucky dips for six pennies your day was made. He used to recite at well spaced intervals over a loud hailer in a booming voice:

'Come and have a go
With your old pal Joe
Your mother won't know
And I won't tell her'.

"It was easy to be hooked. Another little man used to crack this huge whip to attract customers. He had a little ditty too:

'Step right up to see the monkey
The further up the monkey goes
The more you can see of his a....!'
Ah do step up'

"I well remember a fine big woman with well groomed hair neatly tied up in a knot wearing a spotlessly clean and starched white coat in her big tent. She sold the most delicious bacon sandwiches with Colman's mustard nearby should you require same and these would be washed down with a steaming cup of hot tea. She also sold beautiful scones with lashings of butter in between the layers; all those delicacies were displayed on long tables covered with white tablecloths and the best of delph. The outside free area then was very popular and I loved it more than any place else in the early years. Later on I became more interested in seeing the great horses parading. That and the famous trainers and jockeys could be seen in the Stand enclosure.

"*Golden Jack, Swindon Glory, Grecian Victory, Keep Faith, The Gripper* and *King of the Jungle* are the horses I remember best. I had listened to old timers relate the feats of *Yellow Furze, Ring of Gold* and the immortal *Clonsheever* and *East Galway*. Seeing Harry Ussher and Barney Nugent for the first time is a memory. If ever a man and a horse deserve to have a statue erected to them in Ballybrit, then it is Harry Ussher and *Clonsheever*. He trained eight Galway Plate winners between 1919 and 1945 and rode the winner *Ashbrook* in 1910, not to mention all the winners of lesser races and of the Galway Hurdle. The familiar roar of the crowd 'Come on Harry' is alas, a relic of bygone days. He won in 1923 and 1924 with *Clonsheever* and in 1925, with thirteen stone on his back, *Clonsheever* got third in the Plate. What a horse and what a man! Harry really loved his native Galway and Galway loved him.

"Another great Ballybrit trainer was Paddy Sleator, now in retirement. In his familiar hat and equipped with a cigarette holder, he took over the mantle of 'Master of Ballybrit' vacated by Harry Ussher. Like Harry he started off winning the Plate in 1934 as an amateur jockey on *Reviewer*. He trained his first Galway Plate winner in 1948 — *Silent Prayer* ridden by Tim Molony. He followed that up with *Amber Point* in 1954 and 1956 owned by Mrs Ann Bullett Biddle. A half brother of *Amber Point* named *Knight Errant* won for him the Plate in 1957, owned also by Mrs Ann Bullett Biddle. *Knight Errant* showed his versatility in 1958 by winning the Hurdle ridden as in the previous year by another Galway specialist jockey Bobby Beasley. Paddy and Bobby won the Plate again with *Sparkling Fame* in 1960. Sleator as you see was another Galway hero. And then came Phonsie O'Brien, Vincent's brother to win four Plates in a row. That training feat will take beating.

"*Prince Regent*, the greatest steeplechaser of all time got a great reception the one and only time he came to Ballybrit. He was to my generation what *Arkle* was to another and *Golden Miller* was to an earlier one. Tom Dreaper trained both *Prince Regent* and *Arkle*. Barney Nugent and jockey Jimmy Brogan were another great Ballybrit duo. Nugent's *Charles Edward* ridden by Brogan won the Plate in 1947 and Jimmy himself, then a trainer, won the Plate in 1958 with *Hopeful Coleen*. *Workman* who won the Aintree Grand National in 1939 fell in the Galway Plate of 1938. Years after, my cousin Patsy McCartin of Cranmore, Ballinrobe bought him and I had the pleasure of riding him at the Galway Show in College Road.

"I cycled to my second ever Ballybrit meeting on my first bicycle, the price of which I got after fattening a young bonham given to me by my father. Myself and my friend John Coyle, stayed in a Salthill guest house. The memories of this trip are as clear today as if it were yesterday. Bright mornings, up early to get the paper, read the runners and riders and then the trip to the course. *Mardi gras* I suppose you'd call it. I have a few suggestions for Ballybrit apart from the statue to Harry Ussher and *Clonsheever*. I'd love to see the spirit of the old time races — the mardi gras atmosphere which permeated the whole city then — return to Galway. People come to Galway now and many of them leave the city at night. They should be encouraged to return. The atmosphere of revelry is gone. There should be at least three Hunt Balls. Discos and pubs you still have but no real catering for the punter as such. Out in the Course itself I'd like to see the establishment of a Galway Racegoers Association, which would help to complement the wonderful work done by the Galway Race Committee. I'd love to see a Galway Racing Museum established in Ballybrit to honour the great men and horses from the past. People to be remembered like Maxwell Arnott, Atty Perrsse who rode in Galway and later became trainer to the King of England and of course our own Mickey Tully. The Racegoer's Club would help to raise funds for the establishment of such a suggested memorial to *Clonsheever* and Harry Ussher, all to be coordinated with John Moloney and the Galway Committee. Galway is lucky to have John who is all for progress and who succeeded a great man in Luke Mullins. One final suggestion is a special Jockey's Benevolent Fund Dance on the night of the Plate to be inaugurated. This could be staged in a big Marquee either in Town or at the Course and could well develop into the Racing Social event of the year. Imagine such a night when men like T P Burns, Bunny Cox, Martin Molony, Joe Canty, Liam Ward would rub shoulders with the Adrian Maguires, Richard Dunwoodys and Mick Kinanes of today. You could have a 'This is Your Life' presentation for one of the greats annually. We are crying out for such a night. I'd like too to see a Home for Retired Steeplechasers and Hurdlers established here in the West to give these animals who are of no further use after racing a chance to retire and live a comfortable life being well cared for. Most of these horses have been gelded unlike the great flat horses. Such a home could be open to the public for visits at a fee. It's something I've thought of a lot. It is now left to the trainers and owners to look after them and some of them aren't as kind as others. Perhaps the idea is unmanageable but it surely will open discussion. I'm all for being able to see the heroes of the past. It's a thought."

TOMMY GODWIN, DUNDALK AND GALWAY

"It is nearly impossible to diagnose the attraction of Galway's Festival meeting. People from all walks of life come to Galway annually and time their holidays for the meeting. The good humour of the crowd and the foreign visitors mingling together give it a special atmosphere.

"Now it has gone to six-day with every race a competitive one due in no small way to good sponsorship, and four days of TV exposure has been a big boost. It is beginning to attract horses from across the water and that is good. As to memories of good horses. I have been coming since 1961 and have been living here since 1968. My Dad and all the family used to come with Bunny Cox. We always were racegoers. *Hindhope* and *Hard Tarquin* under Jonjo O'Neill in 1979. *Spanner* and *Tirconderoga* in the early days of Weld. Good horses who ran in Galway included *Cairn Rouge*, later to win the Champion Stakes and *Blue Wind* who was only fifth in a maiden in Galway one September, then went on to win her maiden in Gowran Park before winning both Oaks Stakes. Both *Pinch Hitter* and *Steel Duke* won twice in the same week for Noel Meade. The great trainers were Paddy Mullins, Paddy Sleator, Edward O'Grady, Noel Meade and Dermot Weld.

Wally Swinburn rode it best of all that I have seen in his era. Mick Kinane is now the top man and Stephen Craine also made his mark when Noel Meade's horses were flying. Paddy Prendergast (The Long Fellow) used to train for the O'Malleys and their best horse was *Corrib Chieftain* which got second in the Colonial Cup in Camden, USA. As for local horses the ones I remember best were *Lesabelle* (Gort), *I'm Confident* (McDonagh's) and *Natalie's Fancy* (Kelly's). Socially Festival week is a hard slog when you have to be the perfect host for all your friends and your house has to have plenty of spare beds. But it's a brilliant week."

BRIAN GERAGHTY, CHURCHTOWN AND OUGHTERARD

He is better known as Garach to his friends. Brian Geraghty works with Bórd Fáilte and since his gaelic football days with Galway (he won five All-Ireland medals, three senior and two junior), has been a racing *aficionado*. Well-known in racing circles, I have seen him literally hold court before the Stands in Cheltenham. A great man to spin a yarn or two in any company, he is the life and soul of any party and he really loves his native Galway.

"If there is a better gathering of nice people in the valley of Jehosephat on Judgment Day than at the Galway Race Festival then I won't mind being there. The Galway Races is the greatest sporting and social occasion and landmark for me annually. It takes on a very special meaning for migrants and emigrants from the West and I have been a migrant since 1963. It is a time when you renew acquaintance with old friends and bump into all the people who grew up with you. Personally, I get a great kick out of the lilt of the Western accent and everybody you meet has the kind word such as, 'You're looking great', or 'You haven't changed a bit', and so on and there is always a genuine céad míle fáilte.

"My very first visit to Ballybrit was in 1946 and I saw *Keep Faith* win the Galway Plate owned by J V Rank, trained by Tom Dreaper and ridden by Tim Hyde. My Dad it was, who first brought me. He wasn't a great racing man but he made a point of just going to see the two main races, the Plate and the Hurdle every year, driving into the free infield area, thus avoiding the crowds and going home afterwards. He wasn't a betting man really and preferred the Hurdle as a race to the Plate. My mother was a keen racing follower and always went for the day. She used to stand beside the £10 Tote window and listen to the bets being put on and often got a few good pointers that way. I suppose I took the gambling instinct from her. Another big influence in my life then was Uncle Seán Donnellan who never missed the Races.

"My earliest of all memories is of *King of the Jungle* winning the Galway Hurdle in 1945, ridden to victory by Danny Morgan. You see a few doors up the street from us in Oughterard lived a family called the Conneelys and to distinguish them from all the other Conneelys in the area, they were known locally as the Morgan Conneelys and the father's name was Danny. The morning of the Galway Hurdle I had seen Danny Morgan Conneely set off in his lovely horse and trap and when I heard Mícheál O'Hehir describe the race I raced up to Mrs Conneely to inform her that Danny her husband had ridden the winner of the Galway Hurdle. I can still see her startled expression! I always thought that *Keep Faith* won the Plate in 1949 until my good friend Jim Dreaper presented me with a copy of the book *Tom Dreaper and His Horses* and in the book was a photo of *Keep Faith* winning the Plate, date and all.

"I have gone to the Races annually ever since. The most outstanding occasion of all for me was in 1957. That was a good year anyhow. I played for Galway minor footballers in Roscommon that year and lost a fine overcoat somewhere in Roscommon. I was a clerical student in Maynooth at the time and when I reported the matter to my Dad he told me in no uncertain terms he was fed up buying clothes for me and that I'd have to earn the price of a new overcoat myself some way or other. That year I went to the Races with the late Michael Carty TD from Loughrea, an old friend of our family. He had had his card marked for him in the Dáil. I followed his tips, put a pound on every horse. They all obliged including *Tymon Castle* in the Galway Hurdle who came home at 40/1. In all I made £110, a lot of money then and I could afford to buy ten overcoats if I wanted!

"One of my great ambitions is to win a race in Galway, with one of my own horses. I have run two or three horses there and the best I have done so far is fourth. I'd even prefer to win a race in Galway to Cheltenham if I had the choice because Galway is home. It is a dream I hope to realise.

"When I think of Galway so many memories shoot back. One concerns my good friend, John Queally of Waterford. He rode *The Highace Driver* to a short head victory in a Galway bumper and in the process didn't spare anything, either himself or the horse to get a nose in front. As he rode into the winner's enclosure, he threw the reins over his neck and said to the owner, 'Take him, I don't think he likes me anymore!'

"I think too of the late Pat Black, the former jockey, who had many fine successes for Bunny Cox in Galway not least his Galway Hurdle success in 1971 with *Highway View* owned by Charlie Carr of Down whose colours were the well-known Down GAA colours red and black and I will never forget *The Gooser* winning the Plate in 1992 for old friends Margaret and the late Tom O'Leary. In earlier times all the Grangecon people, the Sleators and the Floods used to stay in my Aunt Catherine's Hotel, the Banba in Salthill, a great place to be then during the Races. Others to stay in the Banba were the Quinns of Baltinglass, lovely people whose horse *Firion's Law* won the Plate in 1991. Nowadays I tend to get excited about it all long beforehand. I usually travel now with my teacher friend Jody Glynn from Kilconly, who looks forward to it just as much as myself."

AIDAN MALONE

Aidan is a Director of Geraghty's Menswear and Casual Wear next to the Saturday Market.

"I got the interest from my Dad, a Westport man originally, and always a keen punter. He'd always be sitting at the table picking his horses for the following day. We lived in Augustine Street and my mother's name was Betty Geraghty. Herself and her mother, Mary Jane, brought me out by bus as a four-year-old when we used to have picnics down in the Dip. My next memory is going myself to enjoy the swinging boats and the chairoplanes and the crack in the free infield area.

"After that I used to meet my Dad in the enclosure — U-14's got in for 50p then. The first good bet I remember winning was on *Spittin Image* in the Plate in 1977, £3 win at good odds early in the day. *Pinch Hitter* and *Steel Duke* were great Galway horses. Johnny Roe was so reliable as a jockey. Also Stephen Craine, Tommy Carmody and my boyhood hero Tommy Carberry.

"Until two years ago Galway business life accommodated the Races with two half days on the big days but that has gone now unfortunately. Commercialism has taken over and I'm lucky now to get four days racing. It would be super if two or three big TV screens were placed at strategic points in Ballybrit as happens in Cheltenham and other sporting events to accommodate punters. Finally, Geraldine, my wife and I brought our young son, Jeff along last year to continue the tradition passed on to me."

 From The Horse's Mouth

Mr Thomas Waters

Mr Thomas Waters was a 'professional racing engineer' and as well as designing Ballybrit, also designed Cork Park, Tramore and Punchestown. He constructed at Ballybrit a complete new hunter's course with a 'rattling double bank similar to the Punchestown bank' (the two fences close together at the Moneen).

*— **Irish Horse-racing** by J Welcome (Gill and MacMillan).*

The Fringe

From The Horse's Mouth

Summary of 1946 Connacht Tribune Report of Races

"Keep Faith wins the Plate. Brilliant sunshine on opening day. Record crowds. Fastest run Plate for ten years says Tim Hyde. Attendance records broken according to Mr C J Kerins. Day's aggregate betting thirteen thousand five hundred and thirty-two pounds (previous record seven thousand five hundred and forty-seven pounds in 1945). Swindon Glory aiming for a three-timer on the trot second, ridden by Aubrey Brabazon. Seán Ogue third, Fair Pearl a most popular Hurdle winner, winning at 10/1 ridden by M J Tully."

The following is the complete written tribute to Mickey Tully's success.

"Up the hill with about one hundred yards to go, Fair Pearl's jockey M J Tully put in some superb jockeyship to win. It was the most popular victory ever and great credit is due to our Galway boy for bringing off such a great win against terrific odds. Congratulations Mick."

The last race in Tuam on the Friday that year was won by Magic Memory ridden also by M J Tully. Fair Pearl was owned by Mr John McGreal of Tuam before being sold to M J Tully. For the record, Fair Pearl beat King of the Jungle second and Submarine third, while unplaced was the fancied Point d'Atout.

18

Ladies' Day

"Dress up to suit the weather and the races and have a bit of fun"
— *Fergus Foley*

$\mathcal{G}$alway Hurdle Day — Thursday — has always been Ladies' Day in Galway, traditionally. Fashion and glamour were always part of the Galway racing scene at Festival time. Well-known photographer of the time Jimmy Walshe (*Connacht Tribune*) had a field day. There were ladies who just loved to be photographed and as the years went by you tended to recognise familiar faces in the papers both national and local. And then along came Fergus Foley of the Blue Cloak in Galway to formalise the Best Dressed Lady scene some years back. He takes up the story here.

"We started in 1988 but had planned it years beforehand. I wrote to the Secretary suggesting the idea in the early eighties. The Secretary then, Captain Luke Mullins, invited me in to discuss it early in 1988. And it took off from there. The Racecourse then hadn't the facilities it has now. So selecting a location for a Best Dressed Lady event was very important. The Mayor's Garden was suggested and though a long way off the action, it had a television camera conveniently close and suited us grand for a start.

THE BLUE CLOAK

"We don't call ourselves a boutique. It is a Ladies' Fashion shop. We started off in Lower Abbeygate Street in 1971. My intention at the start was to have a craft shop-cum-coffee shop-cum-fashion store something like the House of James now, having been involved in Tourism most of my life and having worked with Jimmy Lydon's Restaurants. On a visit to Dublin at the time I was sold on the idea of fashion only. Des McNally came in and set off the shop. From the beginning we were in and out of sponsorship but the one which really cued us into it was the Galway Rose of Tralee occasion which we have sponsored from the second year of its inception. The Galway Races idea was a natural successor to that. In the first one we have had two outright winners of the Rose of Tralee, Sheila Hanrahan and Niamh Grogan and both sponsorships have done us proud. The Galway Race Committee are a super committee to work with and have been absolutely supportive.

"Ladies' Day had always been there. There were people like Mrs Cahill from Salthill and others, who traditionally dressed up for the occasion, and had been much photographed over the years. Thursday was known all over Ireland as Ladies' Day. Galway Plate day was always number one. Then you had Galway Hurdle day which was always fashionable. But it is unbelievable the way Ladies' Day has taken off to become the number one day of Galway racing now. That isn't accidental. The fashion has helped. Paddy Ryan was Chairman when we started and he made everything that was difficult seem easy. We were worried about the weather and being new to it didn't know how many finalists we'd have and if it would catch on.

"We have a team of selectors and judges of from ten to twelve people following a carefully laid out plan. We start at least two hours before racing and our selectors patrol randomly concentrating on special areas like the vicinity adjacent to the main entrances and outside the main ladies' loos because all have to attend to makeup and final adjustments. It was Stan Shields (*Connacht Tribune* photographer) who wised me up to that one. We cover all areas. We always have two spotters covering the late arrivals. We have three to four judges usually, many of our own staff, experienced in the business of fashion as spotters and in the last few years a few independent people interested in fashion and representative of the Galway Races Ladies' Committee. It helps variety of choice.

RACING MISS

"We go for a combined look. It started off with a double prize of Best Dressed Lady and Runner-up. Now we have four separate sections. The first extra one was 'Racing Miss' an idea we got from the Ladies' Committee, from people like Breda Ryan and Margaret Naughton, this one to appeal to younger people in their teens and early twenties. The third was the 'The Best Hat'. The number one was the Best Dressed Lady and the overall look determines this major one. The prize is five hundred pounds. The others were for two hundred and fifty pounds. The latest one we brought in in 1993 was the 'Look to Our Own', a development out of our work with An Bórd Tráchtála, if you like a runner in the Buy Irish Campaign of old which we always supported but a slogan now outlawed because of our EC involvement. The prize for this is five hundred pounds too for an Irish design, and this has been an unqualified success. A girl from Ballinrobe named Paula Walsh won it first, the epitome of Irish fashion. A beautifully long knitted garment from a Dublin designer Deirdre Fitzgerald worn over an Irish woven skirt, an Irish blouse and a knitted hat. If you were to pick somebody to show off Irish fashion abroad, you'd pick Paula. Fantastic.

"Now we operate our own marquee at the back of the main Tote buildings in the hub of it all. That developed due to the good will of the Race Committee. One year we had an old Barna shed in the Mayor's Garden and it rained that year and tended to spoil things. It didn't work and two years ago after moving up to the corporate area, we got a tent of our own. Hundreds of people crowd around to watch it now and we always have about fifty or sixty finalists. Three times the Taoiseach of the day Albert Reynolds, came down to visit us. Last year, he gave up with the crowds. The previous year the Mayor of Galway, Henry O'Connor had to climb over the fence to get in. It certainly is a big added attraction. We get on very well with the sponsors of the Galway Hurdle (Guinness) and it is a relationship with no conflict on either side.

"The expense of it all runs into several thousand, up to seven thousand. It isn't a great time of the year for us but we get a lot of local and national publicity as a result. A lot of credibility and it certainly keeps us on our toes. The overall publicity is unbelievable, international as well. A Danish radio station did intensive coverage of the event last year. We also have the national media, *Raidio na Gaeltachta* and *Galway Bay FM*, who are very helpful. The lady who won in 1994 was from Carlow and the local radio station took her story up, prompted by *Galway Bay FM*. The latter people Keith Finnegan, Jarlath McDonagh, Kevin Dwyer and Paul McGinley really hone in on us and are quite adept on the fashion scene. The local radio stations have become a new media dimension. *RTE* television has always been exceptionally good to us and supportive. The format of the television coverage has changed dramatically lately. There is much more emphasis on the racing now and less coverage of the fringe events, but they still cover it and usually show it on the highlights that night. That of course gives it status but the local radio station is much more personal. You get great feedback from the local scene. Usually beforehand on local radio shows I'd advise the ladies what to wear. Telling them not to fuss, and not to drive their boyfriends or husbands mad by arriving late and so dressed up as not to enjoy themselves. My advice to each one is to go out dressed to enjoy oneself. Not to turn oneself into a Christmas cracker or a Christmas tree or a decorating stage so that you can't walk around. Dress up for a lovely day to enjoy yourself and be able to move around comfortably. Dress up to suit the weather and the races and have a bit of fun. That's what the judges are looking for.

JUDGING

"Celia Holman-Lee has been the backbone of our judging panel. A model from Limerick she has been with us all along (missing just one year) and Barbara McMahon (of RTE's *Head to Toe* programme) is another of our judges. They are top people in this area. Sometimes we vary our judging panel but a major coup for us was getting Philip Treacy on to our panel three years ago. Philip, the well-known hat designer is based now in London and Paris and is proud of his Galway roots. A most sought after man, Philip, who is so extrovert in his colours, hails from Ahascragh, County Galway.

"I have two funny memories. Back in 1989 this elderly lady came into the middle of us just as we were judging (won that year by Arlene Capot from France) and proceeded to go for me with an umbrella, I was shocked but realised it was a theatrical plant that added excitement, to which I was not privy. I never found out who was behind it. Another year one of the street theatre lads dressed up as a women crashed the party and came over and kissed and hugged me wanting to be in the finals but I wasn't as shocked that time. The last two years there was an old lady from Ennistymon, Mrs Curran who has been coming to the Races for over seventy years and she wore a hat and produced a hat and an old photograph showing her wearing the same which she had purchased in Moon's many moons ago (our pun!). We made special presentations to her. It is that kind of thing which makes our day. Not to mention the Cahill family. One of the girls from that family actually designed, dyed, cut and made up the material for her own creation to win the hat competition one year. So the tradition is carried on. Every year on the national papers you'll find photos of the Cahill family.

PHOTOGRAPHERS

"In the old days Jimmy Walshe and Johnny McMahon were the great local press people in Galway. Add on Sean Fahy another backbone of journalism. The photographers of today, Stan Shields, Joe Shaughnessy, Mike Shaughnessy and Ray Ryan snap the girls and the celebrities for the media. We get great support from the Gardai who give great support to Ann Hogan, our co-ordinator, and handle problems for us. We have always got great support from Brian Beggan, of Libra Designs, a horse lover himself and a co-sponsor. Brian actually breeds these dray horses of the Budweiser advert as a hobby. He has been one of our judging panel. Yes, I'll keep the sponsorship going as long as they will have me and as long as I'm able. Then I'll get Ray, my son, to take over along with Mary Niland here in the office and I'll be placing it in good hands. My staff are absolutely brilliant. The competition as such has improved in quality, design, standard and participation and people are now coming to study the way we organise it. So we are proud of it and we have had no controversies so far. No fighting and no fixing. Really good fashion from the youngest people to the glamorous grannies. Innovative styles in antique costumes modern and Irish fashion and getting better."

ADDENDUM

Less than two weeks after this interview, Galway city was shocked with the sad news of the sudden passing of Fergus Foley. I taped the interview in his

Blue Cloak premises and he provided me with all the photographs I have used. At the time, he was his old jovial bouncy self, eager to talk with pride of this very popular promotion of his. It is a monument to him which I hope will continue and flourish under the same banner.

— Author.

From The Horse's Mouth

Tipperary Boy and Golden Fleece

"In 1938 the value of the Galway Plate was augmented to one thousand and twenty sovereigns and so became worth as much to the winner as the Irish Grand National. The race had always enjoyed great prestige, particularly in the West of Ireland; and because it took place in late July or early August, it kept interest in steeplechasing alive at a time of the year when it might otherwise have tended to lapse. Only one horse has won the Galway Plate three times — this was Mr T Holmes's Tipperary Boy in 1899, 1901 and 1902. Another notable winner was Golden Fleece in 1918 whose consistent performances during World War I elicited from Mr R J Duggan the wry comment that it would have paid him, as a bookmaker to have bought this horse as a yearling for as much as thirty thousand pounds — and then to have had him shot! The winner of the Plate in 1919 was a versatile performer Picture Saint, who in that year won the Cesarewitch in the Curragh, a feat repeated by Miss E L M Barbour's Blancona in 1925"

— **Between the Flags** by Colonel S J Watson (Published 1969)

19

Racecourse Architect

"Just before the Pope arrived by helicopter I was struck by terror and excitement."

— *Simon Kelly, Galway Racecourse Architect*

Simon, who was born in Westport, came to Galway in the mid-fifties commencing practice in general architecture from a small office in Eyre Square. Married to Ann O'Malley, daughter of well-known eye surgeon Conor O'Malley, Simon makes no secret of the fact that his years as an architect in the West have been in the boom years. His hand is to be seen in the building of over ten new Churches and over twenty reconstructions to existing ones in different dioceses — the most recent being the new Knocknacarra Church. Add to all that a long list of schools, Vocational, Secondary and National in Counties Galway, Mayo and Clare. In 1969 he became advisor to the Galway Race Committee and since then has been involved as well in development work at the racecourses in Leopardstown, Roscommon and Listowel.

He starts his development work story thus.

"By 1971 it was decided to construct a large new Stand to replace one which had already been condemned as being unsafe. Lord Killanin was the new Chairman and he approached the future at Ballybrit with enthusiasm, having a view of Galway as a great growth area for business, tourism and recreation, all of which would justify a long term major development of the Ballybrit Race Track on a phased basis. This view I strongly supported as I foresaw Galway as the major Regional Capital of the West. The design was for a reinforced concrete structure made from precast, prestressed units which could be efficiently assembled on site and so reduce considerably the time needed for construction. Time has always been of the essence — works had to be always timed to be done between September and the following July and be ready in good time for race week. A new administration centre was also provided then to include accommodation of the highest standard for jockeys, judges, office staff and management, and the best medical facilities. The new Stand completed in 1972 was most successful, accommodated five thousand people and contained the Tote layout at ground floor level. Some six months after this I was asked by the Racing Board to design a new Stand at Leopardstown based on similar lines which was ready for their Christmas Festival that year. Crowds continued to grow at Galway's Festival meeting. More facilities were needed. We then proposed to fit in a refreshment area under the terracing on the top of the main (East Stand) stand which had been built in 1945. This experiment proved so successful that it is now a special bar and food area. Seating was later provided in the Stand under this area and is now a reserved ticket area which provides a magnificent extended view towards Galway Bay and across the Corrib lake on the opposite side.

"In 1978 I accompanied Lord Killanin and some members of the Committee on a trip to visit race courses in the Paris area to study developments there. By September of that year we refurbished the big Stand (East) by new terracing from the stand to the parade ring and increased the area outwards. New terracing and steps were introduced also in front of the new Stand (West). The west end of the enclosure near the Moneen was extended and the Tote buildings enlarged. All this development created more space and it was very satisfying to see an increase in the attendance and the facilities coping with that increase.

THE PAPAL VISIT

"My association with Galway Racecourse led me into a project which no architect would ever anticipate. This was the projected visited of Pope John Paul II to Galway. In July of 1979 it was announced that the Pope would visit Ireland and would be received by the youth of Ireland at Ballybrit Race Course on September 30.

"I was appointed by the Galway Diocesan Office with the approval of the Galway Race Committee to take charge of the planning for the visit at Ballybrit. It was an honour I gladly accepted, though at the time I had no idea of the extent of time, energy and initiative required. It is now history. Myself and a staff of six were involved in the planning for over six weeks non-stop. Days of sixteen to eighteen hours work and daily visits to Ballybrit.

"The work involved site and Committee meetings, reports, specialist talks with *Teilifís Eireann* engineers, reporters, Army personnel, the Air Corps, helicopter pilots, sound specialists, contractors, timber suppliers for constructing the 'corrals' in which the youthful pilgrims from all over Ireland were controlled in units of one thousand people. Roads were built, toilets and first aid buildings were erected.

"The main focus was a special podium which was constructed over the old Tote building in the infield area of the course. Existing buildings were re-scheduled and adapted for Press rooms, communications, catering, provision for the handicapped and elderly and under the podium a fully equipped emergency hospital with an operating theatre was provided. This was the kind of detail prepared for. It was indeed an exciting time.

"Over two hundred and fifty thousand attended on that lovely morning and the visit was successful in every way. As I heard the helicopter approach I was gripped with terror and excitement and a great fear that perhaps the crowd would surge forward and break down the corral structures. Myself and all my staff were in the VIP top security section beside the podium. I remember pacing around the podium checking everything. Then things started to happen and the whole exercise surpassed all expectations. It would have to be one of my greatest days. There were no major accidents, no need for the temporary operating theatre and Colm Galvin, the Surgeon on duty, recently told me that apart from the birth of a baby, there was no emergency. After the Pope left, I entertained all my subcontractors to breakfast and refreshments in the canteen and we heaved a collective sigh of relief. The clearing up and refurbishing of the site was carried out immediately and took three weeks under the capable hands of Luke Mullins, the Secretary/Manager.

THE SPECIAL UMBRELLAS

I remember this time well. The whole of Ireland was thrilled with the Papal visit and Galway was honoured to be chosen as the location on the Sunday of the Pope's meeting with the youth of Ireland. My son, John, worked on the building of the podium and I remember his great sense of satisfaction and achievement when he arrived home that weekend with the work complete. Myself and three of my sons walked from our home in Salthill through the night to Ballybrit and the atmosphere was unreal. Everything was brilliantly organised. You could feel the air of expectancy. Everybody was jolly. It was like Christmas morning on a huge scale with Santa arriving by helicopter for everybody. The cheer that greeted the Pope's arrival at Ballybrit is one I will never forget. It was a day to remember. One quaint little memory is of the moving black and white topped umbrellas, a very inventive scheme conceived by Bishop Eamonn Casey to identify and locate the many priests giving out Holy Communion. That and the terrible sense of anticlimax when the Pope took off again. The Popemobile came quite close to our corral. The trek home was wearisome enough but the conviviality of the huge crowd lived on.

FURTHER DEVELOPMENTS

"During the early eighties, attendances continually increased and much thought was given to a master plan of further improvements and enlargements to meet requirements up to 2000 AD at least. The scheme decided upon was a very brave one which showed confidence in the expansion of Galway and of the Races themselves. The major scheme prepared after much discussion with the Building Committee provided for the demolition of the majority of old buildings, and the enlarging of the enclosure area. A new amenity building incorporates restaurants, the trainers' and owners' bar, stewards' facilities, new toilets, first aid and a major central kitchen. This required complete new drainage and water supplies and a new water tower. The enclosure area provided a street for shops/bars entertainment and here marquees are used for the main Festival meeting. These marquees can be enlarged and adapted to the needs of clients. John Moloney, since his appointment, has brought considerable experience and racing knowledge to Ballybrit. His advice and guidance on the major project completed in 1991 must be acknowledged, the main contractors of which were Messers James Stewart Ltd., of Galway.

"The most recent improvements in 1994 initiated by Lord Hemphill and John Moloney provided terraced viewing in the space around the Parade Ring, getting rid of the grassy mounds and also providing seating at the rails of the Ring. For the parade of horses now, the facilities, which also cater for the handicapped, can accommodate over two thousand five hundred people. Over the years I have noticed that the more facilities, space and comfort provided at Ballybrit, the greater the attendance. The patrons now have a vast area of circulation compared to some years ago and due to large crowds it is desirable to have focal points and so we provided the Clock Tower and the Cross Road sign. An attractive design was produced for a new judges stand. This is reinforced concrete carried on two supports and gives clear viewing to 360°. In all the projects, besides those people already mentioned, I'd like to acknowledge the support of Paddy Ryan and Tim Naughton both very experienced in business decisions and the needs of racegoers. Long may Galway Race Committee continue improving facilities for a growing number of patrons."

From The Horse's Mouth

Sheltered Under Bushes

"The 'father' of Galway Corporation, ninety-year-old Councillor Jim Reddington will be in Ballybrit as usual on Wednesday. He still remembers the first time he was there eighty-two years ago. It was the day his mother gave an older boy sixpence to mind him while she was busy on the course. The two wandered off, wide-eyed. When a shower came, they sheltered under some 'bushes'. They were still there when a dozen horses thundered over them. The 'bushes' formed one of the jumps on the course."

—— From a press cutting of the fifties.

159

20

Catering

"Our philosophy is to keep the customer happy always."
— John Sherry, Managing Director, Lydon House Catering
(Caterers at Ballybrit)

$\mathcal{J}$ohn Sherry is a big man. Fond of sport, he comes of Mayo stock interested in racing and was introduced to Galway Races at an early stage.

"My mother was a great racegoer in the West of Ireland tradition. Galway was critical on the agenda; Roscommon, Ballinrobe, Sligo and Tuam. As a child, my father used to call me my mother's sheepdog as I followed her everywhere. A trip to the Galway Races was just part of the natural life in our house. Weather didn't matter. Nothing mattered. She was a great woman to put together a picnic. We got to a stage where relatives would come home from America and elsewhere and their visits always seemed to coincide with the timing of the Galway Races. The car would leave early from Foxford and we'd be in the carpark with the first fifty cars. And there and then we'd have a big picnic. Always it seems in good summer weather. When the meal was washed down she took up her position in what was known then as the Mayor's Garden, an area near the Moneen. It was an old green, timber and galvanised building with a little bit of grass in front of it. My main job was to run up to the Tote to place the bets for all. It was a profitable business because when any of them won, there was always something for me. I could go to the Races then and make money without ever betting on a horse.

MICHEAL O'HEHIR

"On my first trip to the Galway Races, Jack Feeney, my uncle, asked me did I know Mícheál O'Hehir and would I like to meet him. As an eight-year-old, I was brought up the steps of the radio commentary box and Mícheál was instructed to mark this boy's racecard. It was a great honour to meet the great Mícheál. The year was 1956. There was a horse called *Woodbine Cottage* running that year and I learnt a very fundamental lesson that day in Ballybrit. Pay particular attention to horses which run twice in the same week. If you can see them making no effort in the first outing, be sure to have a few bob on them in the second. I don't know what happens to them when they get one run over the Galway course but their form improves dramatically between Monday and Friday. In those days, Tuam was on the Friday and we always went there too. It was an adjunct to Galway, a place to recoup losses. Galway was a big meeting even then. Big crowds. A car park jam full of black cars. Every car then was black. There was a well established routine. People go to the Races now and can stay in the same spot all day. In those days everybody had to go down to the Parade Ring. Everybody considered him or herself to be a judge of horseflesh. I remember one bad incident when I was sent to collect my mother's winnings and I ran into a three-card-trick man on my way and it all looked so easy. And I couldn't understand how the dummy beside me didn't know where the queen was. So I put up ten shillings and promptly lost it and then the table was folded as the Gárdaí came into sight. The various two shilling tips had to go into the kitty to repay my mother's winnings. That was nearly thirty years ago and I have never been tempted since to try my luck with the three-card-trick man again.

LYDON HOUSE'S INVOLVEMENT

"The man that gives me the history of it all is ex-Sergeant Pat Anglim. It used to be done by Lawlors of Naas, who were famous Racecourse Caterers. Mrs Lawlor was the woman in charge, a strong personality and always in evidence. The catering in Mrs Lawlor's time was done in marquees in the free area. After Mrs Lawlor, a company called Bearcroft took it over for a number of years. About fifteen years ago, Lydons were asked to do the catering, when because of some hiccup, a caterer was needed at short notice and Lydon House has been in charge of catering ever since. At the time they were very much into catering, looking after the catering for factories, weddings, special occasions and outdoor marquee type functions. I still have the planning files of their first involvement at the Festival meeting. Things may be more sophisticated today but the same basic plan still remains. I came home from the Middle East and joined Lydon House in September 1984. I went up to observe the September meeting and I was very impressed by the activity, commitment and team spirit of the crew that day. Afterwards I was told that the September meeting is only about one twentieth the size of the Festival meeting. So I knew what was in store.

GROWTH

"It has grown over the years. The growth is a result of the philosophy of the Race Committee which is that the customer comes first and is treated as he/she should be treated. They expect everybody involved in the Races to follow their lead and is the reason why Galway has tended to grow and grow. All the time they think ahead and keep re-investing. One of their recent excellent developments was the building of a road to the Course from the Tuam/Galway road and which gives access to all the spacious carparks. Now people can leave Galway forty-five minutes before the first race and be in time to place a bet. I would still give myself more time on the two big days. Going to and coming home from the Races isn't at all the big chore it used to be, something that is very appropriate to modern life. The car parking facility is second to none. I know of no other Racecourse where you can park with such ease close to the Course. The days of the huge tailbacks are over.

GROWTH IN CATERING

"The food has grown continually. The drink is static, at best. People are now much more careful about drink. The number of outlets where we sell drink has grown, again with the customer in mind. The staple drink at the races is the pint of Guinness. We have a great mix of customers, many from Connemara. In many racecourses you take whatever drink is available and don't complain. We take particular pride in the quality of the Guinness we sell and the Guinness Company bends over backwards for days beforehand to ensure the product is right. They keep a container in their own yard where the Guinness is cooled down and delivered to the course at 6.30 in the morning. That is the meticulous attention to detail we all engage in. To try and take some pressure off the numbers and the draught section of the Long Bar under the stand we decided we would erect a Guinness and Oyster tent just inside the gate. It took a little while to take off but now it has become a great meeting place which is very convenient for those entering or leaving the course. We launched that about four years ago.

THE VARIETY OF OUTLETS

"Our outlets include the Tea Pavilion in the Mayor's Garden, a Hot-Dog Stand mainly for young people, a Tea Room with light meals provided, a Fast Food Restaurant again mainly for young people, the Carvery —reputed to be very good value, a Self-Service Restaurant, the Seafood Restaurant in the Owners' and Trainers' Bar, the traditional Seafood Bar in the Corrib stand, the Hot Beef Huts, one down beside the Parade Ring and one in the middle of the enclosure, special facilities for both the stable boys and the jockeys and an Owners' and Trainers' Tea room and finally a Restaurant for the Committee in its own special rooms, fourteen outlets in all. So you can get anything you want from a hot-dog to a burger to a four-course sit down meal, to the most recent addition of the hospitality catering for corporate groups.

CORPORATE CATERING

"We sell a package which is divided into two. You can have a private suite for groups of forty and upwards. Or you can take a table in the Public Pavilion if your group is smaller. People take tables for two, four, six, eight, ten, sixteen or twenty. They get a package which comprises car parking, entry ticket, the use of the table for the whole day, which is important for the ladies in particular who like to have a seat to come back to to sit down on, champagne reception on arrival, four-course meal, afternoon tea, waiter service and table service from the bar plus a Tote in the pavilion and close circuit television right beside them. You can spend the day there if you like. Last year the prices varied from sixty-five pounds on the Monday to seventy-five pounds on the Wednesday for such a package and the Private Suite went from eighty-five per head on the Monday or Tuesday to one hundred pounds on the Wednesday or Thursday. We recommend that you don't bring a group of less than forty to the Private Suite. We have all sorts of variations on that.

DALLAS

"Two years ago an American who was a retired millionaire visited us on the Monday. We had only four small parties on the Monday night. So we have a trellised off area in the Champagne Tent where we place the smaller groups on a Monday so that they are part of the action and not in an island on their own. I was happy to tell the American on the Tuesday night that we would be putting him in the big Pavilion on the Wednesday because of the numbers, where he'd have more comfort and luxury but he refused to move. 'I'm happy here, I'm not moving. I didn't come all the way from Dallas to be sitting on my own. So I don't care if I'm trampled on!' The whole corporate idea was slow enough to take off. The Committee insisted that the price structure be such as to encourage small groups to participate. And local people started to come. So that now we have a lot of repeat business. It isn't a very expensive day out for a man and his wife to indulge themselves in comfort. We have one girl who coordinates the hospitality section of our catering. She takes all the orders, which come to us from advertisements we place and we mail our current brochure annually to all our previous clients.

PECULIAR REQUESTS

"You'd get some peculiar requests. Somebody coming for three days would ask for a change of menu. We don't overly encourage it but we tend to try and keep the customer happy. You might have vegetarians, coeliacs — you learn to deal with them all. To put it in perspective the whole tented area in 1994 amounted to about twenty-five thousand square feet, equivalent to an apartment block of thirty apartments. So it is our biggest catering event of the year by a long shot. It also gets most of our attention annually. The planning for the Galway Races starts with us immediately after the Festival. We'd have a big post mortem. Things do go wrong. You're dealing with food and with people and you'd like to correct anything that went wrong. We tend to review the hiccups and to look at the individual's performance in the week gone by. Some show great potential for more responsibility. Others aren't able for it. But the main focus is to try to avoid identifiable mistakes.

"We'd employ about three hundred for Festival week. We are structured in this way with a team of six on the top rung — Paul Kerr my co-Director and myself, Liam Payne the Catering Manager, Hilary Molloy, the Catering Controller, Willie Cooke the Head Chef and Tommy Glynn the Bar Controller. If anything happens to any one, the others will take over his/her job. Underneath that tier we'd have about forty-five supervisors, some full-time, others part-time. It's a bit like a maternity hospital where the nurse says, 'We'll see you again next year madam' and the lady says, 'No way'. A lot of our staff swear at the end of every race meeting, it is their last but they tend to show up again the following year. We tend to stay loyal to them too. In some cases daughters have taken over from the mothers. I suppose it is a bit of an extension of the way the Galway Races embraces the whole town. The work is hard, the hours are long but somehow people don't want to be out of the action.

JOHN'S TYPICAL RACE DAY

"The most difficult day for us is the Wednesday. The first two days are evening meetings. The two critical days are Monday and Wednesday. The numbers increase for Wednesday. We'd leave the course about midnight on Tuesday. There would be a team of cleaners in action all night and before they would leave at 6 a.m. our crew would be back in at about 5 a.m. And we'd be there till about 10 p.m. on Wednesday evening. You can relax and have a bit of fun as well. The atmosphere is good and the staff are coming into contact with racing people all the time. If you have no interest in placing a bet it can get a wee bit monotonous. I'd take ten minutes out and mark my card, picking a horse per race for a pound each way bet and maybe two horses for the big races and I'd get somebody to place my bets. It means that you are part of the excitement and you'd be looking out for your own horse. There are over seventy television sets all around the course. When the race is on all the punters face the telly. All you are looking at are people's backs. That is an opportunity for the staff to get food redisplayed. You get a little break from the pressure. If I want to walk from one end of the course to the other, I just wait for the off announcement and set off on my way. You have the whole course to yourself but don't ever try and make headway when the race is over and they are coming down from the Stands. Thursday has become as busy a day as Wednesday. Friday is an evening meeting so we all get a breather. Here one of the problems you have to guard against on the Friday is complacency and the human reaction of feeling the worst is over. If you succumb to that temptation, disaster could happen. The racing isn't over for me until I get to Flannery's Hotel for the little staff celebration we always have after it is all over. Some years ago I was late arriving at Flannery's but when I arrived I got a barman to organise a round for all of Lydon's staff present, asking him to do the same again twice. At that stage I had to go to the toilet. The barman happened to be a temporary barman and didn't know me. So when he noticed I was gone he questioned one of my staff as to who was the man who placed the triple order and where was he gone to. Quick as a wink they perceived his discomfiture and worried him further by saying, 'We haven't a clue. He just came over to us and asked us would we have a drink. He seems to be gone a good while now.' His face was a deathly pallor when I returned but a big smile spread across it!

DRINK OR FOOD

"The Galway Races is subject to whatever is the prevalent marketing exposure and pressure as anywhere else. Some years ago the Course Manager mentioned to me that the Trainers were finding it awkward to come from the Parade Ring up to the Owners' and Trainers' Bar which is permanently packed! If a horse wins the Trainer likes to stand a drink for the Owner and his/her entourage. So we provided a facility right down beside the Parade Ring. We wanted to keep it relatively simple, so we set up a Budweiser tent selling Budweiser beer and the growth in sales there has been very impressive. There is the thrill of victory and the punters tend to like rubbing shoulders with the winning teams. The most popular food outlet is the Self Service Restaurant — chicken casserole, plaice, a regular lunch and we would have six or seven menus there every day. The Carvery is at the end of the Self Service Restaurant. The punters tend to pick their time for a meal. We have consciously promoted the concept of arriving early for the Races especially on the big days. We would serve food to our own staff and the Tote staff at 11a.m.

Then the punters start to arrive at noon and long before racing would begin we would have fed many punters. We would have just as many customers who would come into the Carvery for a sit down meal after the last race is run. That spreads the day out more.

"Seafood is fairly static. We sell it in two areas. Up in the Corrib stand where you can get food, drink, there are toilets and a Tote and you just walk out the door to get a magnificent view of every race. The champagne sales have crept up and up over the years. We have tried to hold the price for the last four or five years. Compared to other race meetings our champagne would not be expensive. The excitement in the champagne tent can vary. A good local winner coming in at long odds generates great excitement. Kevin McDonagh's *I'm Confident* win of the Galway Hurdle is one such memory. I wouldn't remember the specific winners but I can tell when I walk into the champagne tent that there was a local winner or a winner owned by a consortium or syndicate, who tend to buy a horse as a hobby and hope to have a winner in Galway especially.

ANECDOTES

"Little things happen over which you have no control. One year I remember there was a particularly bad storm and every light in the place went out. All the cooking stopped, every till jammed and there was pandemonium. There was a downpour of rain at the time and everybody sought refuge in one of the sheltered areas. Acts of God really in insurance terms and you have to put up with them. We had a minor fire once but these challenges were much greater when the catering facilities were of the old variety. With our new facilities water is always on tap and there is a complete ESB sub-station manned by ESB personnel for the week. So the excitement generated by facilities failing is a thing of the past.

"You can relax of course. In fact you're of no benefit to your staff if you are going around with a long face. And you do get the odd laugh. Sometimes a runner from the stores would be sent to one end of the course with a tray of buns. He'd be gone for fifteen minutes. And would arrive back complete with tray having gone to the other end. The catering has to look after the stable boys, the jockeys (you won't sell any cream cakes here, Ryvita yes!) the hospitality, the children and the tea room which I feel very strongly about. There is nothing better than sitting down and getting a cup of hot sweet tea as you take the weight off your feet. It appeals to people and there is a continuous throughput of people there all day.

MEETING THE STARS

"You get to recognise and know them all. A few years ago I hired a man to mark the cards for the hospitality people in the Pavilion and I picked a winner. This is very much the fashion of corporate hospitality at sporting events. Mark Dwyer was very nervous doing it at the start and has made a very good job of it. All the punters want is a few each way bets and a winner or two if possible. In 1994 Mark, who rode the Galway Hurdle winner *Oh So Grumpy* to victory, had to return to England for the Friday and Saturday and recommended Graham Bradley as a substitute. Graham was a great success too. The punters are delighted to see top jockeys dressed for riding giving them the tips literally from the jockey's mouth. They take it seriously, are alert, listen to what the other jockeys are saying in the jockey's room. Graham was so successful on the Friday that he got an ovation when he arrived on the Saturday. So the pressure was on him to do as well again. Mark, the man who has ridden *Jodami* to such success, has become very good at it. If we have four different tents, he visits them all and runs through the card with them all. Afterwards he will return and have the chat and perhaps a beer. He has become a popular figure in Galway since he started. Of course, he gives no guarantees. It is always nice to have a few winners.

CONTINUING THE CATERING

"We renew the contract with the Committee three years at a time. I believe that as long as we continue to improve our service, that they will continue to invite us to cater in Ballybrit. We like the buzz. Much of our year is built around it and we are based in Galway itself. We are as local as you can get. One of my earliest memories was a visit to the bar at the Races and seeing these strange minerals that you couldn't ever get in Mayo, Clada Orange and Corrib Orange. If we didn't have these local minerals on sale, punters would feel we were forgetting our roots. Galway Water is very much available. Kerry Water had to be on sale because they sponsored a race. The Tipperary Water people had booked a table in the hospitality section and they had to see their product. And some punters call for Ballygowan. You must keep the customer happy!

"Our planning now would entail such peculiar things as the staff you see, the backroom staff, the cleaning staff, hiring buses to transport them all to and from, close circuit televisions, PA systems, provision of ice, flowers, bouquets daily. We have to change the menus on a daily basis, arrange for the printing of them. In the Carvery for example, there are fourteen different menu choices everyday — everything from lamb to salmon cutlets. Vouchers for staff and suppliers to have meals. Plumbers and electricians on site. The provision of mobile washrooms, kitchens and dishwashing units. Making sure that the security and fire officer is involved. It's a huge operation and it is the little things which make it. I mentioned ice. We use three tonnes of ice a day. We are making ice for the Festival about fourteen weeks beforehand. Last year's flower order had eight hundred table centre arrangements.

PLANS FOR 1995

"I'm going to Cheltenham to see what they do there and to see how they cope. I have been there before. Danno Heaslip, owner of *For Auction* a former Champion Hurdle winner, once told me we were wasting our time if we expected fellows like him to sit down or queue for a meal. So he suggested we provide a hot steak sandwich like they do in Cheltenham, where there is a hut, a chef who carves the beef and puts it in a roll with four dressings available which you can lather on yourself. The advantage is that you can eat it standing up and waste no time between races. We introduced that about five years ago, the same customers come every day. When I'm hungry myself and I'm on the run I find it very appetising.

"We have many meetings beforehand. Our first meeting would be an all day meeting in March. Once a fortnight for a time, then once a week down to once a day for a fortnight before the Festival. I'm associated with the Galway Races for eight years now and have eight great memories, especially with the Saturday night and the end of the Festival week. The job is successfully accomplished, there is a sense of relief, but there is also a sense of pride. We depend on teamwork and like the cogs in any wheel, there is no cog more or less important than the other. Pride and relief and the relaxing pint after it is all over, that is the best feeling of all."

From The Horse's Mouth

1958, a wet Ballybrit and the Ryndam

In 1957 I travelled home to Cobh on the SS Ryndam from Hoboken Pier in New Year. The following year on Galway Hurdle Day, the Holland-America liner mainly through the efforts of Galwegian Willie Fahy, then working with Bórd Fáilte in New York had the liner sail into Galway Bay depositing seven hundred passengers in Galway for the races. This is how the late John Healy described the event in the Evening Press over a photograph of a very mud splattered Bobbie Beasley who rode Knight Errant to victory in the Hurdle:

"Despite one of the worst rainfalls in the history of the Galway Races, punters left Ballybrit this evening in a joyful mood which had nothing to do with the last minute bit of sun. They were jubilant over a day's racing that saw Knight Errant complete a double after a year's interval when galloping home to win the Galway Hurdle from Sorrel and Regal Token. The race was a thriller. It gave Mrs A B Biddle the double she lost so narrowly a year ago, her first Galway Hurdle to add to the three Galway Plates she has already won."

21

Hotelier

"Kevin Bell's Bunclody Tiger Gave Rise to a Swell Party."
— *Tom McCarthy O'Hea, Manager of the Ardilaun House Hotel,
Taylors Hill, Galway.*

Tom McCarthy O'Hea has been General Manager of the Ardilaun Hotel for over twenty-seven years. He is in a perfect position to observe the effect Galway Races has on tourism generally. In 1992 Eamonn O Muirí (RTE Radio 1) did a documentary on a day in the life of Tom McCarthy O'Hea, the day being Galway Hurdle Day or Ladies' Day.

"The first real racing people I remember coming here were blood-stock agent Jack Doyle and well-known trainer Kevin Bell — the first people of the racing fraternity who came here when we opened. After that we built up our own racing clientele over the years but they were the pioneers. Kevin's horse *Bunclody Tiger* won the Plate in 1974. Before the race Kevin said to me, 'Mac, have a bet and go back and get ready for a real party tonight'. That was one of the greatest parties we ever had here. It was the year the Plate was postponed and run on the Friday with one fence taken out of the dip. I had a bet on, too, though I'm not a gambling man. Kevin told a great story that night about a waiter and the Ailesbury duck he was serving which I won't repeat. It is a great story but it did nothing for the duckling we had on the menu that night. No one wanted it!"

I ramble up to the Ardilaun from time to time during the Races. Last year, 1994, at the next table I met two owners, Tommy Doran, a Mayoman from London and his friend Tommy Scanlon from Clonard both of whom had horses trained by Michael Hourigan. Tommy Doran, whose colours are the green and red of Mayo owns *Doran's Pride* among others.

"One year (1992) Donal Kinsella owned two of the favourites in the Hurdle *Beau Beauchamp* and *Cock Cockburn*, trained by different trainers Noel Meade and John Queally both of whom stayed here. They were the two co-favourites and figuring out which horse to back was the rage then. Neither of them won it. One of the extraordinary things about that story is that one of Noel Meade's greatest winners in Galway *Steel Duke* was ridden to victory in the Amateur Handicap in 1981 by John Queally. *Steel Duke* was a great Galway horse.

OTHER CHARACTERS

"In those early days we had a great character from Waterford, Paddy Power, known as 'Daddy' Power, one of the biggest bookies in the country. His nephew David runs the chain of Power's Bookie shops in Ireland."

Whenever I come to the Ardilaun, I often see the same faces year in year out such as former Kerry footballer Dave Geaney from Castleisland.

"We get great support from Kerry and we have had a lot of winners of the lesser races and these celebrations can be just as much fun and coated in champagne as the big ones. To them it is better than winning the Plate or Hurdle. Other areas to support us besides Kerry are North Cork, Tipperary, Waterford and a big contingent from Meath and the North. The Northern punters are really a wonderful group of people. They come down here and have great fun. They are also a very charitable bunch. I'm not big into racing myself but I will say this. After twenty-seven years as Manager and there are times when we would have a thousand people on the ground floor for sixteen hours of the day during the Race period, I have never yet had to experience any trouble, vulgarity, bad language, or nonsense of any kind. They tell stories, have fun. They come to have fun. That is the nicest aspect of it all. We put in very long hours and get satisfaction out of seeing them enjoy it all.

HECTIC WEEK

"No question about it it is our best week of the year. It would be the equivalent of two to three weeks at any other time. It is the start of the adult holiday period. You have the repeat business then. Some of them come back for the September race meeting or for the Oyster Festival or at other times during the year. The Festival meeting is special. They come from all over the world, Australia, the Irish in Boston, catering people from the States. They book from year to year, look for the same rooms. The rooms are almost named for Race week now! It's a long week for myself. It's a fun week too. They make it easy for us. I go out for the third, fourth and fifth race every day. No traffic problems either way. I usually meet many of my guests out at the course with conflicting tips. I remember John Moynihan, the Head Porter in the Great Southern Hotel, who used to give us a lot of business in the early days, never backed a horse during Galway Race week and John, a gambling man himself, was a wise man if ever I met one. The show pretty well runs itself. We have postmortems every year to study the scene. We meet with the heads of all the departments and go through the details, see how we can improve on the product from year to year, see how we can cope if there is bad weather, staffing etc. We have the special race menu running ten days in advance of the Races. So everybody is totally *au fait* with all the dishes before Race Week comes. I don't like to create a hype coming into Race week. We take it as it comes and flow through it.

MEMORIES

"Late night gambling sessions are *sub judice*! There are some but the extent is largely exaggerated. We used to have more of it in the past. Not much, if any, now. The victories of Noel Meade's *Pinch Hitter* ridden by Jonjo O'Neill in successive Galway Hurdles are great memories. Earlier than that we had *Paddy Bouler* trained by Pat Rooney and owned by former Mayo footballer Jimmy Curran, like *Pinch Hitter* a Galway specialist. We had great nights. I remember a night one winning owner when I was trying to close the bar begged me to leave it open if he could shatter a three hundred watt bulb shining overhead by popping corks at it from two cases of champagne sitting beside him. He failed miserably but the champagne was shared by all and sundry and we managed to close the bar! At one stage he had five or six helping him to pop the bulb. The liberality of champagne is not as much as in years gone by. Celebrations are more subdued. In the past perhaps it was the frustration of not being able to get to the bar and it was so handy to order a bottle of champagne and six glasses. Drinking has become far more sane nowadays.

CORPORATE?

"Like other sports, it is perhaps becoming too corporate. That's the lovely aspect of Galway still, everybody rubs shoulders together in Galway. Longchamps is totally corporate and devoid of fun. You go to a box and you're literally under house arrest for the day. That is what separates Galway. Everybody mixes. I hope Galway doesn't go that road. I'm happy that the Galway Race Committee will safeguard that aspect of the Galway scene. Cheltenham is much the same. When I go to Cheltenham I go to the same pub, stay in the same hotel, meet very much the same people and we have fun.

SONNY MOLLOY

"Sonny Molloy was a great bookmaker and marvellous for a sing song and getting a party going especially if the buzz was low. He'd start with 'Cockles and Mussels' or 'Dublin in the Rare Ould Times' and before long he'd have a few hundred involved. Finbarr Cahill and his wife Mairéad have been very lucky owners in Galway. When they had winners and that was often, we had some great nights. The two big days are Plate and Hurdle Day. The Plate was always the day. The busiest night of all for us. In latter years since Fergus Foley RIP started sponsoring a Best Dressed Competition for ladies in different categories on Galway Hurdle Day, the Hurdle Day is now the biggest day of all. It is an incredible day and adds colour and gaiety to the scene. The late Fergus did a wonderful publicity campaign for the Races as well as for his own product the Blue Cloak. He gave Galway a new image in all the glossy magazines. He brought a new dimension to the Galway Races. Let that be his legacy. I hope it is continued."

22
Security

"The Ladies with their stalls worked a long day for an honest living"
— *Pat Anglim (former Sergeant of the Guards and Security Coordinator at the Course).*

*P*at Anglim from Kilmihill, County Clare joined the Gardaí in 1953 and took up duty first in Oughterard in 1954, when he remembers doing duty in the Grand Stand avenue for the two days of racing then. As a Garda he moved around the country in his work but came back to Galway again in 1968 and became associated with the Galway Races in 1969. From then until his retirement from the force in 1993 he was in charge of the coordination of security and the arrangement of Garda duties at the Racecourse and its environs. During that time he attended all the traffic coordination meetings held by the Committee usually around June every year with all the other services involved.

"Luke Mullins was in charge when I started and I finished off with John Moloney. As the years went by the work load got much greater with the increased attendance, more cars and consequently more duties. It was easy to work with the Committee and they always complied with our demands. The outstanding people I met then were Luke Mullins, the Ryans (Paddy and Breda), John Brennan, a man of great foresight and Mrs Gillen, a brilliant anchor woman.

"We caught pickpockets galore, sometimes the same people. The three-card-trick men usually start to operate at the back of the Stands just as the Races finish but we never had much trouble with them as the punters always were eager for another gamble. The same three-card-trick people come back annually mostly from Limerick. Often the women with the stalls were their wives. So they had a double pay day! I always admired the stalls people who work so hard and so long to make an honest living. They sleep in their old vans at night, with their families, cause no trouble and pay all their bills before they leave Galway. Even though they aren't allowed into the course they usually get in before the day is out.

A TRIER

"When the gates are locked at night, nobody gets in. I remember one morning Luke spotted a van early in the morning parked behind one of the toilets and was furious. He accosted the trespasser as quickly as possible in most unfriendly tones but was completely disarmed when he was asked, 'Please don't throw me out, even God loves a trier'. He let him stay, under certain conditions of course.

"If we have VIPs, like the Taoiseach or the President or any Northern Ireland dignitaries we are on our toes and extra vigilant. It is a long tense week. We relax only when it is all over and things go well. As a rule we finish up the Races in the Stewards' Room with the Committee for about an hour and then it is all over for another year.

"When John Moloney came to Galway he sought me out and we discussed the security, etc. in reference to the past and to the future. He too was most helpful. Now I go to the Races every year and enjoy them not having the worry of other days. Still I'm always on the lookout, call it a sixth sense if you like, but it wouldn't pay for a pickpocket to be in my vicinity as I can still almost smell anything sinister."

Local Successes

From The Horse's Mouth

The Start of Ballybrit

The following is an extract from the history of the Turf Club 1790-1990 entitled **Horses, Lords and Racing Men.**

"The Galway Races reflected the rise of racing hopes in the 1860s. In fact from 1869 Galway began its unbroken history of one of the great festival meetings. The Midland Great Western Railway Company played an important role in bringing the crowds and in endowing a race. As one journal put it 'A great feature towards the success of the Galway meeting is the unbounded liberality of the Midland Railway Company who, in carrying horses free to and from the meeting, have struck the keynote of success'.

"The successful establishment of the venue, however, owed most to the enthusiasm of the local people, the Ussher family prominent among them, and to the drive of the Earl of Howth, his son the Viscount Saint Lawrence and his friend Christopher Saint George. Saint Lawrence was MP for Galway Borough from 1868-1874 when he succeeded the Fourth Earl of Howth. He employed the services of the talented racecourse designer and fence-maker, Thomas Garrett Waters, to produce the finest course in the West. While the local racing official W H Halliday, may have been too generous with his praise when he observed 'but for your Lordship there never would be any races in Galway unless mere country runs of the Ennis and Roscommon type', there is no denying the important contribution made by the Lords of Howth to Galway's foundation and success as a meeting."

23
To Afford a King

"Charlie fed him on garlic, royal jelly and Guinness"
— Mary King, Athenry, County Galway.

*C*harlie King from Bawnmore, Athenry comes from a farming background and with that came a love of horses, whom he used to work on the land. When he returned from a ten-year stint in Canada he set up his own business and started to ride out with the Galway Blazers. Mary, his wife, who hails from Galway City, takes up the story.

"The Galway Blazers hold a point-to-point every year and one of their races was known as the Farmers' Race where each member could ride up their own horse. Charlie had a horse called *Esker* and he got second in the race one year with *Esker*. After that he decided to get a thoroughbred and train him for the Track. He had land in Carnmore so he prepared the way there when he got a permit to train. First of all he decided to concentrate on point-to-points and he was pretty successful having had several winners in the early 1980s. After these successes we usually sold the horses off. Then he got a full license to train and decided to buy one for the Track and train it himself. So he bought a three-year-old from Liam Niland in Kilcolgan, a lovely looking animal of seventeen hands and the horse was given time to mature. When he was about six years old we started to point-to-point him and he was, as Ted Walsh would say 'a great lepper'. This was *Afford A King*.

TRAINING AFFORD A KING

"Charlie had various friends, who were interested in horses and one of them was Sir Henry Grattan Bellew from Ardrahan who used to hunt also with the Galway Blazers. They used to school horses together and they made a pact in 1987 that they would bring off their double dream as it were, of Sir Henry winning the La Touche at the Punchestown Festival and Charlie winning the Galway Plate. They schooled together, brought their horses to the sea and gave them special feeds, etc. Charlie was absolutely particular on this. He felt *Afford A King* was allergic to dust so he got paper bedding which was pretty novel then, he fed him on big strips of garlic, one in the morning and one in the evening and it seemed to help the dust allergy. The horse got Royal Jelly and a bottle of Guinness every day. Winning the Plate was his big dream and nothing was going to stand in the way. He always believed in the horse. Sir Henry won the La Touche in April 1987. So it was now up to Charlie. Gerry Lynch, a young local lad rode the horse in all the point-to-points and was still riding the horse in 1987 when he got third in the Galway Plate. We celebrated in a big way then too. Sir Henry believed Charlie could still do it and at this stage he set off for Africa wishing Charlie the best in 1988.

"*Afford A King* had a pretty unenviable record of eight second places in a row and we were fed up of the 222 in the form sheet. Then in 1988 the successes started to come first in Clonmel then in Roscommon and some six weeks before the Galway Plate he gave him to Tony Mullins to bring him on in the company of other horses with strict instructions to keep the horse on the diet he was used to. We got Paudge Gill to do the weights and were all set for Plate Day 1988.

THE FAMOUS DAY

"We all left Athenry at about 12.30, in plenty of time and feeling confident. I remember telling our good friend Gerry Crowe, home from his teaching post in Toronto, that today was the day. We had the feeling in our bones. Charlie was exceedingly calm. The friends around us wouldn't believe I was a co-owner when *Afford A King* started in front and led all the way to win. I couldn't get down after the race but somehow floated all the way down to the Parade Ring. It was an unbelievable feeling — interviews with Robert Hall, the Ring was packed with about three hundred friends. It was a real local success and the return of the horse brought a cheer something like that *Danoli* and *Doran's Pride* received recently in Cheltenham. Then the presentation and receptions all the way after that. I was very happy for Charlie especially.

"That night we had a swell party in the Oranmore Lodge Hotel where Brian O'Higgins was the perfect host. We seemed to party the whole night long with our friends and had a wonderful night. The Plate was passed from guest to guest. Went racing next day. Back to the Ardilaun the next night with many of the same people plus Tony Mullins who was able to be with us that night, but minus Paudge Gill who had riding engagements on the morrow. We hosted the stable lads that night and it was another great party.

THE LOCAL PRIDE

"They were very proud of the achievement in Athenry. The local people got a banner and put it right across the street near our house in Cross Street reading '*Afford A King, A Hero*' for all to see. It was a dream come true, beating the best trainers and the best of horses. Charlie is in the U.S. at the moment and he rang me this morning to remind me of the pact he had with Sir Henry and how the telegram from Africa about two weeks after the Plate saying, 'You did it Charlie' told it all. Nobody really felt Charlie could do it except himself, so it was a great triumph for him.

"Our local is Grealish's Pub in Carnmore and the crack was great there even prior to the race. On our way home with the Plate before going to the Oranmore Lodge we called at Grealish's Bar and the place went mad. We did the same at Egan's of Coshla nearby, another friendly local. They were all in Ballybrit that day. Bertie Burns, a well-known local man from nearby Newcastle recorded the event in verse for posterity.

> *Athenry has crowned another king*
> *This year at Ballybrit*
> *Where Paudge Gill was in the saddle*
> *And 'Afford A King' was on the bit*
> *The last two jumps he hit them hard*

But the Bookies had no fears
And as he passed the winning post
We'll ne'er forget the cheers

I'm sure there were great celebrations
Round Athenry and Oranmore
So I'll raise my glass to little Patch*
At the house around Bawnmore"

*A reference to Charlie's Dad, the late Patrick known locally as 'Patch'.

From The Horse's Mouth

Not all good vibes!

Vaughan Biscoe of the **Daily Mail** had this to say on Wednesday August 5 1959 under a sub heading 'Galway Grumbles'.

"Galway, from now on, is a three-day meeting, in view of the obvious success of last week's experiment. But something must be done about the racing there. One decent race per day is just too short a ration. It does not justify that most of the other events being of minimal prize value are attracting some of the worst animals in training. There were eleven contests worth a miserable one hundred and thirty-three pounds to the winner. An even more general complaint concerns the layout of the betting ring. Bookmakers and gamblers alike grumble about it annually. With improvements Galway's popularity can be increased."

Obviously the Race Committee were listening. Sponsorship has helped in a big way.

24
I'm Confident

"It was like bringing the County Cup to Turloughmore."
— *Kevin McDonagh, Glencree Riding Stables.*

*K*evin McDonagh and his family run the Glencree Riding Stables on the main Galway Roscommon road near the village of Lackagh in Turloughmore, County Galway, a hurling stronghold which produced Galway hurlers down the years. Kevin's brother Senator Jarlath is no mean judge of a horse either and has, since the beginning of official local radio, been the main tipster on *Galway Bay FM* and the top linkman between the Racecourse and the Galway public on local radio during Festival week. Kevin's interest began early.

"I was interested in horses all my life. When we were young we had ponies at home here in Turloughmore. My father was keen on horses and it was he who brought me to the Galway Races first about forty-five years ago. It became an annual event. That time if we put five pence (or a bob) on a horse we were lucky. We'd be brought to the Bazaar in the evening in Eyre Square. It was always in the free area then and I remember having tea and sandwiches in one of the many marquees out there. Swinging boats and chairoplanes and hobby horses. We'd have more interest in them then than the races. Then I got interested in horses more as I grew up. In owning race horses first. The first horse I bought was off Pat McNamara, a horse called *Mr Cool* and Paddy Sleator trained him. He won a maiden hurdle in Tralee and was then sold to England. *Turloughmore Lad* was my next acquisition trained by Paddy Norris and he won ten races in all for me, never in Galway though he ran in a bumper there. We brought him to Tralee afterwards and he was backed from 20/1 to 5/4 on and there was an enquiry at the payout. Barney Curley had laid a fair few pounds on him I understand! That, of course, was his winning bumper. He went on to win the BMW Steeplechase in Punchestown. I was always keen on becoming a trainer myself and winning one of the big ones in Galway. Galway is the daddy of them all. Like winning in Cheltenham, especially for a local. Everybody loves to win in Galway. There is a buzz to it. After that I had *Mr Vernon*, a half brother of *Turloughmore Lad*. He won two races for me, one in Listowel, another fine fixture but not blest with the same ancillary facilities as Galway or the same quality of racing. However it is the last holiday fixture of the year, everyone goes and is guaranteed a week's great crack. I lost *Mr Vernon* then after a fall. That is a big set back but you have to be prepared for losses like that and you have to accept it. The lows and the highs of racing. Then we set up here in Glencree with a training establishment of our own. Liam Brennan trained for a few years in these stables before I started myself in 1985. We built the stables from scratch ourselves. Training was a new dimension. My biggest number of horses training at any one time was twelve to fourteen. *Red Oyster* was my first winner. A novice chase in Naas. That was historic. Frank Berry rode him. The achievement is so much greater when you are training the horse yourself. It is all hard work and the wins you get are your satisfaction. There are lots of ups and downs in it and many heartbreaks. After that in Sligo I had a double with *Bold Monarch* (owned by Tony Murphy of Athenry) and *Abilene Girl* (owned by Pat Hurley of Limerick) in June 1986. *Bold Monarch* was my first Galway winner in a handicap hurdle. *Concessionaire,* a horse I bought for nineteen hundred pounds in Doncaster, won a bumper for me before I sold him to Herb Stanley, owner of *Merry Gale*.

I'M CONFIDENT

"Tony Murphy owned *I'm Confident* and sent him to be trained only to be told he was no good. So he brought him home and I bought a half share in him and I started to train him. We trained him for about a year and we ran him as a two-year-old in Galway in a flat race and he did well enough. Then the horse got a cut in his leg and was off for a year, so I bought Tony's share in him for a song in 1987. He won a maiden hurdle in Ballinrobe in 1988, and the Amstel Lager Handicap Hurdle in Killarney. Early on in 1989 he was disappointing enough on the soft ground. Then we brought him to Killarney for the Amstel again and he hit a hurdle and finished lame. Just two weeks before Galway. He was a tough horse. Hopeless in the gallops at home. But loved to race. We nursed him back and ran him in Ballinrobe the week before Galway and got placed in a bad race, but he seemed on his way back. Then Galway in the Barna Handicap two-mile flat race on the Wednesday, where he was beaten a short head in a big field. Next morning he was fresh as a daisy and we knew he had a great chance in the Galway Hurdle. We were fifteen pounds wrong in the handicap and some people said we were crazy to run him. But he ran and won and I had a good bet on him at 66/1 on the morning of the race in Dublin. Everyone here at home had a flutter on him, which of course brought the price down. Everyone from the riding school backed him. Winning the Galway Hurdle was the realisation of a great dream. Catherine, my wife, led the horse in but I wasn't very far behind. It was a lovely sunny day and he came from behind on the way up to win by a head. He beat an English trained horse called *Capa II* owned by the Careys from Cartymore, Coolarne, County Galway. Afterwards he ran in Limerick in the Munster Grand National and got second, came out again next day and won a handicap chase by fifteen lengths. He was a great horse really. Won a flat race, a hurdle race and a steeplechase in the same season. The Galway Hurdle in July, a flat race in August in Sligo and a novice steeplechase in Gowran Park in October 1989. Some achievement that. Pretty unique.

THE CELEBRATIONS

"The celebrations began immediately. First it was into the Committee Rooms for a champagne celebration. Once we got to Claregalway the bonfires started and it was like bringing home the County Cup to Turloughmore. The home place was packed and the party continued in the Copper Beech, about two miles from here. Of the people there, Dave McNally, who used to ride out for me here deserves a lot of credit, and my own daughter, Yvonne, who took great care of the horse. She lives for the horses. The bonfires were still ablaze as darkness closed in. The Copper Beech was still packed. They wouldn't leave when time was called. So the Guards came and raided it and took a host of names. An understanding judge just fined them a tenner apiece, exonerating them on the pretext as he said of 'a joyous occasion'. The day *I'm Confident* won the Hurdle, someone from Turloughmore whose identity is still secret around here won the Jackpot with *I'm Confident* the banker. The amount was £21,652.50 for an outlay of five pounds. He doesn't live too far from here and as you know things like that aren't secrets at all in rural areas! But it was some scoop. The following year *I'm Confident* won the Golden Years Hurdle in Galway. I sold him to England where he ran in the Stayers Hurdle in Cheltenham and got injured and never ran again. That's the story of *I'm Confident.*

SLEEPERS

"Sleepers was a different kettle of fish. Her unique achievements happened in 1990. She was bought for a very small amount of money at the Newmarket sales. She ran forty-eight times before we got her and never came into the frame. Martin Hickey from London, originally from Connemara, owned her and put her in foal. She found new reserves and won two five-furlong events for us in the same week in Tralee in August 1990. She won first on a Sunday and the second on the Friday. A good outsider the first day and 6/4 favourite next time out. Then a month later we brought her to Chepstow where she won another five furlong event in Chepstow, another beautifully hot day, and a great party was had by all the owners friends from London and Martin Hickey himself, all of whom had a touch on the horse. Then on to Beverley a week afterwards and won yet another five-furlong event. Within one lunar month, a small unknown West of Ireland trainer had landed four five-furlong events, two in Ireland and two across the water with the same mare — an achievement I'm proud of.

CELLYPH

"Cellyph was a French bred horse which I bought in Newmarket for eight hundred pounds. He won his maiden hurdle race in Roscommon, a handicap hurdle in Limerick on Saint Stephen's Day. All this on soft ground and he loved firm going. Then to Sligo where he won a flat race. All this in 1992! So I laid him out for the Galway Hurdle of that year —

the big objective. Just one more hurdle race before the big event. We went to Gowran Park. Coming to the last he was cruising but he fell, broke his neck and that was the end of *Cellyph* and our Galway Hurdle hopes. That's the ups and downs of racing.

THE FUTURE

"We have nine horses in training at the moment and we have a full brother of *I'm Confident* with us called *Omesmacjoy*. He has run twice but will not be running again until September at the earliest. I'll always have horses for Galway. I'm just after getting one called *Entitled Lady*. A nice horse and I have a full brother of *Knocknacarra Lad* and the *Earl of Cong* here too.

The Glencree Riding Establishment is a full family run business and we are all involved. Yvonne is a qualified riding instructor and is in charge of the riding school. All the others get stuck in in different ways. In the Summer we offer a Pony Trekking service from a base at Spiddal that is very successful. We use about fifteen horses there and the potential for this leisure pursuit is great. You can go for a full day's trekking or for less and the scenery is quite enthralling. Michael Francis is in charge of that operation which is very big for July-August, reaching its peak around the Galway Races. You have no idea the amount of people who stay in the Connemara area for the races. The Galway Races mean an awful lot to Connemara. And they are getting bigger."

 From The Horse's Mouth

Knight Errant, a Galway Specialist

In the first race in Galway in 1956 — the Corrib Hurdle — Knight Errant was the winner. A brother to Mrs A Bullett-Biddle's Amber Point which twice won the Galway Plate, Knight Errant subsequently won the Plate in 1957 and the Hurdle in 1958. In that Corrib Hurdle win of 1956 the Aintree hero Mr What lost narrowly.

25
Natalie's Fancy

"My big ambition now is to win the Plate."
— *Pat Kelly, Trainer.*

*P*at Kelly, a local County Galway trainer has his stables at Cahercrin, Athenry, County Galway, a little over a mile outside Craughwell in a lovely sylvan rural area so conducive to training horses. When I called to see him in his well run establishment, he had just seven horses in training, a string which might go up as far as fifteen at times.

Pat is a young trainer in his thirties and has been associated with horses all his life. First with the Galway Blazers, then as an apprentice with another local trainer Tommy O'Brien and later with Pat Hughes of Carlow. He was an amateur jockey up till over a year ago when weight problems took over but he still loves to ride out and is a fit young man with ambitions. For five years now he has been operating his own yard at Cahercrin. Pat takes up his story.

"To me Galway Races are the biggest in Ireland, next to Cheltenham in stature. From the beginning I always wanted to win in Galway. My first horse ran there in 1990. *Madame Vitesse* finished a creditable sixth at the Festival meeting that year. I had already ridden in Galway for Pat Hughes and Tommy O'Brien, my first winner being *Xandora's Path* which I rode for Pat Connolly at the September meeting of 1988.

NATALIE'S FANCY

"*Natalie's Fancy* is a horse I purchased for Tim Crowe, a businessman here in Craughwell. I bought her and her half-brother *Killian my Boy*. Both of them were very good to me. *Natalie* won eight times (four of these successes in Galway) and *Killian* won six. The first time *Natalie* won in Galway was in 1991 and I rode her myself that day in the O'Malley Handicap Hurdle at the Festival. I thought then there was a lot more to come from her. After I dismounted I told Mr Crowe she would win the Galway Hurdle for him the following year, 1992, and she did. At the time the media condemned her performance as a fluke win. In winning you have to have some luck, but in racing flukes don't often happen. Pluck and luck is what you need in life. Our tactics were for jockey Jason Titley to hold her up at the back and you need the luck in the running of the race. She won by two and a half lengths from *Natural Ability*. Jason Titley did a fine job and is a good lad. Geraldine Geoghegan, who used to work for me then and now works with Jonjo O'Neill in England led her in to the winner's enclosure and as you see the occasion is well photographed in my office here. Tim called the horse after his daughter Natalie. At the September meeting in the same year against much the same opposition, she defended her status in winning style in a Grade two listed race. There was no talk of flukes then. Her last success in Ballybrit was in winning the Winners' Chase in Galway after winning a Novice Chase in Tralee earlier.

NO TAG

"*No Tag*, who was third in the 1994 Galway Hurdle has been a good horse to me. Owned by Paddy Hynes from Beltra, *No Tag* has never been out of the money in any race for us. Always in the first four. Before last year's Galway Hurdle he had won four Hurdle races on the trot including the Murphy's £10,000 Hurdle Race in Killarney. He is a very good horse and we had great hopes.

"Like *Natalie's Fancy* he has to be ridden from the rear end. But this time we hadn't the luck. Pat Flynn's horse *Onomatopoeia*, which had won earlier in the week fell in front of him. Our lad had to gallop out over him and slit his tendon in the process. In one way we were fortunate enough to finish third to *Oh So Grumpy* and collect £5,000 even though we were disappointed he didn't win. It would have been a lot worse if he had fallen. His injury has meant he has not run since but he comes back into training today. And we will keep our fingers crossed.

"I don't get carried away with success. I enjoy every winner that comes. It was great to win the Hurdle but the Galway Plate is definitely the race I want to win most of all — more than the Gold Cup or the Aintree Grand National. The Plate is special. Always was since I was young. I love it. I think, or rather I hope, I have a horse to do it. Maybe *Natalie* in 1995 or *No Tag* in 1996. If I don't achieve it with them, I'll keep on trying. But luck plays its part too.

ART TRAIL/KILLIAN MY BOY

"Charlie King, whose horse *Afford A King* won the Plate in 1988 lives just four miles down the road from me. I enjoy my life training horses. It has its up and downs. You need the odd success to give you the buzz and let you know that you are doing things reasonably well. My saddest moment in racing was in 1990. The best horse I ever rode was *Art Trail* which won for me on Jan 1. That was a Winner's Bumper in a big gamble the first time out for me at Fairyhouse. A great start to 1990 and I rode him myself that day. Unfortunately, we brought him to Cheltenham and he ran a blinder in the Supreme Novices Hurdle surprising many but not ourselves. He broke his leg there coming down the hill. That was very sad. He was a great horse.

"*Killian My Boy*, has also been a great servant and won for me in Galway too, in the September meeting of 1993. Subsequently he won in Mallow. From a small string of horses I have done well. We work here as a team. The two lads are very good. My belief is that no more than in a game of hurling there has to be team effort with horses. First of all you need good owners. Also good staff which I have. Thirdly you need a good veterinary surgeon and mine are Billy Gibbons (Craughwell), Humphrey Murphy (Athlone) and Meadow Flynn (Oranmore). Finally you need a good farrier and mine is Hugh Behan from The Curragh. That's my A team. It costs a lot but you have to have the best, and you won't get rich with it."

As I left Pat I felt he'd achieve his big ambition sooner rather than later. I hope to be there for the celebrations. Good luck Pat!

Tradition

A P O'Brien and Galway 1994

The up-and-coming man of Irish racing is A P O'Brien, who is just twenty-five years of age and in 1994, for the second year running, became top Irish trainer in terms of numbers of winners. Aidan, who shuns the limelight, is beginning to make his mark in Galway and was next to course specialist Dermot Weld during Festival week 1994 with five winners. It was in Galway at the October meeting 1994 that he equalled Dermot Weld's all time record of one hundred and fifty winners in a calendar year when Double Symphony ridden by Charlie Swan won the Bank of Ireland Ascent Novice Hurdle, the opener that day. To mark the occasion, Galway Race Committee Chairman Lord Hemphill made a presentation to the Piltown, County Kilkenny trainer, who later that day in Leopardstown broke Dermot's record when Holiday Star became his one hundred and fifty-first winner.

26
Insight

In all my research of the Galway Races, its history and significance over the years, I have come across many historical insights which I feel must be included in this book if I am to build a rounded picture of the tradition which has created the Galway Races. Each of these is a window on the past of some person, place or circumstance that went to build up the Galway Races of today. Enjoy these with me.

MOORE v. CLANMORRIS

Tom Bourke, the Mervue Pharmacist, who was reared in his mother's home place Beechgrove, Newbrook near Hollymount, County Mayo, famous for horses and horsemen, tells of a famous cross-country match between Augustus Moore of Moore Hall and Lord Clanmorris of Newbrook.

"Moore had bought a fifteen hands scraggy little horse and mounted on his little steed *Fág an Bealach* did battle with the Lord on his beautiful black horse. They met at Ballyglass and after negotiating many stone walls and other obstacles came to a stone wall six foot high with an uphill approach and the ground so broken in front as to make it impossible to jump. The chase was now going on for over two hours and it was Moore's turn to lead and he scanned the terrain looking for a suitable crossing. In the corner was a large rock half the height of the stone wall and he rode at this to everybody's amazement, the little horse changed his feet on the rock and using it as a stepping stone landed safely the far side. Clanmorris's big horse refused and Moore won the wager. Clanmorris and Moore who were neighbours died shortly after this. Moore died from a fall at the Aintree Grand National in 1845. Clanmorris died at the early age of thirty-nine and at one stage owned *Jerry* the 1840 Aintree Grand National hero."

MR C J BLAKE

"Just as the courses were changing, new names and faces were becoming prominent in both branches of the sport. The most notable of these, as an owner and Turf administrator, was Mr C J Blake of Galway, elected to the Turf Club in 1866, becoming a steward for the first time in 1876."

— *Irish Horse-racing* by J Welcome (Gill and MacMillan).

STATISTICS OF RACE MEETINGS IN PERIOD 1850-1910

Course	Date	Days	Races	Starters
Curragh	April 1850	4	15	82
	April 1870	3	15	73
	April 1890	3	15	78
	April 1910	3	18	143
Down Royal	July 1850	3	7	24
	July 1870	2	12	46
	July 1890	2	10	49
	July 1910	2	12	61
Galway	Sept 1850	2	3	10
	August 1870	2	10	90
	August 1890	2	10	43
	August 1910	2	12	67

— From *Horses, Lords and Racing Men* by F A D'Arcy

AT GALWAY RACES

There where the course is,
Delight makes all of one mind,
The riders upon the galloping horses,
The crowd that closes in behind.
We, too, had good attendance once,
Hearers and hearteners of the work,
Aye, horsemen for companions,
Before the merchant and the clerk
Breathed on the world with timid breath,
Sing on: somewhere at some new moon,
We'll learn that sleeping is not death,
Hearing the whole earth change its tune,
Its flesh being wild, and it again
Crying aloud, as the racecourse is,
And we find hearteners among men
That ride upon horses.

W B Yeats

THE FIRST EVER GALWAY HURDLE

The Galway Hurdle was first run in 1913 and from a field of sixteen runners. *Red Damsell* ridden by F Morgan won for his owner Baron F de Tuyil the two hundred sovereigns stake. The stakes were increased in 1921 to three hundred pounds, in 1939 to five hundred and ten pounds and again in 1947 to one thousand. In 1956 the race was changed to a sweepstake with eight hundred pounds added bringing the value at the time of writing to the winner of twelve hundred pounds (1958).

(The Guinness Galway Hurdle Handicap (Grade B) — guaranteed value of not less than £40,000 — 1994)

1920

"At Galway a threat to cancellation was avoided by the successful efforts of two of its directors. Mr Martin McDonogh and Mr C Kerins, who arranged the necessary transport. On the first day of the meeting Harry Ussher trained the winners of all the races except the Plate which was won by *Clonree*, trained and ridden by Frank Morgan from Waterford, who had been champion jockey in 1917."

— *Irish Horse-racing* by J Welcome (Gill and MacMillan).

DAN BREEN AT GALWAY RACES

"The truce of 1921 imposed an uneasy peace in the country and enabled those of the occupying forces and their erstwhile enemies to mingle on the racecourse and elsewhere. Brigadier-General Ormonde Winter, the Deputy Chief of Police in Dublin Castle and a racing man himself, has left in his memoirs a vignette which captures something of the air of unreality which hung over that strange interregnum. He had been anxious to catch Dan Breen, one of the leading guerrilla leaders, but had failed to do so. However, he wrote 'I once rubbed shoulders with him, after the Truce when we were both making a bet with Dan Leahy, the well-known bookmaker, at the Galway Races. I wonder if he had an automatic in his pocket at the time? I know I had'".

— *Irish Horse-racing* by J Welcome.

GALWAY'S ONLY EVER ABANDONMENT

"The civil war which erupted in 1922 after the departure of the British, in fact caused more disruption than all that had gone before. Thirty-nine meetings were abandoned; even Galway had to admit defeat and no meeting was held that year for the first time since the inauguration of Ballybrit racecourse. But Fairyhouse and Punchestown went ahead."

— *Irish Horse-racing* by J Welcome.

MR JOSEPH S YOUNG

Mr J S Young in 1956 celebrated twenty-one years of being Chairman of the Galway Race Committee and fifty years of membership since 1907 by leading an inspection of the course in a walkabout the Sunday before the Festival. Almost ninety years old, Mr Young succeeded Mr Máirtín Mór McDonagh as Chairman in 1935. In that year he was attending his fifty-fifth successive Ballybrit meeting.

AFTER 1922

"Shortly after the only ever abandonment of the Galway Races in 1922 the Stewards, as part of a general plan of improvement and consolidation acquired outright ownership of the course thereby making it available 'for all time for the people of Galway'.

"When Mr Martin McDonagh (Máirtín Mór) died in December 1934, having been Chairman of the Stewards for twenty-seven years, his passing was mourned in every quarter where the success of the Galway fixture was discussed. With such able colleagues as Mr George Mack, a former Secretary and Treasurer, and Mr C Kerins (died 1955) and Mr J S Young (died 1958) he used all his energies, influence and business acumen towards ensuring the quality and standard of the annual meeting in Galway was of the highest order. Everybody shared his joy at the success of his entry *Kyleclare* in the Galway Hurdle in 1931."

— From Christopher Townley's *History of Galway Races* written for the Races Centenary Year of 1969.

REQUEST FOR INCREASES IN STAKES 1920

Letter from M T Donnellan to Mr P M K Waters on April 20, 1920.

"It was decided to make the following alterations on last year's programme:

The Stakes for the Galway Plate to be increased to £750 and for the Galway Hurdle to be increased to £300 and the Maiden Steeplechase be increased to £250."

CLONSHEEVER AND EAST GALWAY

"During the 1920s steeplechasing in England was in much the same doldrums as flat racing in Ireland." Because of the decline all the good steeplechasers stayed in Ireland. "Mr J E Tyrrell's *Clonsheever* was one of these. Trained by Harry Ussher he won the Galway Plate in 1923 and 1924 (read Matt Connolly's comment on page 132). In 1924 he was ridden by the Welsh jockey F B Rees, probably the finest rider of steeple-chasers in a decade of great jockeys. In 1925 when attempting a third successive success and burdened with thirteen stone, *Clonsheever* strug-gled gallantly into third place proving himself one of the immortals of Ballybrit. Three years later *East Galway* shouldered twelve stone seven pounds to win the Plate and in 1928 with twelve stone ten pounds was just beaten into second place."

— *Irish Horse-racing* by J Welcome (Gill and MacMillan).

SEAVIEW AND KNUCKLEDUSTER IN 1932

Connacht Tribune Saturday July 30, 1932 under a heading 'Galway's Greatest Races — Fields, Crowds and Odds make New Record — Epic Events in Plate and Hurdle — All Round Excellent Racing. I have chosen 1932 as it is the year of my birth and the report began:

"'And he played the ukulele though the horse went down'. So they all sang on Wednesday and Thursday nights to the mad and merry music of steam organs and jazz bands. For the crowd who gathered for the epic races of Galway are sportsmen. Even the ladies are sports when it comes to enjoying a first class race meeting under the smiles of friends and fortunes. The Grand Stand held more than it ever held before, there was a bigger attendance outside the sticks, bigger fields, better going and a more complete feeling that the event was absolutely square. The Plate valued at six hundred sovereigns was won by *Seaview* trained by E Cunningham of Youghal. No such excellent racing as Thursday's has been seen at Ballybrit since *Shady Girl* won the Plate twenty-five years ago. The Hurdle valued at three hundred sovereigns was won by Major H D Beamish's *Knuckleduster*."

1936 CONSTITUTION OF GALWAY RACE COMMITTEE

"The Galway Races are run by a Committee of local sportsmen — usually seven or eight in number purely for sport and incidentally for the benefit of Galway, by attracting visitors to the City. They give their services free and any profits resulting from the Race Meetings are expended solely on improvements on the Course or in payment of increased taxes.

The Race Committee are the owners of the property on which the Races are run and with the exception of entry to the Grand Stand and Carriage Enclosure there is no charge for admission to any other part of the grounds. All the grounds are the property of the Race Committee and there is no right of way.

1. The average attendance each day in the Grand Stand enclosure is about four thousand and the races are held each year on the Wednesday and Thursday prior to August Bank Holiday. The charge for admission to the carriage enclosure is made solely for use as a car park.

2. There are six races each day and the number of horses racing would average sixty per day.

3. I am enclosing a plan of the Course showing the portion actually railed off and the part in process of being enclosed. Practically the whole track will be enclosed before this year's meeting. The grounds included in the Grand Stand enclosure, in which the horse parade enclosure is situated, comprise about two acres. Every effort is made to protect the spectators and nobody is allowed on the Race Track during the progress of the races. A staff of roughly one hundred and thirty is employed each day to run the meeting in addition to the stewards. A large force of Civic Guards (police) are also on the course and their services are available if required.

The Races are run under Irish Turf Club and National Hunt Rules whose officials visit the Race Course prior to each meeting and every-thing must be in order for their approval.

The Catering is done by Messers Mills, Dublin who are responsible to their patrons for any refreshments supplied and all our staff are insured. Any further information will be readily supplied."

— From a letter dated June 12, 1936 from M T Donnellan, Secretary Galway Race Committee to Messers Price Forbes and Company from an address Committee Rooms, Race Office, 1 Eyre Street, Galway.

1938 PLATE

Twenty-three runners ran in the Galway Plate of 1938, the winner being six-year-old *Symaethis*, ridden by Don Butchers and owned by Lieutenant Colonel S S Hill-Dillon. *Yellow Furze* also won the Plate for him in 1936. One of the horses to fall in the race in 1938 was *Workman* who had three months earlier been third in the Grand National and went on in 1939 to win the big Aintree event ridden by Tim Hyde.

GLAMOROUS GALWAY

As told by P D Mehigan in Sean Kilfeather's book *'Vintage Carbery'*, published in 1984. The title of this particular essay is 'Glamorous Galway'. It was Galway Plate glamour which first drew him to Galway and for twenty-five years he retraced his steps from the time in 1915 when *Hill of Camas* won the Plate to the year he wrote the essay, 1941, when *Saint Martin* won it.

"Galway City and Eyre Square were packed on race eve. A carload of us secured bed and breakfast in a comfortable drawing-room at a fair price. The breakfast itself was worth half the sum — trout, salmon, home-cured streaky bacon, fresh eggs, crisp toast, marmalade, bastible cake — that woman kept a great table. 'Why is the Galway Plate so popular?' I once asked a well-known breeder of thoroughbreds and hunters from Limerick. His answer was satisfying and complete — 'Only a rale good horse can win it'. And an examination of the records shows no bad horse or middling one has ever won the Plate!

"When you walk the searching course the reasons are clear. The undulating surface, the formidable jumps, the fine galloping stretches, the steep fall and demanding rise with two firm leaps one behind the other when horses are tired, that pinch into the straight, the slope and fast finishing flat — all these test the best qualities of a true chaser. He must be a clever fencer, with speed and stamina to get home in front of a field that always includes the best horses in Ireland.

"The Galway Races are unique in Irish Sport. For this is a rich Connacht holiday. Caravans and their picturesque owners are making the trek weeks ahead. Urgent farm work is abandoned for the hour. Business and professional men, regular racegoers, hunting folk, farmers of all ranges of acreage, holiday trippers from the Eastern cities, Connemara and Aran Island men and maids who speak Gaelic only are here in colourful buoyant groups. All the fun of the fair, huge fields of beautiful horses, thrilling finishes and good priced winners — all lend glamour and life to this great outdoor festival of the West.

"Eyre Square on Race nights is a midnight bivouac. Taverns are open all night. Open turf fires everywhere. Dancing, singing, carousing everywhere — and all in the great good humour of glad holiday spirit — the huckster's harvest. The salt tang of the Atlantic fortifies us all against indispensable late hours. The morning brings no ill results that a dash to Salthill cannot dissolve. And the bright spirit of these mingling throngs is contagious. Even the bookmakers cease to grumble in Galway."

— It hasn't changed much has it!

PRINCE REGENT AND GOLDEN JACK

Golden Jack won the Galway Plate in 1942 and the following year won the Irish Grand National for Miss Dorothy Paget beating the great *Prince Regent* by four lengths but in receipt of thirty-three pounds. The order had been reversed in 1942. *Prince Regent* was one of the great all time Irish chasers, and but for the war which meant no racing in Cheltenham or Aintree or elsewhere, may have become as celebrated as *Golden Miller, Cottage Rake* or *Arkle*. In the year of 1943, his greatest, he never carried less than twelve stone one pound.

FIFTY YEARS AGO

The *Connacht Tribune* heading read "Attendance breaks all records in brilliant sunshine".

"Danny Morgan brought off a great double on Harry Ussher's last ever Plate winner *Grecian Victory,* the grey who got up by half a length in a great finish to beat *Sun Bird* and *Pongo.* The Plate and Hurdle double was achieved by Morgan on *King of the Jungle,* a brilliant hurdler who held off *Destichado* ridden by Aubrey Brabazon and *Belted Monarch* ridden by Mr J Cox Junior. Unplaced in the Plate were previous heroes *Swindon Glory, Keep Faith* who won in 1946 and *Caughoo* who later won the English Grand National."

CARRANTRYLA WINS HURDLE 1948

The Gleesons of Galway, whose drapery shop at the Four Corners was so much part of old Galway, later became known as O'Máille's when Sal married into that other well-known Galway drapery family. The Gleesons originally came from outside Dunmore and one of them M J became very successful in the building industry in England. He brought his horse *Carrantryla*, called after a well-known great house in his local area, to Galway in 1948 to win the Hurdle under Tim Molony who was bringing off the double of Plate and Hurdle that year. M J's nephew Frank led in the winner in 1948.

BEN HUR

"Out in the enclosure, one can find almost any kind of diversion imaginable, from fortune tellers to musicians, three-card-trick men and find-the-lady; la boule and roulette are to be found there in almost the same profusion that one might expect to find in Monte Carlo, Deauville or Las Vegas.

"During the war it was a great thing to come and stay in Galway for the week, as there were no cars about and it was not possible to get here just for the day if you happened to live more than a few miles away. The horse came into his own in those days and I remember well hundreds of side cars going day and night from Eyre Square to Salthill. There were stage coaches and shooting brakes with one horse and six horses. There were races from Salthill to the Square in the middle of the night with six and eight people perched perilously atop sidecars, jarred out of their minds, goading on equally jarred jarveys to feats that would have done justice to Ben Hur."

— Dickie Byrne from *West Awake*, 1979.

MORE SPECIAL TRAINS REQUESTED FOR 1941

The war years caused problems for Galway Races but the Races were run annually despite many traffic restrictions. This is a letter sent by J Gavin, Secretary Galway Race Committee to P J Floyd, Traffic Manager, Kingsbridge Station, Dublin on May 21, 1941.

"As the Galway Race Meeting will be held as usual this year on July 30 and 31, provided nothing unforeseen happens, my Committee have instructed me to write you with a view to having as many special trains as possible to Galway on these days. Due to the shortage of petrol my Committee are of the opinion that the majority of racing people who come to Galway by car will this year avail of the train service."

RACES DOUBTFUL IN 1944

The following letters sent to A D Comyn Esq LLD and to Mr O'Sullivan and to The Secretary, General Racing Advisory Committee, by Mr Joe Gavin, Secretary Galway Race Committee show how near to postponement the 1944 fixture came. Dated May 20, 1944 it read:

"Your letter of 17th inst. received with thanks. I placed your letter before my Committee at its meeting on the 20th inst. and I have been instructed to inform you that the Galway Race Committee is very anxious to hold its annual fixture but consider it impossible to do so unless:

1. Horses from the province of Munster and the Counties of Kilkenny, Wexford and Offaly are allowed to enter.

2. If permission is given to hold the fixture, that the value of the Galway Plate be £500, the Galway Hurdle £250 and all other races £100 each. An early reply would be appreciated."

In the letter to Mr O'Sullivan, Mr Gavin stated "The Committee are most anxious to hold the meeting but see little likelihood of doing so unless facilities are provided to carry horses to the meeting and that horses from the whole of Ireland are allowed to race. The Southern owners and trainers have always been great patrons of Galway and the elimination of their horses would have a very serious effect on our meeting.

With the exception of 1922 the Galway meeting has been held continuously since 1869 and it would be very serious if this continuity was broken and the West deprived of this annual holiday fixture."

The meeting took place. Things were worked out and *Swindon Glory* retained the Galway Plate that year ridden again, of course, by Aubrey Brabazon. The Committee deserves credit for sticking to its guns and maintaining the fixture despite the wartime difficulties. In many ways these wartime years are still the most talked about years of them all.

HUNT BALL IN ASTAIRE

In the late forties and early fifties Tommy Nevin and Paddy Ward ran a very successful Hunt Ball in the Astaire Ballroom (near where the Tourist Office is today). Plate night was the date and this was a social occasion not to be missed. The Astaire is long since gone. Tommy Nevin recalls, "We discontinued this when Seapoint took over but it was a great occasion. Paddy Cawley ex-Fine Gael TD ran the bar for which we got an extension in those days. One night Sean McEntee and his niece were refused minerals by Paddy as the shutters were closed and no special treatment was offered to the then Senior Fianna Fáil Minister by his Fine Gael adversary. Civil war politics died even harder in those days!"

"SALTHILL OR THE DOGS"

That catch cry came into being in the war years when petrol was rationed and it was not permissible to drive a car or bus to the races. Every horse drawn vehicle available it seemed was brought into action to convey the masses of people to Ballybrit and back again after racing. Later in the evening the same hordes of sidecars, traps et al converged on Eyre Square soliciting customers to taste the night life in Salthill or to be driven to the Greyhound Track in College Road. Then "Salthill or The Dogs" as an expression was born. This can still be heard wherever Galwegians assemble.

THE BEASLEY TRADITION IN GALWAY

Beasley is a famous name in Irish and English racing. Like the Brabazons it has continued for three generations. In all the Beasley name is associated with Galway Plate wins nine times as winning jockeys going back as far as 1881. The last one was the legendary H "Bobby" Beasley who rode the Plate winner four times, *Knight Errant* in 1957, *Sparkling Flame* in 1960, *Clipador* in 1961 and *Blunt's Cross* in 1963 all trained by the famous Paddy Sleator of Grange Con. Bobby Beasley was a marvellous jockey both here in Ireland and across the water. He had in fact two careers. His early first career earned him rave notices for his marvellous jockeyship and dedication. With fame came an addiction to booze and the good life when he sank to an all time low, then quit riding before joining Alcoholics Anonymous with the great help of the late Nicky Rackard, former Wexford hurler and Mr Austin Darragh. After this came the second career when all the old skills resurfaced and Bobby re-shot to fame on Pat Taaffe's *Captain Christy.* His early career is best remembered for his exploits on *Roddy Owen* and Champion Hurdler *Another Flash.* And, of course, all his Galway triumphs including the Galway Hurdle on *Knight Errant* in 1958. He told his story in a remarkable book about his two lives in racing *Bobby Beasley's Second Start* published by W H Allen (London, 1976), a book to be recommended. This is how he described his first ever Galway Plate success on *Knight Errant.*

"He was a hard horse to ride and it gave me great satisfaction when I won the Dundalk Hurdle on him on July 12. We followed up with a double at Killarney and then on the last day of the month, we went to Galway to run *Knight Errant* in one of Ireland's biggest and most competitive chases, the two and half mile Galway Plate, worth even then, £1160 to the winner.

"Although my mount, a hunter-chaser of the previous season, had never before run in an open chase, he was backed down to favouritism at 4/1. It was a strange race on a lovely day in front of a record crowd at this historic Ballybrit course. There were fifteen starters, including *Nickleby,* one of those horses that I had ridden to win 'bumper' races, when he was trained by my father for Dorothy Paget and which was now trained in England by Bryan Marshall. He was ridden by Michael Scudamore, Peter's father. As the starting tape went up, it caught in *Nickleby's* mouth and we were all recalled because it was declared a false start.

"When eventually we were dispatched, I took the lead, but *Knight Errant* was jumping so stickily that he soon lost it. In fact, I had some awkward moments as he made a mess of nearly every fence and we were way behind the leaders. This was lucky in fact, because five fences from home *Southern Dago* and *Box On* were involved in a collision, which brought about the falls of both of them, knocked down Pat Taaffe's mount, the innocent passer-by *Villian of Lyons*, who was going well and interfered with several other runners.

"I was still pushing and struggling too far in the rear of the field to be involved. But suddenly *Knight Errant* seemed to warm to his task, took hold of his bit and started to jump like a stag. Two fences out, where *Nickleby* was leading from *Brookling*, I had moved up into third place and knew I had the beating of both of them! I jumped the last upsides with *Nickleby*, soon had his measure and had no difficulty in holding off the late challenge of *New Hope* to win by three lengths.

"This race, well illustrated, was splashed all over the Irish papers. It was splendid for me and a wonderful start to my new job. It also set the seal on my partnership with Paddy Sleator, which was to last ten years."

So Galway and Ballybrit played an important part in the Beasley-Sleator combination which took on and beat everybody in Ireland and England for many years afterwards.

WERE YOU THERE FORTY YEARS AGO IN 1955?

Then if you were, Louis Gunning's account of proceedings in the *Irish Press* in July 1955 will refresh your memory.

"In the blazing heat and swirling dust of one of the hottest Galway Plate Days in history and before the greatest ever crowds to pack the vast stands at Ballybrit, Pat Taaffe completed a unique treble in this the most marvellous year of his life to win the Galway Plate on *Umm*.

"The hero of this year's Grand National win on *Quare Times* and of *Umm's* Fairyhouse win in the Irish Grand National rode what was I think the cleverest and most forceful finish of his spectacular career in turning what looked like certain defeat into sweet victory. The vast crowd applauded more exultantly than the huge Aintree and Fairyhouse crowds had done as the well-backed *Umm* snatched victory in the last few strides from *Athenian* and enriched his supporters to the tune of thousands of pounds in as fine a Galway Plate finish as I have seen. *Skateaway* was third in an eleven horse field. The day's Tote aggregate was £31,638.15 shillings (previous year £27,240.13 shillings)."

FIRST EVER THREE-DAY FESTIVAL IN 1959

Ballybrit's first ever three days of racing at the Festival came into being in 1959 with the races starting on a very rainy Tuesday when Mr Kevin Prendergast, son of the winning trainer Paddy, who was in Goodwood that day, won the initial running of the Corinthian Stakes, the most valuable race for amateurs in Ireland worth £500, for American owner Mrs J Forrestal on the favourite *Rising Spring*. Unobtrusive but warmly welcomed visitors were former President Sean T O'Kelly and Mrs O'Kelly. The Taoiseach, Mr Sean Lemass was guest of honour of the Committee on Plate day. The Tote returns for the first ever Tuesday meeting was £21,375/12/6. Also present at the meeting was the American Ambassador to Ireland Mr Scott McLeod.

JOSEPH F COSTELLOE, ELECTED CHAIRMAN IN 1959

"Mr Joseph F Costelloe has been elected Chairman of the Galway Race Committee in succession to the late Mr J S Young. New members co-opted are Surgeon M G O'Malley, medical officer for the course for many years; Mr Thomas McDonogh of T McDonogh and Sons Limited, whose uncle Máirtín Mór was Chairman for many years; Mr Patrick D Ryan, President of Galway Chamber of Commerce and Baron Hemphill of Tulira Castle, Ardrahan."

— *Irish Press,* January 8 1959.

"HELP THE BLIND"

On the road into Ballybrit, especially on the pedestrian way immediately outside the entrance gates, punters are assailed with cries of "Racecards", "Timeform Sheets"and "Biros" from vendors, mostly with Dublin accents, plus the usual vendors led by Lily who sell everything from fruit to chocolate. And the odd appeal from handicapped people who set themselves up on some kind of seat with an appealing notice like "Help the Blind or Handicapped" and an equally appealing spiel about their affliction. It is hard to pass them by and even if there is a doubt betimes about the genuineness of it all, their caps or tin boxes are never empty. Such is the generous spirit of the Galway Races.

SIGNIFICANT DATES

1959 First three-day Festival and first ever sponsorship.

1963 First television coverage of Races.

1969 First Autumn meeting.

1970 September meeting extended to two day.

1971 First four-day meeting.

1974 Extended to five days.

1979 September meeting extended to three days.

First sponsorship of Galway Plate in 1979 also (Hygeia).

1982 Summer Festival extended to six days.

"OVER TO YOU MICHEAL"

The above was the link phrase when Noel Reid used to hand over to Mícheál O'Hehir. Now it is Tracy Piggott or Ted Walshe or Robert Hall handing over to Tony O'Hehir. Noel had some embarrassing encounters during his Galway Race interviews. He recalls this one.

"I was interviewing in the enclosure area and from the corner of my eye I spotted a drunk making for the television interview position. A sixth sense warned me. He moved closer. I wrapped up the interview with a hurried 'Over to you, Mícheál'. 'You're only a f.....' said the drunk just as the camera switched away. He very nearly made television history in Galway."

WERE YOU THERE THIRTY YEARS AGO?

Under a heading "Weather Spoil Sport for Galway Races. Outsider takes Player's Trophy. *Ross Sea's* second Galway Plate" the *Connacht Tribune* (the national newspapers were all on strike then) reported:

"The most dramatic success of the meeting came on Wednesday when trainer A S O'Brien (Phonsie) won his fourth consecutive Galway Plate with *Ross Sea* (8/1) ridden by English star jockey Stan Mellor bringing off his second successive Plate win. The weather improved on the Wednesday evening and continued fine on Thursday. *Troubled Sole,* ridden by Mr W P Browne (10/1) won the Players Amateur beating *Panic* and *Agrippina*. The Galway Hurdle was won by Charlie Weld's *Tirconderoga*."

ALBERT REYNOLDS, REGULAR GALWAY RACEGOER

He has been coming to Galway for over thirty years, as TD, Minister, Taoiseach or ex-Taoiseach now.

"I got the last winner today thanks to Victor Bowens. I enjoyed the day. Great crowd here, but it is back to the desk tomorrow. I enjoy it here every year. It's a great break and a great start to winding down for the holidays. Racing is my relaxation. I don't play golf. What attracts me to Galway is because Galway has an atmosphere all its own. Day and night it goes on in Galway. For years my wife, Kathleen, used to accompany me but she needed a holiday after Galway with me. Everybody comes to Galway to enjoy themselves and come from one year to another. Some people meet annually, some exiles from near and far. It is a great social event. A great place to go out and meet people. When in cabinet there are times when you can easily lose touch with what the real world is all about. Come to the Galway Races for a few days and you'll meet the real world and know what it's about. Nobody would ever criticise you at the Galway Races. They never talk politics to you, nobody would be looking for a grant or a Social Welfare pension or anything like that. No it is not that kind of atmosphere at all. You forget everything when you're at the Galway Races and they usually have glorious weather for it."

— Albert Reynolds TD, from a documentary done by RTE Radio on a day in the life of Tom McCarthy O'Hea (Manager Ardilaun Hotel) at the Galway Hurdle Day 1992, presented by Eamonn O Muirí.

GALWAY RACES

As I rode down to Galway town to seek for recreation,
On the seventeenth of August, me mind being elevated,
There were multitudes assembled with their tickets at the station,
Me eyes began to dazzle and I'm going to the races,
With me whack folda da folda diddly-ida-day.

It's there you see the jockeys and they're mounted out so stately,
The pink, the blue, the orange and green, the emblem of our
Nation.
When the bell was rung for starting, all the horses seemed impa-
tient,
I thought they never stood on ground their speed was so amazing,
With me whack folda da folda diddly-ida-day.

WERE YOU THERE TWENTY YEARS AGO IN 1975?

Well if you were the following extracts from Michael O'Farrell of *The Irish Times* accounts of events will serve as a reminder.

"*Spanner* and *Double Default*, the first two past the post in Tuesday's Players Wills Amateur Handicap won exciting divisions of the Galway Hurdle yesterday. *Spanner* covered the course in 3 minutes 45.5 seconds to *Double Default's* 3 minutes 48.7 seconds. It was quite a remarkable feat from both horses to pull out so fresh and well after Tuesday's race to win these competitive hurdle races. *Spanner* who has won the Player Wills Handicap on three occasions finished fourth in last year's Plate, fourth in a previous Galway Hurdle and was brought down when going like a winner two years ago, has clearly the best record on the track in post war years."

The Tote Aggregate on Galway Hurdle day 1975 was a record £142,432 (previous year £84,630). The Plate that year was won by *Our Albert* trained by Mick O'Toole. That day's Tote Aggregate was £131,855.75 (previous record was £90,900 from Plate day 1972 compared to the Curragh Derby record of £150,000). 'Now for the double,' said Mick O'Toole after *Our Albert* came cruising home. Michael O'Farrell, the senior of the racing press corps picked up on that "Only two trainers, the late Barney Nugent and Paddy Sleator have achieved that distinction. Nugent with *Point d'Atout* and *Charles Edward* in 1947 and Sleator with *Tymon Castle* and *Knight Errant* ten years later. Dessie Hughes, who was riding his first Galway Plate winner rides *Silent Prayer* in the Hurdle. Only three jockeys have completed the double, Danny Morgan in 1945, Tim Molony in 1948, and Frank McKenna in 1950."

Some good statistics there. For the record *Our Albert* beat *Colonial Prince* and *I'm Happy* with *Spittin' Image* fourth. *Leap Frog* who won the Plate with twelve stone seven pounds on his back two years before, was unplaced in 1975, with twelve stone on his back.

TEN YEARS AGO (1985)

Michael O'Farrell (*The Irish Times*) described the Galway Hurdle thus "Winning was sweet compensation for owner Michael Smurfit, trainer Dermot Weld and jockey Tommy Carmody who were unlucky not to have won the first leg of the double with *Greasepaint*. And to think that the Galway Hurdle winner *Strathline* won his maiden over hurdles only two weeks ago. 'He loves fast ground, a real summer horse' was how trainer Weld described the winner who came in at 8/1 to beat *Derryvale* and *William Crump*. Tote receipts were £340,000."

The previous day's Tote returns topped over £400,000 for Galway for the first time (an Irish record). The actual record was £404,594. Michael described the Plate thus: "The winning post arrived just in time for *Chow Mein*, who, in winning the Galway Plate, held by a diminishing length the furious late challenge of the top weight *Greasepaint*. The stands all but erupted when *Greasepaint* arrived on the scene. 'He was in front too soon,' said a relieved Dessie Hughes who rode the Mick O'Toole trained *Our Albert* to win the Plate just ten years before."

GEORGE KIRWAN, PRO FOR THE RACING BOARD 1992

"Galway Races, possibly one of the racing highlights of the year. The last thing you do when leaving the Ardilaun Hotel every year is to book yourself in for the following year in the same section. It is a marvellous mix, the atmosphere great and a good mix of racing. This year they are very lucky with (a) the weather and (b) the ground so good. Galway is unique for its atmosphere within the crowds themselves. Everybody knows everybody else. And if a really good horse wins, everybody seems to own him or everybody had a pound on him."

— Eamonn O Muirí's Radio documentary 1992.

CITY JET FROM LONDON IN 1994

All forty-two races during the Summer Festival meeting of 1994 were sponsored and total prize money amounted to £316,000. The value of the Digital Galway Plate went from £40,000 to £50,000. The value of the Guinness Galway Hurdle was £40,000. City Jet organised a direct flight service from London's Docklands to Galway Airport on the Wednesday and the Thursday, returning each day after racing at an all in cost of £149 for flight, transfer to and from the races, admission and race card.

ANNOUNCEMENT FEBRUARY 1995

The Galway Race Committee is never prepared to rest on its oars. Always expanding, always with an eye to the future. Early in February the Committee issued this announcement:

"Galway Race Committee is pleased to announce, as part of their ongoing development plan, the purchase of five acres of land adjacent to the Racecourse Avenue. These lands have been leased in the past for horsebox parking, and have played a vital role in overall traffic control during race meetings. The purchase of these lands has been under negotiation for quite some time, and it was felt that this land is vital for any future expansion. Over the past number of years, the emphasis at Galway racecourse has been to develop the amenities within the enclosure, and we are delighted to be able to announce this new acquisition of land, which will also benefit our patrons by allowing smoother access and egress to and from the Racecourse."

UTTOXETER TRIALS

The Galway Race Committee broke new ground in 1995 by sponsoring two races in Uttoxeter on June 29, namely the Lichfield Cathedral Digital Galway Plate Trial and the Guinness Galway Hurdle Trial. Yet another imaginative piece of marketing.

Appendices

GALWAY PLATE WINNERS 1869-1994

This table follows the pattern: Date, Horse, (Owner), Trainer...Rider, Prize money, Horse's Age, Handicap Weight, and number of starters.

1869   *Absentee* (Mr Bell), n/a...W Bell, £100 5yrs, 9-11, 13 ran

1870   *Comet* (Mr Moffatt), n/a...Mr J D Whyte, £150, 6yrs, 10-2, 23 ran

1871   *Aster* (Mr H S Chester), n/a...Mr R Exshaw, £300, a, 11-1, 19 ran

1872   *Belle* (Mr Maher), n/a...W Bell £360, 6yrs, 11-5, 15 ran

1873   *Lancet* (Mr St George), n/a...M Connolly, £400, 6yrs, 10-0, 20 ran

1874   *Revoke* (Mr St James'), n/a...T Miller, £365, 6yrs, 10-13, 19 ran

1875   *The Liberator* (Mr C Hawkes), n/a...T Ryan, £365, 6yrs, 11-2, 12 ran

1876   *Martha*(Mr T Wade), n/a...Mr Beasley, £275, 5yrs, 10-9, 11 ran

1877   *Tattoo* (Mr J G Blake), n/a...W Canavan, £270, 5yrs, 10-7, 13 ran

1878   *Jupiter Tonans* (Mr J F Lee-Barber), n/a...Owner, £220, 5yrs, 10-7, 10 ran

1879   *Rocksavage* (Mr Wilsea), n/a...Mr Lee-Barber, £140, a, 11-8, 12 ran

1880   *Lady Newman* (Mr J Monehan), n/a...D Meany, £160, a, 10-7, 9 ran

1881   *Night Fall* (Mr H E Linde, n/a...Mr T Beasley, £140, a, 10-1, 8 ran

1882   *Sugar Plum* (Capt. Kirkwood), n/a...Mr H Beasley, £138, 4yrs, 9-7, 8 ran

1883   *Ventriloquist* (Capt. Walker), n/a...Mr H Beasley, £138, 6yrs, 10-7, 4 ran

1884   *New Meadow* (Mr P N Fitzgerald)), n/a...Mr R Brabazon, £138, a, 10-7, 5 ran

1885   *Erin's Star* (Mr F Fawcett), n/a...Mr W P Cullen, £137, 6yrs, 10-10, 7 ran

1886   *Zulu II* (Capt. St Lawrence), n/a...T Kavanagh, £137, a, 12-7, 7 ran

1887   *Victrix* (Mr C W Bagge), n/a...Mr W P Cullen, £132, a, 11-0, 6 ran

1888   *Fethard* (Mr J A Cassidy), n/a...J Hoysted, £132, 4yrs, 10-6, 9 ran

1889   *Alexande* (Mr E Frazer), n/a...T Kavanagh, £132, a, 11-7, 6 ran

1890   *Lakefield* (Mr J Brady), n/a...T Walsh, £137, a, 10-8, 6 ran

1891   *Queen of the May* (Col Thomson), n/a...Mr W Beasley, £137, a, 11-13, 7 ran

1892   *Springfield Maid* (Mr S A Leonard), n/a...E Reilly, £137, 6yrs, 11-0, 6 ran

1893   *Lady Pat* (Mr R G Alexander), n/a...T Bailey, £132, 6yrs, 10-10, 7 ran

1894   *Star One* (Mr G V Briscoe), n/a...E Reilly, £132, 6yrs, 11-3, 12 ran

1895 *Double Primrose* (Mr H E Linde), n/a...W Hoysted, £132, 4yrs, 10-10, 13 ran

1896 *Castle Warden* (Mr R C Dawson), n/a...Mr W P Cullen, £132, 5yrs, 11-9, 9 ran

1897 *Drogheda* (Mr G F Gradwell), n/a...Dowdall, £166, 5yrs, 11-9, 7 ran

1898 *Boreenchreeogue* (Mr T Cleary), n/a...J Cheshire, £166, 6yrs, 10-13, 10 ran

1899 *Tipperary Boy* (Mr T Holmes), n/a...T Moran, £166, 5yrs, 11-9, 20 ran

1900 *Ivanoff* (Mr Leybuck), n/a...J O'Brien, £166, 5yrs, 9-7, 19 ran

1901 *Tipperary Boy* (Mr T B Holmes), n/a...T Moran, £166, a, 12-10, 13 ran

1902 *Tipperary Boy* (Mr T B Holmes), n/a...T Kavanagh, £166, a, 12-7, 9 ran

1903 *Hampton Boy* (Mr T McMahon), n/a...A Anthony, £166, 6yrs, 11-0, 12 ran

1904 *Strategy* (Mr E C Byrne), n/a...A Magee, £166, 5yrs, 11-0, 12 ran

1905 *Goldfield II* (Mr A Buckley jun), n/a...M Walsh, £166, 6yrs, 11-6, 10 ran

1906 *Royal Tan* (Mr J Reid), n/a...R Morgan, £166, 6yrs, 11-0, 13 ran

1907 *Apollo Belvedere* (Colonel Kirkwood), n/a...Mr P O'B Butler, £182, 6yrs, 11-4, 11 ran

1908 *Shady Girl* (Mr M Arnott), n/a...G Brown, £181, a, 12-4, 16 ran

1909 *Schwarmer* (Mr M Farrell), n/a...A Anthony, £181, 6yrs, 12-0, 14 ran

1910 *Ashbrooke* (Mr R M Liddell), n/a...Mr H Ussher, £181, 5yrs, 12-4, 11 ran

1911 *Dear Sonny* (Mr H L Fitzpatrick), n/a...E Lawn, £216, a, 10-5, 7 ran

1912 *Noble Grecian* (Sir G Abercromby), n/a...G Brown, £201, a, 12-5, 18 ran

1913 *George B* (Sir T Dixon), n/a...Mr G Harty, £246, 6yrs, 10-9, 15 ran

1914 *Alice Rockthorn* (Mr J Nugent), n/a...Mr P Nugent, £246, 6yrs, 10-12, 17 ran

1915 *Hill of Camas* (Mr W Molony), n/a...G Harty, £246, 5yrs, 10-0, 13 ran

1916 *Never Fear* (Mr T Nolan), Walker...F Morgan, £441, a, 11-8, 16 ran

1917 *Privit* (Major McCalmont), M Arnott...W Smith, £422, a, 11-11, 14 ran

1918 *Golden Fleece* (Mr W Parrish), Rogers...A Stubbs, £422, a, 11-8, 21 ran

1919 *Picture Saint* (Colonel Croft), H Ussher...M Colbert, £422, a, 10-6, 17 ran

1920 *Clonree* (Major Owen Toole), Morgan...F Morgan, £592, 6yrs, 12-7, 21 ran

1921   *Max* (Mrs Croft), H Ussher...F Wootton, £592, 5yrs, 11-0, 14 ran

1922   No Meeting   -   -   -

1923   *Clonsheever* (Mr J E Tyrrell), H Ussher...J Hogan jun, £392, a, 10-12, 10 ran

1924   *Clonsheever* (Mr J E Tyrrell), H Ussher...F B Rees, £442, a, 12-7, 13 ran

1925   *Blancona* (Miss E L M Barbour), Bracebridge...C Donnelly, £442, 5yrs, 10-7, 11 ran

1926   *Fair Richard* (Mr M Arnott), M Arnott...D Ward, £442, 5yrs, 11-4, 9 ran

1927   *Tony Lad* (Mr J J O'Ryan), H Ussher...J Moloney, £442, a, 10-5, 6 ran

1928   *East Galway* (Mr J S Shepherd), M Arnott...D Ward, £442, a, 12-7, 11 ran

1929   *Guiding Light* (Mr J B D'Ardenne), Dawson...P Powell, £442, a, 10-5, 13 ran

1930   *East Galway* (Mr J S Shepherd), M Arnott...J McNeill, £442, a, 12-7, 12 ran

1931   *Pucka Shikhari* (Mr J A Mangan), Owner...Mr J A Mangan, £442, 6yrs, 10-10, 11 ran

1932   *Seaview* (Mr E Cunningham), Cunningham...T Regan, £442, a, 11-2, 17 ran

1933   *Red Park* (Lady Helen McCalmont), Barry...D Kirwan, £442, a, 12-1, 13 ran

1934   *Reviewer* (Mrs C O'Neill), M Deegan...Mr P Sleator Jun, £442, 6yrs, 11-12, 9 ran

1935   *Southernmore* (Capt E A Gargan), Capt E A Gargan...J Harney, £517, 6yrs, 11-6, 18 ran

1936   *Yellow Furze* (Lieut -Col S S Hill-Dillon), J P Loughran...J McNeill, £517, 6yrs, 9-12, 14 ran

1937   *Brighter Cottage* (Capt. D W Daly), H I Ussher...W T O'Grady, £517, a, 10-8, 16 ran

1938   *Symaethis* (Lieut Col S S Hill-Dillon), R Fetherstonhaugh...D Butchers, £740, 6yrs, 9-7, 23 ran

1939   *Pulcher* (Col Scott Moore), R Fetherstonhaugh...J Costello, £740, a, 10-6, 18 ran

1940   *Ring of Gold* (Col D W Daly), H I Ussher...T McNeill, £740, 5yrs, 9-7, 17 ran

1941   *St Martin* (Miss M O Mathieson), C Brabazon...A Brabazon, £740, a, 11-9, 13 ran

1942   *Golden Jack* (The Hon. Dorothy Paget), C A Rogers...D L Moore, £444, a, 12-5, 9 ran

1943   *Swindon Glory* (Mr J A Mangan), Owner...A Brabazon, £444, a, 10-1, 7 ran

1944   *Swindon Glory* (Mr J A Mangan), Owner...A Brabazon, £444, a, 10-13, 8 ran

1945   *Grecian Victory* (Mr G Cheney), H I Ussher...D Morgan, £740, a, 9-7, 14 ran

1946   *Keep Faith* (Mr J V Rank), T W Dreaper...T Hyde, £740, a, 11-6, 18 ran

1947   *Charles Edward* (Mr W Hide), B Nugent...J Brogan, £1110, a, 9-9, 21 ran

1948   *Silent Prayer* (Mr A J Cope), P Sleator...T Molony, £1110, a, 11-6, 17 ran

1949   *Result* (Mr H Freeman-Jackson), Owner...Owner, £1110, a, 10-11, 15 ran

1950   *Derrinstown* (Mr P Digney), G Flood...F McKenna, £1110, a, 9-11, 15 ran

1951   *St Kathleen II* (Mrs Adam Bell), W T O'Grady...P J Doyle, £1110, a, 9-12, 19 ran

1952   *Alberoni* (Mr H H M Stanley), M V O'Brien...L Stephens, £1110, a, 11-9, 14 ran

1953   *Gallant Wolf* (Mr H R D McCarrick), T J Taaffe...T Taaffe, £1110, a, 11-1, 12 ran

1954   *Amber Point* (Mrs A M B Biddle), P Sleator...C Sleator, £1110, 6yrs, 10-6, 17 ran

1955   *Umm* (Mr C Rooney), G Wells...P Taaffe, £1110, a, 12-2, 11 ran

1956   *Amber Point* (Mrs R More O'Farrell), P Sleator...P A Farrell, £1160, a, 10-11, 11 ran

1957   *Knight Errant* (Mrs Ann Bullett Biddle), P Sleator...H Beasley, £1160, a, 9-12, 15 ran

1958   *Hopeful Colleen* (Mr J Graham), J Brogan...J A Mahony, £1160, a, 9-2, 10 ran

1959   *Highfield Lad* (Mr C L Weld), C L Weld...J Lehane, £1160, 7yrs, 9-10, 18 ran

1960   *Sparkling Flame* (Mr C Balding), P Sleator...H Beasley, £1160, 9yrs, 9-13, 12 ran

1961   *Clipador* (Mr F L Vickerman), C Collins...H Beasley, £1160, 10yrs, 10-4, 12 ran

1962   *Carraroe* (Mrs Miles Valentine), A S O'Brien...F Winter, £1160, 10yrs, 10-0, 10 ran

1963   *Blunt's Cross* (Lord Fermoy), A S O'Brien...H Beasley, £1530, 10yrs, 11-0, 13 ran

1964   *Ross Sea* (Mrs G Buchanan), A S O'Brien...S Mellor, £1530, 8yrs, 9-11, 13 ran

1965   *Ross Sea* (Mrs G Buchanan), A S O'Brien...S Mellor, £1900, 9yrs, 10-8, 15 ran

1966   *Cappawhite* (Mrs Denis Murphy), G Spencer...T Finn, £1900, 8yrs, 9-7, 11 ran

1967   *Royal Day* (Mr P Dunne Cullinan), P Sleator...R Coonan, £1900, 10yrs, 11-6, 13 ran

1968   *Terossian* (Mr R McIlhagga), G H Wells...G W Robinson, £1900, 8yrs, 10-9, 14 ran

1969   *Royal Day* (Mr P Dunne Cullinan), P Sleator...R Coonan, £2120, 12yrs, 10-13, 13 ran

1970   *Lisnaree* (Mr T H Moore), A Watson...F Shortt, £3000, 7yrs, 9-7, 14 ran

1971   *Sarejay Day* (Mrs E R Farrell), Eugene Farrell...S Shiels, £4000, a, 9-7, 17 ran

1972   *Persian Lark* (Mr J F Clifton), Jeremy Maxwell...J P Harty, £4000, 7yrs, 11-0, 17 ran

1973   *Leap Frog* (Mr P F Burrell), J Dreaper...T Carberry, £4000, 9yrs, 12-7, 10 ran

1974   *Bunclody Tiger* (Mr A Redmond), Kevin Bell...T Brown, £4000, 7yrs, 11-2, 11 ran

1975   *Our Albert* (Mr Charles Lewis), Mick O'Toole...D T Hughes, £4000, 9yrs, 11-3, 11 ran

1976   *O'Leary* (D Jackson), P Sleator...R Coonan, £5000, 8yrs, 11-7, 15 ran

1977   *Spittin' Image* (Joseph Walsh Jnr), J R Bryce-Smith...M Cummins, £5000, 11yrs, 9-11, 14 ran

1978   *Shining Flame* (J P McManus), E J O'Grady...Mr N Madden, £7000, 8yrs, 10-10, 24 ran

1979   *Hindhope* (David Louthan), E J O'Grady...Jonjo O'Neill, £15000, 9yrs, 11-1, 20 ran

1980   *Sir Barry* (Paul Clarke), J W Boyers...P Kiely, £15000, 9yrs, 10-11, 22 ran

1981   *Rugged Lucy* (Jeremiah Dunne), E J O'Grady...T J Ryan, £15000, 7yrs, 10-6, 22 ran

1982   *The Lady's Master* (M C Duggan (P)), M C Duggan (P)...N Madden, £20000, 11yrs, 11-9, 16 ran

1983   *Hamer's Flame* (Edward Farrell), M Neville...J Brassil , £20000, 7yrs, 9-13, 21 ran

1984   *Master Player* (Mrs R Eastwood), Thomas Bergin...J P Byrne, £25000, 7yrs, 9-7, 19 ran

1985   *Chow Mein* (Mrs Josephine Downey), D T Hughes...T Morgan, £25000, 8yrs, 11-0, 22 ran

1986   *Boro Quarter* (Mrs C D Hill), P Mullins...P Kavanagh, £30000, 7yrs, 11-3, 22 ran

1987   *Randoss* (Standish Collen), Miss Anne Collen...K Morgan, £40000, 8yrs, 8-5, 22 ran

1988   *Afford A King* (Charles King), Anthony Mullins...P Gill, £40000, 8yrs, 9-10, 22 ran

1989   *Bold Flyer* (Standish Collen), Jim Dreaper...Miss S G Collen, £40000, 6yrs, 9-7, 18 ran

1990   *Kiichi* (M W J Smurfit), D K Weld...B Sheridan, £40000, 5yrs, 11-3, 17 ran

1991   *Firion's Law* (Mrs M T Quinn), V Bowens...M Flynn, £40000, 6yrs, 10-8, 21 ran

1992   *The Gooser* (Mrs M O'Leary), P Mullins...A Maguire, £40000, 9yrs, 10-11, 21 ran

1993   *General Idea* (M W J Smurfit), D K Weld...A Maguire, £40000, 8yrs, 12-0, 21 ran

1994   *Feathered Gale* (E P King), A L T Moore...F Woods, £50000, 7yrs, 9-11, 21 ran

GALWAY HURDLE WINNERS 1913-1994

This table follows the pattern: Date, Horse, (Owner), Trainer...Rider, Horse's Age, and Handicap Weight.

1913   *Red Damsel* (Baron F de Tuyll), M Arnott...F Morgan, 5yrs, 11.4

1914   *Clonmeen* (S Grehan), M Arnott...F Morgan, 5yrs, 11.10

1915   *Naughty Earl* (G M Dennehy), M Dawson...C Hawkins, 4yrs, 10.12

1916   *Elgon* (F Barbour), R H Walker...Mr H S Harrison, 5yrs, 12.0

1917   *Happy Moments* (P D Coen), P Behan...Jos Canty, 6yrs, 10.11

1918   *Maroc* (Mrs Croft), H Ussher...H Harty, 6yrs, 10.2

1919   *Jenny Jones* (J C McKeever), R H Walker...Mr H S Harrison, a, 11.9

1920   *King Eber* (Lord Lascelles), M Arnott...T Burns, 4yrs, 11.13

1921   *King Michael* (J J Moore), Owner...Jos Canty, a, 12.7

1922   No Meeting

1923   *Smoke Cloud* (Col. O'Malley-Keyes), J J Parkinson...T Burns, 4yrs, 11.2

1924   *Holy Fooks* (F Burke), M Dawson...Jos Canty, a, 11.3

1925   *Alroi* (Miss M D Barbour), G P Bracebridge...C Donnelly, 5yrs, 11.5

1926   *Blancona* (Miss E L M Barbour), A Bickley...E Foster, 6yrs, 12.8

1927   *Southern Prince* (M Cunningham), Owner...J H Harty,

1928   *Prudent Pat* (W R Read), M Dawson...J Moloney, a, 12.6

1929   *Shrewd King* (H M Hartigan), Owner...Jos Canty, 5yrs, 10.11

1930   *Pucka Ranee* (J A Mangan), Owner...Owner, 5yrs, 11.7

1931   *Kyleclare* (M McDonogh), J J Parkinson...C O'Connor, 4yrs, 11.4

1932   *Knuckleduster* (Major H D Beamish), Owner...Mr F E McKeever, 6yrs, 12.7

1933   *Knuckleduster* (Major H D Beamish), Owner...Mr F E McKeever, 7yrs, 12.7

1934   *Red Hillman* (E T O'Meara), A P Harris...Tim Regan, 6yrs, 11.0

1935   *Kate Carlin* (D W H Garde), M Cunningham...Tim Regan, 4yrs, 9.13

1936   *Bachelor's Lane* (E T O'Meara), Owner...L C Keating, a, 11.6

1937   *Gorgia* (E T O'Meara), Owner...L C Keating, 5yrs, 10.2

1938   *Serpolettte* (E Delany), Owner...D Butchers, a, 9.11

1939   *Honor's Choice* (M McDonogh), J J Parkinson...J Barrett, 4yrs, 10.2

1940   *Red Shaft* (Col D W Daly), R More O'Farrell...S Magee, 4yrs, 10.8

1941   *Amor de Cuba* (Mrs M Mitchell), W J Kelly...T Hyde, 6yrs, 10.0

1942   *Point d'Atout* (Miss A E Hall), B Nugent...J Lenehan, 6yrs, 11.9

1943   *Erinox* (J C Landy), J Kirwan...J P Maguire, a, 10.2

1944   *Cockasnook* (W Barry), Owner...J Fitzgerald, 6yrs, 9.10

1945   *King of the Jungle* (R Mc Illhagga), B Nugent...D Morgan, 5yrs, 11.7

1946   *Fair Pearl** (Mickey Tully), Owner....Owner, 8yrs, 10.7

(forfeited the race subsequently due to a technicality. Race awarded to 2nd. horse)

King of the Jungle(R McIllhagga), B Nugent...D Morgan, 6yrs, 11.11

1947   *Point d'Atout* (Miss A E Hall), B Nugent...Mr A O'Scannell, 12yrs, 10.6

1948   *Carrantryla* (M J Gleeson), D Ruttle...T Molony, 4yrs, 10.6

1949   *Barberstown Prince* (P L Heron), Owner...Mr P C Heron

1950   *Lady's Find* (H E Rawson), C Brabazon...F McKenna, a, 9.7

1951   *Wye Fly* (Mrs E J Lewis), M V O'Brien...M Molony, 6yrs, 12.6

1952   *Warrenscourt Lad* (D J Duggan), D J Duggan...T P Burns, 6yrs, 9.7

1953   *Prince of Devon* (Mrs C Magnier), C Magnier...E Newman, a, 10.11

1954   *Cloudless Days* (Mrs F Blacker), M Dawson...E Newman, a, 9.8

1955   *Antigue II* (T Doyle), D L Moore...P Powell Jnr, a, 9.10

1956   *Ivy Green* (J G Duggan), J W Osborne...P Taaffe, 6yrs, 11.0

1957   *Tymon Castle* (Mrs P Meehan), P Sleator...G W Robinson, a, 9.7

1958   *Knight Errant* (Mrs A B Biddle), P Sleator...Bobby Beasley, 8yrs, 9.13

1959   *Cashel View* (Duchess of Westminster), T W Dreaper...P Taaffe, 6yrs, 10,3

1960   *Commutering* (Maj L Gardner), D L Moore...G W Robinson, 5yrs, 10.10

1961   *Newgrove* DH(J V Leavy),V Leavy Jnr...C Kinane, 9yrs, 9.7

Cygne Noir DH(M Sayers), J Lenehan...P Taaffe, 6yrs, 10.5

1962   *Tripacer* (Lady Honor Svedjar), D L Moore...T Carberry, 4yrs, 10.9

1963   *Snow Trix* (J Cox), Owner...B Hannon, 8yrs, 10.1

1964   *Extra Stout* (J F Hoey), R A Hoey...T Taaffe, 5yrs, 10.5

1965   *Tirconderoga* (Col J Reid), C L Weld...P Powell Jnr, 6yrs, 10.7

1966   *Warkey* (Mrs P J Hume), K Prendergast...F Carroll, 7yrs, 9.9

1967   *Muir* (A Willis), T W Dreaper...B Hannon, 8yrs, 11.3

1968   *Annalong* (Mrs B Eastwood), J Cox...P Black, 5yrs, 9.7

**Fair Pearl* came in at 10.1 and many local punters went home happy at the local success.

1969   *Bonne* (S P Muldoon), P D McCreery...P Taaffe, 8yrs, 11.11

1970   *Dictora* (Mrs M Egan) C Magnier...T Murphy, 5yrs, 9.12

1971   *Highway View* (Charles Carr), J Cox...P Black, 6yrs, 10.13

1972   *Hardboy* (Gene H Kruger), R J McCormick...T Murphy, 4yrs, 10.1

1973   *Lesabelle* (C D Lee), M A Scully...L O'Donnell, 6yrs, 9.10

1974   *Just for Fun* (P Deere), T Bergin...J Cullen, 5yrs, 10.9

1975   Div 1 *Spanner* (Mrs M T Jackson), D K Weld...P Russell, 8yrs, 12.0

          Div ll *Double Default* (Col Sir D Clague), C Magnier...Mr C P Magnier, 5yrs, 10.8

1976   *Negrada* (Capt L Mullins), P Mullins...S Treacy, 5yrs, 9.12

1977   *Paddy Bouler* (P Rooney), P Rooney...S Lynch, 4yrs, 9.10

1978   *Prince Tammy* (D O'Donnell), P Mullins...S Treacy, 8yrs, 11.2

1979   *Hard Tarquin* (W K Hosford), E J O'Grady...J J O'Neill, 7yrs, 10.0

1980   *Pearlstone* (W W Brainard Jnr), P Mullins...T V Finn, 4yrs, 9.12

1981   *Double Wrapped* (C P Magnier), C Magnier...D O'Gorman, 5yrs, 10.11

1982   *Pinch Hitter* (B Carolan), N Meade...J J O'Neill, 4yrs, 9.9

1983   *Pinch Hitter* (B Carolan), N Meade...J J O'Neill, 5yrs, 10.12

1984   *Tara Lee* (P Durkan), W Durkan...J P Byrne, 7yrs, 11.4

1985   *Strathline* (M W Smurfit), D K Weld...T Carmody, 5yrs, 10.12

1986   *Rushmoor* (J Ennis), R Peacock...P Scudamore, 8yrs, 10.6

1987   *Belsir* (P Anglim), R Nevin...P Gill, 5yrs, 9.11

1988   *Try A Brandy* (M Dunne), Owner (P)...H Rogers, 6yrs, 9.7

1989   *I'm Confident* (M McDonagh), Owner...Mr F J Flood, 5yrs, 9.7

1990   *Athy Spirit* (W Fennin), Owner...T J Taaffe, 5yrs, 10.11

1991   *Sagaman* (M Doocey), L J Codd...Mr P Fenton, 5yrs, 10.12

1992   *Natalie's Fancy* (Mrs E Crowe), P G Kelly...J Titley, 6yrs, 10.3

1993   *Camden Buzz* (Miss C Byrne), P Mullins...C F Swan, 5yrs, 10.12

1994   *Oh So Grumpy* (Mrs E Queally) Mrs J Harrington...M Dwyer, 6yrs, 10.9

WINNERS OF THE AMATEUR HANDICAP —1962-94

This table follows the pattern: Date, Horse, (Owner), Trainer...Rider, Prize money and Handicap Weight.

1962   *Bahrain*, (Mr E Sturman), D Moore...Sir Wm Pigott-Browne, 11. 2

1963.   *Maigret*, (Mr F Launder), D Brennan...Mr J R Cox, 11.7

1964   *Tirconderoga*, (Col. J Reid), C Weld...Mr D K Weld, 11.11

1965   *Troubled Sole*, (Mr R M V Willington), Owner...Mr W P Browne, 11.3

1966   *Many Mansions*, (Mrs J Bennett), Mr M Connolly...Mr C Ronaldson, 11.3

1967   *Evilo*, (Mr T J Tormey), Owner...Owner, 10.10

1968   *Bonne*, (Mr S P Muldoon)...Mr W McLernon, 12.0

1969   *Musty Penny*, (Mr John A O'Connor), Mr M Connolly...Mr W McLernon, 10.10

1970   *Swing Low*, (Mr T H Moore), Mr P Sleator...Mr R Barry, 10.10

1971   *Vector*, (Lady Honor Svjedar), Mr G Wells...Mr M F Turner, 11.9

1972   *Spanner*, (Mrs M T Jackson), Mr D K Weld...Mr D K Weld, 11.0

1973   *Spanner*, (Mrs M T Jackson), Mr D K Weld...Mr D K Weld, 11.3

1974   *Intended*, (Mrs E Doyle), Mr P V Doyle...Mr M J Grassick, 10.0

1975   *Spanner*, (Mrs M T Jackson), Mr D K Weld...Mr D K Weld, 10.10

1976   *Irish Fashion*, (Mrs M O'Dowd), Mr M Cunningham...Mr J Fowler, 10.0

1977   *The Lady's Master*, (Mrs Gabriel Mulholland), Mr T Bergin...Mr N Madden, 10.12

1978   *Double Default*, (Mr C P Magnier), Mr C Magnier...Mr C P Magnier, 10.0

1979   *Pigeon's Nest*, (Mr Berni McDonnell), J S Bolger...Mr P Scudamore, 10.2

1980   *Hamer's Flame*, (Mr Edward Farrell), Michael Neville...William Cronin, 11.9

1981   *Steel Duke*, (Mr H N Kavanagh), N Meade...Mr J Queally, 11.0

1982   *Double Wrapped*, (Mr C P Magnier), Mr C Magnier...Mr C P Magnier, 11.1

1983   *Double Wrapped*, (Mr A N Durkan), William Durkan...Mr C P Magnier, 11.11

1984   *Street Angel*, (Mr 0 Freaney), P Mullins...Mr J Shortt, 10.1

1985   *Pargan*, (Mrs P Mullins), P Mullins...Mr W P Mullins, 12.7

1986   *Shoubad Melody*, (Mr J Morrison), J Morrison(P)...Mr J A Flynn, 10.1

1987   *Coolcullen*, (Miss Una Bolgers), Jim Bolger...Mr A J Martin, 11.4

1988   *Try A Brandy*, (Mr Martin Dunne), Martin Dunne(P)...Mr F J Flood, 10.10

1989   *Nameloc*, (Mr Edmund Coleman), J E Kiely...Mr J A Flynn, 11.10

1990   *Athy Spirit*, (Mr W Fennin), Mr W Fennin...Mr J P Banahan, 10.7

1991   *Breyani*, (Mrs David Nagle), T Stack...Mr K Whelan, 11.13

1992   *Beau Beauchamp*, (Mr Donal Kinsella), Noel Meade...Mr S R Murphy,.10.1

1993   *Shankorak*, (Mr E O'Mahony), Frank Berry...Mr P J Kelly, 10.13

1994   *Onomatopoeia*, (Mr David O'Reilly), P J Flynn...Mr D Murnane, 10.5

 From The Horse's Mouth

Curran's Yard

Prior to the 1950s, the racehorses were stabled in various yards around the city. One of these was Curran's Yard at Prospect Hill, site of Curran's Hotel of today. Proprietor, Michael John, tells me his father, John, never stopped talking about the most famous horse stabled in his yard. That horse was East Galway, winner of the Galway Plate of 1928 and 1930.